ORIGINAL
FERRARI V12
1965-73

ORIGINAL
FERRARI V12
1965–1973

by Keith Bluemel

MOTORBOOKS
INTERNATIONAL

This edition published in 2003 by Motorbooks International, an imprint of MBI Publishing Company, Galtier Plaza, Suite 200, 380 Jackson Street, St. Paul, MN 55101-3885 USA

First published in 1999 by Bay View Books Ltd.

Motorbooks International titles are also available at discounts in bulk quantity for industrial or sales-promotional use. For details write to Special Sales Manager at Motorbooks International Wholesalers & Distributors, Galtier Plaza, Suite 200, 380 Jackson Street, St. Paul, MN 55101-3885 USA.

ISBN 0-7603-1752-6

Front cover: 275 GTB/4

Frontis: 500 Superfast

Title page: 365 GTS

Contents page: 275 GTS/4

Back cover: 365 GTB/4

Designed by Chris Fayers
Sub-edited by Warren Allport

Printed in China

Contents

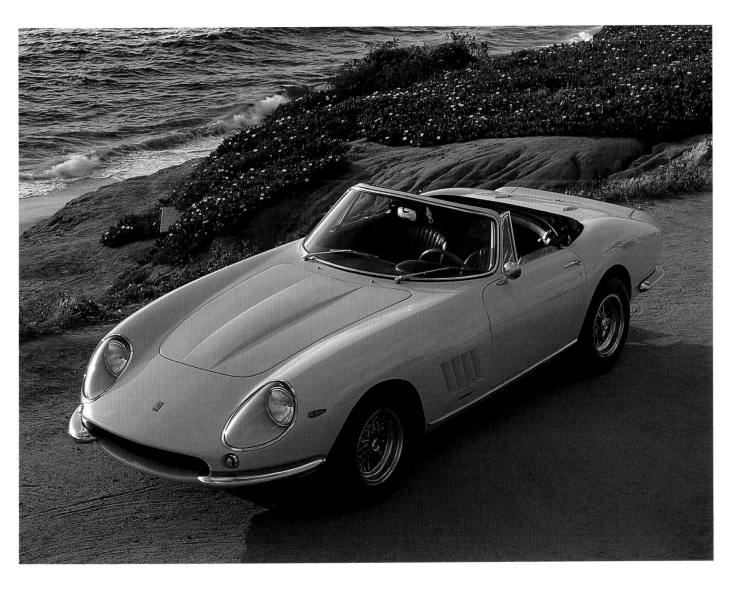

Introduction

In 1964 a 10-year span of Ferrari 250 GT model production, which had started with the 250 Europa GT, came to an end with the 250 GT Lusso and the 250 GTO. The Ferrari 3-litre V12 production engine had reached the end of a long and successful career.

The 1965-73 period of Ferrari road car production covered within these pages embraces the last of the limited-production series, the 500 Superfast and 365 California, together with the front-engined models that followed the 250 GT series – from the 3.3-litre 275 GT series, through the 4-litre 330 GT models, to the 4.4-litre 365 GT series. In 1963 the final 50 examples of the 250 GTE 2+2 had been fitted with 4-litre V12 engines and the model was known as the 330 America. However, as it was more a derivative of the 250 GT, rather than a completely new 330 GT, it falls outside the focus of this book but is illustrated in the *Close Relatives* chapter (page 114).

Apart from the 500 Superfast, where the model type number referred to the total cubic capacity of the engine (5 litres), all the other models used the same designation system as the 250 GT series, where the number referred to the swept volume of a single cylinder in cubic centimetres. Although some of the models started production prior to 1965 and the 365 GT4 2+2 continued in production after 1973, the span of 1965-73 has been chosen specifically so as not to impinge on models outside the scope of this volume, such as the 330 America mentioned earlier and the mid-engined 250/275 LM. The latter was a competition car disguised as a road car and was included in Ferrari's 'odd number' road car chassis sequence in an unsuccessful attempt to get it homologated as an evolution of the front-engined 250 GT series. Ferrari competition cars used a parallel 'even number' system and Dino models had their own 'even number' sequence. The system did not change until the road car numbers reached 75,000, after which both odd and even numbers were used for road cars, with individual model range number sequences used for competition cars.

At the beginning of the period covered in this book all the models were sold world-wide, with the only significant differences being the location of the steering wheel. Left- or right-hand drive was available on all models, except for the left-hand-drive only 275 GTS/4 NART spider, which was specifically a US model. A minor difference was the provision of yellow headlamp bulbs for French-market cars. However, in the late 1960s the USA introduced a succession of safety and exhaust emissions standards with which cars sold in that market had to comply. Thus US-specification versions had to be produced by Ferrari, where viable, for this important market.

The progressive tightening of these regulations meant that the mid-engined 365 GT4/BB, launched in 1973 as the replacement for the 365 GTB/4, was never produced in a US-market version. This was one reason why Ferrari extended the life of the 365 GTB/4, giving breathing space until the V8 Dino 308 GT4 joined the V6 Dino 246 GT/GTS in US showrooms at the beginning of 1974. Such was the cost of complying with US legislation for a relatively small sales volume that, incredibly, Americans would have to wait another ten years for the next 12-cylinder Ferrari for their market. That came in 1984 with the Testarossa, which was designed as a world-market car from the outset and thus needed only minor changes to comply with US legislation.

ACKNOWLEDGMENTS

Stuart Adams, Paul Baber, Robert Beecham, Mario Bernardi, Gordon Bruce, David Cottingham, Graham Earl, Peter and Suzanne Everingham, Ferrari SpA, Michitake Isobe, Kevin Jones, Ian Kuah, Lucas Laureys, Steve Lay, Seamus McKeown, Allan Mapp, Marcel Massini, Michael Phillips, Dyke W. Ridgley, Kevin O'Rourke, Rob O'Rourke, Jess G. Pourret, Gregor Schulz, Nicolaus Springer, Jacques Swaters, Guy Tedder, Brandon Wang, Malcolm West, Mike Wheeler and Miles Wilkins.

PHOTOGRAPHIC CREDITS

Dennis Adler, Tim Andrew, Keith Bluemel, Simon Clay, Michitake Isobe, Ian Kuah, Marcel Massini, Dieter Rebmann and Gregor Schulz.

Chapter 1

500 Superfast

The original Pininfarina show and press photograph car, chassis number 05951SF, with the side/turn indicator light treatment unique to this example and the 11-louvre engine bay exhaust air vent found on early cars. Despite the car's length, the proportions are very elegant.

Introduced to the public at the 1964 Geneva Salon, the 500 Superfast was the last in a line of Superfast coupés dating back to 1956, when the first model bearing the Superfast name was exhibited at the Paris Salon. All the previous cars carrying this name had been one-off show cars, which influenced the lines of the 410/400 Superamerica series. The 500 Superfast was the final link in the chain of very exclusive, low-volume coupés for a few extremely wealthy customers. To put the exclusivity into perspective, in January 1965 a 500 Superfast cost £11,518 15s in the UK – almost twice the price of a 275 GTB and the same price as a 250LM competition berlinetta. Alternatively you could have bought two Rolls-Royce Silver Cloud IIIs or 24 Minis for the same money! There were obviously customers around with money – including the Aga Khan, the Shah of Iran and actor Peter Sellers – as 36 examples were built between 1964 and 1966, when production ceased.

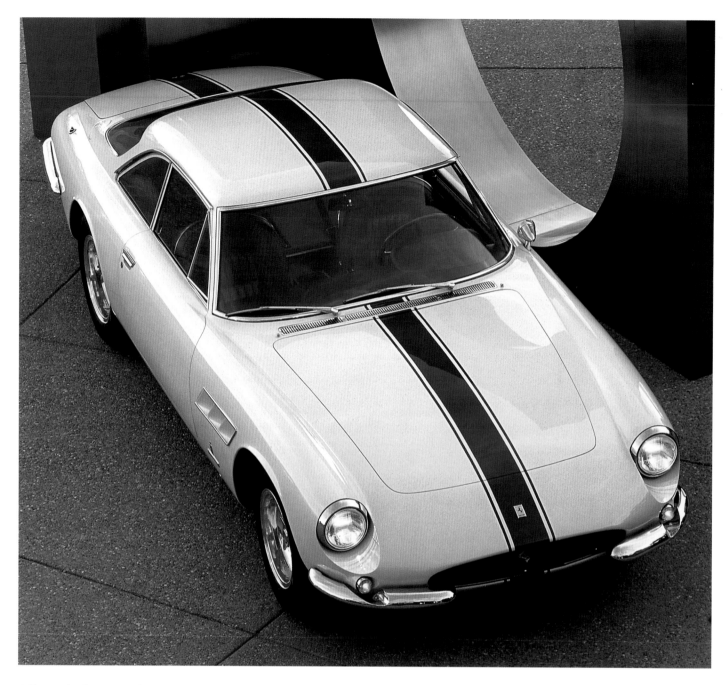

All were built at Pininfarina in Turin before being shipped to the Ferrari factory in Maranello for installation of mechanical components.

The chassis frame was based on that of the concurrently produced 330 GT 2+2. When that car's chassis was modified in 1965, the Superfast incorporated the revisions and thus the designations series I and series II came into being. This distinction is something of an anomaly, as it generally refers to the car having a four-speed gearbox and 11-louvre front wing vents on series I models or a five-speed gearbox and three-louvre front wing vents on series II examples. The general consensus is that there are 24 series I examples and 12 series II cars. Without access to the build sheets, it is impossible to determine the original specification of each car produced. What is certain from the information available to me is that the ninth car produced (06039) was fitted with a four-speed gearbox with overdrive and had triple louvres, that the tenth car (06041) had a four-speed gearbox plus overdrive, and that the 11th (06043) and 13th (06303) cars each had a five-speed gearbox and triple louvres. Thus there was the use of a five-speed gearbox at least ten cars before the second series is supposed to have started, and a four-speed car with triple front wing louvres, leading to the conclusion that there is an overlap of features, or transition stage. I therefore consider it preferable to refer to four-speed examples as early cars and five-speed examples as late cars. Despite being built on the same 2650mm (104.33in) wheelbase chassis as the 330 GT 2+2, the 500 Superfast was a pure two-seater, with an

A mid-series example, chassis number 06307SF, with an unusual paint job, more suitable for a competition car than the top-of-the-range luxury high-speed gran turismo model. Fluidity of line is evident from any angle.

A right-hand-drive British-registered example, chassis number 06661SF, showing the style of triple-louvre engine bay exhaust air vents found on later cars.

Another right-hand-drive example, chassis number 06679SF, with the metallic gold paint finish called Nocciola. This car was displayed at the 1965 London Motor Show prior to delivery to its first owner, renowned comedian and actor Peter Sellers.

DIMENSIONS & WEIGHT

	mm	in
Overall length	4820	189.76
Overall width	1730	68.11
Overall height	1280	50.39
Wheelbase	2650	104.33
Front track	1397	55.00
Rear track	1389	54.68
Weight (dry)	1400kg	3086lb

upholstered luggage platform behind the seats.

The factory never supplied a specific owner's handbook or parts book for the 500 Superfast, only a single typed sheet entitled *Brevi Istruzione Per 'Uso E Manutenzione' Vettura 500/Superfast*. This gave the salient points pertaining to the specification differences relative to the 330 GT 2+2 chassis, on which it was based.

Body & Chassis

The 500 Superfast chassis, type 578, with a 2650mm (104.33in) wheelbase, is essentially that of the 330 GT 2+2 model, with small modifications to the engine mounts for the larger engine and to the body pick-up attachments because of the different body style. From a large shallow U-section front cross-member, the two main longitudinal oval steel tubes of the frame run either side of the engine, under the cabin and rise in an arc over the rear axle. A longitudinal and lateral square-section tubular frame is attached to the two main oval tubes beneath the cabin and to the body support frame, to which the bodyshell is welded. The standard finish of the chassis is satin black paint. Early cars in the series carried the chassis number suffix 'SA' (SuperAmerica) on the factory build sheet but late series cars were provided with an 'SF' (SuperFast) suffix.

The body shape was developed by Pininfarina from the various 400SA and 410SA models, plus Superfast show cars that had been produced over the years. Despite its size – at 4820mm (189.76in) it is 485mm (19.1in) longer than a 'short-nose'

Tail badge treatment varied between individual examples. Chassis number 06673SF has a badge proclaiming 'Ferrari Superfast' beneath the crossed Ferrari/Pininfarina flags; on chassis number 06679SF the wording is '500 Superfast'; and chassis number 06661SF has only the crossed flags with Ferrari script on the tail.

275 GTB – the 500 Superfast is an extremely elegant, light and smooth design. From the elliptical radiator opening in the nose, the lines flow smoothly into the cabin section, with its curved windscreen pillars, large glass area and slim rear pillars either side of the steeply raked rear screen, and then in a continuous line across the boot lid into a slim Kamm tail. The shape exudes speed with supreme elegance, even at rest.

The body is constructed of welded steel panels, with the bonnet, doors and boot lid in aluminium on steel frames. On early cars produced up to around the middle of 1965, the bodies feature an 11-louvre engine bay vent on the side of each front wing. Late-series bodies differ in having three-louvre vents, with polished aluminium surrounds to the upper, lower and front edges. Although the headlamps are deeply recessed in the front wings, Perspex covers were not fitted as standard – but at least one customer asked for them to be provided (on chassis 06039).

Body Trim & Fittings

The front of the 500 Superfast features a shallow elliptical radiator opening and an inset aluminium egg-crate grille carrying a *Cavallino Rampante* (prancing horse) at its centre, with a polished aluminium trim around the opening. Chrome-plated steel wrap-around quarter-bumpers run into the extremities of the radiator grille, with semicircular recesses in their forward top edge to accommodate the wing-mounted sidelamps. The original Pininfarina show car, which featured in press photographs, had plain quarter-bumpers with horizontal elliptical sidelamps between them and the headlamp recess, and also a different tail light treatment. At the rear, a matching pair of wrap-around quarter-bumpers is fitted, with the chrome-plated number plate housing mounted on the inset tail panel lower return edge between them. A rectangular enamel Ferrari badge is fitted on the upper nose panel between the grille and leading edge of the bonnet. Slim horizontal rectangular Pininfarina badges, with Pininfarina enamel shield badges above them, are fitted to the lower rear area of the front wings. The badging at the rear of the car varies, the common thread being a crossed Ferrari and Pininfarina flag badge towards the rear of the boot lid. Some examples have no badge below this, but

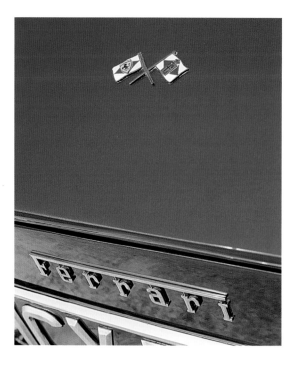

a Ferrari script badge near the centre top edge of the tail panel, while others have badging below the crossed flags. The most common of these is a 'Superfast' script badge, with '500 Superfast' and 'Ferrari Superfast 500' also appearing – but some cars have no badges whatsoever.

The plain flat bonnet is forward hinged and has either a manually-positioned sprung support stay near the left forward edge or mechanical spring support on the hinges. Brightwork is confined to the chrome-plated front and rear screen surrounds, door glass frames, screen wiper arms and blade frames, fresh air inlet grille (between the trailing edge of the bonnet and the base of the windscreen), headlamp rims, polished aluminium front wing louvre surrounds (on late series cars), chrome-plated jacking-point plugs at the front and rear of each sill panel, number plate lamp shroud, plus lift-and-pull chrome-plated cast zinc door handles, with circular keylock below, identical to those found on the 330 GT 2+2.

Plain glass is fitted and the windscreen is laminated. The two-speed self-parking wipers park on the right with left-hand drive and on the left with right-hand drive. The door windows are provided with swivelling quarterlights operated by a catch at the lower front corner on early cars and by a black plastic knurled knob on the inner door panel on late series examples.

Paintwork

A vast range of colours was available for Ferraris at this time and the comments made in the *275 GT Berlinetta* chapter (see page 31) about those models also apply to the 500 Superfast. Being built by Pininfarina, the 500 Superfast should have a paint colour from either the PPG or Duco ranges. The table in the *275 GT Berlinetta* chapter lists the full range of colours offered, although on this exclusive and expensive model the customer's whim was no doubt Ferrari's command.

Interior Trim & Fittings

The standard seat upholstery material is full leather and the range of colours available is shown in the table in the *275 GT Berlinetta* chapter (see page 33). The two seats are mounted on runners with adjustment via a lever under the front edge of the cushion. A knob on the outer lower edge of the seat base alters the rake of the backrest, which can be folded forward to gain access to the luggage platform. The rear luggage platform has triple protective aluminium rubbing strips on the horizontal and vertical faces and a pair of leather luggage retaining straps from the parcels shelf at the rear of the padded top bolster. The parcels shelf was normally in black vinyl, although trimming could

be in the upholstery colour upon request.

The armrests on the doors form the top of map pockets, with an elasticated front panel accessed via a pull-tab and a slim vertical red door-open warning lamp in the rear face. A chrome-plated door handle is at the forward end of the armrest, with matching electric window switchgear (two switches on the driver's side, one on the passenger side) above and in front of it. A plugged circular opening is provided for an emergency winder in case of motor failure. The bottom front portion of the door is fitted with a chrome-plated kick plate, as is the shut face of the sill panel.

The floor, inner sills, firewall and lower vertical face of the rear luggage platform are carpeted, normally with ribbed black rubber heelmats for both driver and passenger. A folding aluminium foot brace bar with a ribbed black rubber sheath is fitted on the passenger side. Carpet colours are listed in the *275 GT Berlinetta* chapter (see page 32). The centre console surround panels, rear transmission tunnel, door panels, rear inner wheelarches and luggage platform are trimmed in leather to match the seat colour. Black vinyl is standard on the facia top, bottom roll, instrument nacelle surround, horizontal inner faces of the centre console and door cappings. The vertical face of the centre console is normally teak veneer to match the facia, but could be finished in black

The interior looks particularly inviting in light-coloured leather, as seen on the right-hand-drive chassis number 06661SF, and provides spacious accommodation in luxury.

vinyl to match the lower centre part of the console and base of the tray between the seats.

The roof lining is ivory-coloured fluted vinyl, although it could also be matched to the interior trim, and is retained by matching vinyl-covered cant rails and quarter panels. Matching vinyl-covered padded sun visors are provided, with a vanity mirror for the passenger. The dipping rear view mirror incorporates an interior light and is mounted on the upper screen rail. Two roof-mounted and two footwell-mounted interior lights are operated automatically by door switches, or manually by a facia switch.

The chrome gear lever is mounted centrally on the transmission tunnel and is topped by a black plastic knob; the gaiter is the same colour as the interior trim. To the rear of this is a chrome ashtray, with a crossed Ferrari and Pininfarina flag badge on the lid, and then a shallow tray between the seats. The handbrake projects from the floor in an upholstery-coloured gaiter and is positioned alongside the front of the transmission tunnel, on the driver's side.

Facia & Instruments

The facia panel and instrument nacelle are teak veneered. The nacelle surround and facia top surface are covered in black vinyl with a padded rolled edge, which matches the lower facia. There are slim demister slots close to the windscreen. A lidded glove compartment, with a lockable push-button catch and an interior light, is provided on the passenger's side.

The wood-rimmed steering wheel has plain aluminium spokes and an aluminium boss with a central horn button. This is yellow with a black plastic rim and contains the *Cavallino Rampante* (prancing horse) emblem. A pair of slender chrome-plated stalks, with black plastic finger pads, project from the left of the steering column; the shorter one controls the indicators and the longer one sidelights, headlamp main beam and flashing. On early cars a stalk on the right of the column operates the overdrive. A floor-mounted push-button for the windscreen washer is sited above the driver's footrest.

The instrument nacelle in front of the driver contains the speedometer and rev counter, plus oil pressure and temperature gauges in the upper part of a triangular arrangement between them and the water temperature gauge central below. The speedometer dial contains an odometer and trip recorder, plus turn indicator and lights-on warning lamps. The rev counter dial has warning lamps for heated rear window, main beam and electric fuel pump. In the top section of the centre console, angled towards the driver, is a clock, an ammeter and the petrol gauge with low-fuel

warning light. Below this bank of dials is a radio. On early cars the speaker is below it; on late cars there are two speakers, one on either side of the forward part of the console below the facia. All gauges have white digits on a black background.

This instrument pattern is common to both early- and late-series models but the heating and ventilation control lever arrangement is different. On both series a pair of circular vent outlets is provided in the centre of the facia. On early series cars a pair of slide levers between these regulate heat input to each side of the car individually, with a further lever at each end of the facia to control the flow of air to that side of the car. On late-series cars there is a pair of outboard levers on the driver's side to control general heat input and air flow to that side of the car; another outboard lever on the passenger's side controls air flow to that side of the car. There is a lever beneath the facia on each side of the car to alter ventilation air flow to either high or low level in the passenger compartment.

Suspended below the facia, between the steering column and door pillar, is a panel containing six rocker switches for the headlamps, electric fuel pump, left and right blower fans, rear screen heated element and interior light. The instrument light rheostat, switch for the two-speed wipers and cigar lighter are in the centre of the facia. The ignition switch is on the lower facia close to and outboard of the steering column. The choke control is a pull-knob beneath the dashboard, between the steering column and centre console. Also below the dashboard are the bonnet release catch (outboard of the steering column) and an aluminium remote-control lever for the passenger door (inboard of the steering column).

The dashboard of chassis number 06661SF, dominated by the elegant Nardi wood-rim steering wheel. Auxiliary gauges on the centre console are angled towards the driver.

Although the shallow boot provides plenty of luggage space, there is also an upholstered platform behind the seats.

Luggage Compartment

The boot contains the fuel tank, which is a rectangular vertical unit mounted at the forward end behind the luggage shelf. Fuel capacity is 100 litres (22.0 Imperial/26.4 US gallons). The filler cap is under a cover flap on the right rear wing, adjacent to the front corner of the boot lid, and is released by a keylock in the cover flap. The spare wheel is

positioned flat in a well in the boot floor and covered with a black-painted metal panel. The tool kit roll is sited in one of the lower wing panel recesses. The boot floor and sides are lined with black carpet and all plain metal surfaces are painted satin black. Two lamps in the ceiling of the boot are actuated by individual switch plates on the hinges when the boot is opened. Access to the boot is via a lever on the outer left side of the forward face of the luggage shelf. The lid is supported when open by a telescopic ratchet stay.

Engine

The 4943cc (301.6cu in) 60° V12 engine is a wet-sump unit with a single overhead camshaft per bank and has the factory type number 208. Power output is a factory-quoted 400bhp (DIN) at 6500rpm, with maximum torque of 48.5kgm (350lb ft) at 4750rpm. The 108mm (4.25in) cylinder centres, plus the bore and stroke of 88x68mm (3.46x2.68in), are the same as the earlier 410 Superamerica series with Lampredi-designed engines, but without the screwed-in cylinder liners of that design. The construction materials, component layout and operation are generally very similar to the other two-camshaft Ferrari engines of the period (ie, the 275 and 330 engines described in later chapters). The cylinder firing order is given on a plate fixed to the top front of the left camshaft cover.

Either three or six Weber 40DCZ/6 carburettors are fitted on individual manifolds, the rear one with a tapping for the vacuum feed to the brake servo, and are fed by a Fispa diaphragm mechanical fuel pump, with a Fispa electric booster pump operated by a facia switch. The twin

The appearance of the 5-litre engine is typical of Ferrari of the period, with the carburettor air filter dominating proceedings and crackle-black camshaft covers flanking it.

ENGINE

Type	60° V12
Type number	208
Cubic capacity	4943cc (301.6cu in)
Bore and stroke	88x68mm (3.46x2.68in)
Compression ratio	8.8:1
Maximum power	400bhp (DIN) at 6500rpm
Maximum torque	48.5kgm (350lb ft) at 4750rpm
Carburettors	3 or 6 Weber 40DCZ/6

TIMING DATA

Inlet valves open	27° BTDC
Inlet valves close	65° ABDC
Exhaust valves open	74° BBDC
Exhaust valves close	16° ATDC
Firing order	1-7-5-11-3-9-6-12-2-8-4-10

Valve clearances with a cold engine should be 0.15mm (0.0059in) inlet and 0.2mm (0.0079in) exhaust, measured between the valve pads and rocker arm.

SYSTEM CAPACITIES

Fuel tank 100 litres (22.0 Imperial/26.4 US gallons)

	Litres	Imp Pints	US Pints
Coolant	14.0	24.7	29.6
Washer bottle	1.0	1.8	2.1
Engine oil	12.0	21.1	25.4
Gearbox oil	3.25	5.7	6.9
Differential oil	1.8	3.2	3.8

12-volt Marelli S85A distributors are of the 15° type, each with a Marelli 12v BZR201A coil. The water pump is mounted on the same shaft as the six-blade cooling fan (on early cars) and driven by a vee-belt from the crankshaft pulley; sometimes there is an auxiliary thermostatically-controlled electric fan in front of the radiator. Instead of the mechanical fan, late series cars have twin electric fans in front of the radiator.

Each bank of cylinders has a pair of triple-branch free-flow steel manifolds, with a heat shield fitted above them. The manifolds are flanged to twin collector pipes that are siamesed into one large-bore pipe for each bank. Each pipe then feeds into its own silencer box assembly, suspended below the cabin floor, from which twin pipes exit. These loop to clear the rear suspension and emerge as a pair of chrome-plated tailpipes on either side, suspended from rubber hangers.

The standard air filter box is of black-painted pressed steel, with the top panel retained by three knurled nuts. Within the casing, which is rectangular with curved ends, are either three separate circular elements (one around each carburettor intake) on early cars or a single perimeter element on later cars. Air is drawn into the box via a pair of rectangular nozzles, which protrude over the cam covers on each side of the casing. Individual pancake filters could be provided as an option.

The normal oil pressure with an oil temperature of 100°C should be 5.5kg/cm² (78psi) at 6500rpm, with a minimum value of 4kg/cm² (57psi) under the same conditions. The minimum slow running pressure (at 700-800rpm) should be 1.0-1.5kg/cm² (14-21psi).

Transmission

The 500 Superfast is fitted with the same gearbox and transmission as the 330 GT 2+2 (see page 56 for a full description) with a conventional location and a live rear axle with limited slip differential. On early series cars the gearbox has four speeds plus overdrive and late series examples have five speeds. The gearbox ratios are also identical, although a different standard 4.00:1 (8:32) rear axle ratio replaces the standard 4.25:1 (8:34) ratio of the 330 GT 2+2.

Early cars with a four-speed gearbox are fitted with a cable-operated Fichtel & Sachs single-plate clutch and later five-speed examples with a hydraulically-operated Borg & Beck assembly.

GEAR RATIOS

	Gearbox		Overall	
	4 Speed O/d	5 Speed	4 Speed O/d	5 Speed
First	2.536:1	2.536:1	10.144:1	10.144:1
Second	1.771:1	1.771:1	7.084:1	7.084:1
Third	1.256:1	1.256:1	5.024:1	5.024:1
Fourth	1.000:1	1.000:1	4.000:1	4.000:1
Fifth[1]	0.778:1	0.796:1	3.112:1	3.184:1
Reverse	3.218:1	3.218:1	12.872:1	12.872:1
Final drive	4.000:1 (8:32)		4.000:1 (8:32)	

[1] Overdrive on series I cars

Electrical Equipment & Lights

The electrical system is 12-volt, served from a 60amp/hour battery sited in the rear corner of the engine bay on the opposite side to the driver, with the fuse and relay board on the firewall adjacent to it. A Marelli GCA-101/B alternator is mounted on the front of the engine and driven by a vee-belt off the crankshaft pulley that also serves the water pump. On both models the starter motor is mounted on the lower right section of the flywheel bellhousing, integral with its solenoid suspended below it. Twin air horns, mounted in the nose forward of the radiator, are actuated by the horn push in the centre of the steering wheel. The overdrive unit on early cars is manufactured by Bianchi and fitted with a Lucas 7615F actuating solenoid. Specifications for the major electrical components are provided in the panel below.

MAJOR ELECTRICAL EQUIPMENT

Battery	12-volt Marelli 6AC11, 60amp/hour
Alternator	Marelli GCA-101/B
Starter motor	Marelli MT21T-1.8/12D9
Ignition	Twin Marelli S85A distributors, each with a Marelli 12v BZR201A coil
Sparking plugs	Marchal HF34F

PRODUCTION

Between 1964 and 1966. Chassis numbers: 05951, 05977, 05979, 05981, 05983, 05985, 05989, 06033, 06039, 06041, 06043, 06049, 06303, 06305, 06307, 06309, 06345[1], 06351[1], 06605, 06615, 06659[1], 06661[1], 06673[1], 06679[1], 07817, 07975, 08019, 08083, 08253, 08273, 08299, 08459[1], 08565, 08739, 08817, 08897[1]. Total production 36.
[1] Denotes right-hand drive.

Rear light arrangement is common to all cars in the series apart from the first, although lens colours vary and the surround panel could be red or orange.

The standard front light arrangement, with the headlight in a shallow recess, the teardrop repeater light on the wing side, and the side/turn indicator light with its semi-circular recess in the quarter bumper.

The engine bay identification plate giving model and engine type, plus chassis number.

The headlamps on early series models are manufactured by Marchal, with later cars in the series having Carello units. Other lighting is all from Carello, throughout the production run. The only market variations were left-hand dipping headlamps for right-hand-drive cars and the provision of yellow headlamp bulbs for France. The headlamps are combined dip/main beam 7in (178mm) diameter units with a chromed trim ring in a deep recess in each front wing, normally without any Perspex cover. Beneath each headlamp is a circular white-lensed sidelamp/indicator unit in the front wing, with a recess in the quarter-bumper top to accommodate it. In the front wing sides are teardrop-shaped orange turn-repeater lamps.

Horizontal combined stop/tail/turn/reversing lamp units, unique to this model, are on the inset tail panel. If the left and right units were butted together, they would replicate the shape of the tail panel at a reduced scale. Within each chrome-rimmed housing are three circular lenses. These normally have a clear red plastic surround, although sometimes the finish is plain chrome. The outer circular lens is an orange turn indicator with a concave face, next to it is the red stop/tail light, also concave, and at the inner end of the assembly is a white reversing light with a circular red reflector in the centre. Number plate

Elegant 7Lx15in Borrani wire wheels with polished aluminium rims were fitted to all 500 Superfasts.

illumination is by two small rectangular lamps in a slim chrome-plated housing, mounted centrally on the lower return edge to the inset tail panel.

Suspension & Steering

The front and rear suspension are virtually identical to the 330 GT 2+2 models (see page 57), as is the steering system and turning circle. The independent front suspension with unequal length upper and lower wishbones is joined by the hub carrier at the outer end and mounted to the chassis via rubber bushes at the inner end, with a coil spring between the wishbones. A telescopic damper is mounted between the top wishbone and a chassis bracket, and there is an anti-roll bar.

Rear suspension is by semi-elliptic leaf springs attached to a bracket on the half-shaft tube at the lower end and a chassis bracket at the upper end, with twin parallel radius arms to each side of the axle to prevent longitudinal movement. Supplementary coil springs have the hydraulic dampers mounted co-axially within them. Worm and roller steering is unassisted and was available in either left- or right-hand drive. The steering box is mounted on the front cross-member.

SUSPENSION SETTINGS

Front toe-in	0 to +1.5mm (0 to +0.059in)
Front camber	+0°40' to +1°10'
Rear toe-in	None
Rear camber	0°
Castor angle	2°30'
Dampers: front	Koni 82H/1321
rear	Koni 82R/1322

Brakes

Dunlop disc brakes are provided to all four wheels and the system is virtually identical to that fitted to the 330 GT 2+2 (see page 58) and underwent the same production changes, which mainly related to the number and type of brake servos.

Wheels & Tyres

Standard equipment is Borrani wire wheels with chrome-plated spokes and polished aluminium 7Lx15in rims with 205-15in tyres. The splined hubs have a triple-eared centre nut. The spare wheel is mounted horizontally in a well, under a removable panel in the boot floor.

WHEELS & TYRES

Wheels, front & rear	7Lx15in Borrani wire wheels with light alloy rims, type RW3812.
Tyres, front & rear	Pirelli HS 205-15in or 210-15in

Chapter 2

365 California

The 365 California was the last of Ferrari's exclusive limited-production models and was unveiled at the 1966 Geneva Salon, with production running through to the middle of 1967, during which time only 14 examples were produced. It was also the only one of this long-running family, which included the 375 America, 410 and 400 Superamericas and the Superfast series, to be manufactured solely in spider form. Actually the term 'spider' is something of an anomaly, as it is in reality a cabriolet with a proper folding soft-top. However, the word has been common practice at Ferrari since the introduction of the 250 GT California spider in 1958 – even the targa-roofed V8 models have been given the letter 'S' for spider in their model type designation – and still continues.

The original prototype, chassis number 08347, was constructed on a standard type 571 chassis as used for the 330 GT 2+2 and is believed to have been built originally with a 4-litre 330 GT engine. It is possible that the first three cars in the series were fitted originally with 4-litre engines but given 4.4-litre type 217B units prior to sale. Cer-

tainly a report by Jonathan Thompson, in the November 1966 issue of the American magazine *Road & Track*, relating to the car displayed at the 1966 Geneva Salon stated that it had a 4-litre engine. The chassis, as with that of the preceding 500 Superfast, was based on the 330 GT 2+2.

While the 500 Superfast had been a pure two-seater, the 365 California provided nominal 2+2 accommodation, despite having a folding soft-top, thus becoming the first series-production open 2+2 Ferrari. Of the 14 cars built, 12 were left-hand drive and two were right-hand drive. At the time of writing, over 30 years later, one of the latter is still in the hands of its first owner – it must be quite a special car! As with the 500 Superfast, the bodies were constructed by Pininfarina in Turin, prior to shipment to Ferrari for fitment of the mechanical components. Similarly no specific owner's handbook or parts manual were produced for this model. The dealer spare parts departments had to refer both to the engine and electrical chapters of the 365 GT 2+2 manual and the gearbox and chassis sections of the 330 GT 2+2 manual.

A British-registered left-hand-drive example, chassis number 09615, with the top down. The styling scallop through the door and rear wing incorporates the door handle within the central chrome strip.

Body & Chassis

DIMENSIONS & WEIGHT		
	mm	in
Overall length	4900	192.91
Overall width	1780	70.08
Overall height	1330	52.36
Wheelbase	2650	104.33
Front track	1405	55.31
Rear track	1397	55.00
Weight (dry)	1320kg	2910lb

The 365 California chassis, type 598 (except for prototype 08347), has a 2650mm (104.33in) wheelbase and is essentially that of the 330 GT 2+2 model. There are small modifications to the engine mounts for the larger engine and to the body pick-up attachments because of the different body style. From a large shallow U-section front cross-member, the two main longitudinal oval steel tubes of the frame run either side of the engine, under the cabin and rise in an arc over the rear axle. A longitudinal and lateral square-section tubular frame is attached to the two main oval tubes beneath the cabin and to the body support frame, to which the bodyshell is welded. The standard chassis finish is satin black paint.

As noted, the 365 California was only ever produced in open form, with the body shape forward of the windscreen very similar to that of the Superfast model but with Perspex-covered headlamps as standard and pop-up driving lights

Two views of 365 California chassis number 10077, resplendant in lustrous deep metallic red, with appropriate California license plate. The curves at the front of the car contrast with the angular tail treatment. This example has a Ferrari script badge fitted to the tail panel.

in the nose panel. However, from the screen rearward there are few similarities apart from accessories such as the quarter-bumpers and triple rear lamp assemblies. The deep arrowhead-shaped scallops on the doors feature a central chrome-plated strip into which the door handle is crafted. These scallops are purely a styling feature on the 365, but they appeared later on the mid-engined Dino and 308/328 series to provide air to the intake system and oil cooler. The smooth curves at the front of the car dissolve into an angular Kamm tail treatment through the rear wings. The body is constructed of welded steel panels, with aluminium bonnet and boot lid on steel frames.

The convertible roof is heavyweight canvas, with a clear Perspex rectangular panel in the rear, on a manually-operated folding steel frame. It is secured to the screen rail by two over-centre fasteners when closed and in its folded position occupies a recess behind the rear seats, where it is protected by a vinyl cover retained by press-studs. Chassis 10369 originally had a standard top, but was later fitted with a powered top at the factory.

Body Trim & Fittings

The front of the 365 California features a shallow elliptical radiator opening with a polished aluminium surround and an inset aluminium egg-crate grille carrying a *Cavallino Rampante* at its centre. Chrome-plated steel wrap-around quarter-bumpers run into the extremities of the radiator grille, with white-lensed rectangular side/turn lights in chrome-plated cases mounted on the lower forward edge. At the rear, two wrap-around quarter-bumpers are fitted, with the number plate lamps mounted in their inner ends. The original Pininfarina show car, which featured in press release photographs, had vertical rectangular number plate lights either side of the number

plate carrier and no turn indicator repeaters on the front wing sides. A rectangular enamel Ferrari badge is fitted on the upper nose panel between the grille and leading edge of the bonnet, while slim horizontal rectangular Pininfarina badges, with Pininfarina enamel shield badges above them, are fitted to the lower sides of the front wings. The badging on the boot lid varies; some examples have no badges, others have a chrome *Cavallino Rampante* with 'California' in script below it, and others a central Ferrari script badge at the rear of the lid. Further brightwork is confined to the chrome-plated front screen surround, window frames, door scallop centre trim incorporating door handle (with circular keylock on the panel below), screen wiper arms and blade frames, and two jacking-point plugs in each sill.

The plain bonnet has a shallow central bulge from front to rear to clear the air filter housing below it, and is forward-hinged with a manually-positioned sprung support on the left.

Low rear three-quarter angle of chassis number 09615 shows how the curves from the front wings flow into the angular tail – a portent of things to come in a more conservative manner on the 365 GT 2+2. The altered tail treatment of chassis number 08631 after its 1970s factory rebuild shows triple circular rear lights, central rectangular reversing light, and full-width rear bumper with number plate light in a chrome-plated housing.

A detail view of the cabin section with erect soft-top, also showing the door handle section of the scallop trim strip.

Interior Trim & Fittings

The standard seat upholstery is full Connolly leather and the range of colours available is shown in the table on page 33 in the *275 GT Berlinetta* chapter. The front seats are mounted on runners with adjustment via a lever under the front edge of the cushion, while a knob on the outer lower edge of the seat base alters the squab's rake. Elasticated map pockets are provided in the rear of the front seats. The door pulls are incorporated in the armrests, with an elliptical chrome-plated opening lever and escutcheon plate in the door panel above it. The electric window switches are either side of the cigar lighter on the centre console, at the forward end of the glove tray. The base of the door trim is fitted with a polished aluminium kick strip, as is the sill panel shut face.

The front seats tilt forwards for access to the rear. Although the doors are wide, entrance and exit are made easier by moving the seats forwards on their runners. The individual rear seats on either side of the transmission tunnel are joined by a shared backrest; a central rear armrest has a chromed ashtray on its top face, over the tunnel.

The floor is carpeted, with black rubber heel-mats for both driver and passenger. The range of carpet colours is provided in the table on page 32 in the *275 GT Berlinetta* chapter. The lower centre console, rear inner wheelarches and door panels are trimmed in leather and vinyl to match the seat colour. There is black vinyl on the facia top, bottom roll, upper centre console, centre firewall, armrest and door cappings as standard, although customers could deviate from this specification.

Padded, vinyl-covered sun visors were provided, with a vanity mirror on the passenger's side.

Plain glass is fitted and the windscreen is laminated. The two-speed self-parking wipers normally park on the right on left-hand-drive cars and on the left on right-hand-drive examples. The door windows are provided with swivelling quarterlights operated by a black plastic knurled knob on the inner door panel.

Paintwork

A vast range of colours was available for Ferraris at this time and the comments made in the *275 GT Berlinetta* chapter also apply to the 365 California. Being built by Pininfarina, it should have a paint colour from either the PPG or Duco ranges. The table on page 30 in the *275 GT Berlinetta* chapter lists the full range of colours available for the 365 California.

The cabin, seen on chassis number 09615, showing the general layout, including rear seats with a degree of legroom. This example originally had a veneer dashboard, but in recent years has been retrimmed in black to match the upholstery.

Between them was a dipping rear-view mirror mounted on the upper screen rail. Two interior lights are fitted under the facia high on the outer walls of the footwells, and operated automatically by door switches or manually via a facia switch.

The chrome gear lever, topped by a black plastic knob with a leather boot in either black or upholstery colour, is central on the transmission tunnel. To the rear of this is a chrome-lidded ashtray, with the electric window switches and cigar lighter on the front edge of the glove tray behind it. The handbrake is in an upholstery-coloured vinyl gaiter and projects from the floor alongside the front of the transmission tunnel.

Facia & Instruments

The facia and forward section of the centre console form a single area with a standard teak veneer finish, which extends along the base of the console to the glove tray, although customers could specify an alternative finish. The main instruments are mounted in two large pods and three small ones, which have a black vinyl finish to match the top of the facia, into which they are integrated. There are slim demister slots at the base the windscreen. A lockable glove compartment, with a push-button catch and a rectangular Pininfarina badge on its face, is provided on the passenger's side and is fitted with an interior light.

The wood-rim steering wheel has aluminium spokes with an engraved pattern and an aluminium boss. The yellow central horn push has a black plastic rim and features the *Cavallino Rampante* emblem. Two slender chrome-plated stalks,

A detail of the folded soft-top mechanism, the chromed bars providing the effect of a piece of art deco sculpture. Boot and fuel filler release levers are located in the trim panel below.

with black plastic finger pads, project from the left of the steering column; the shorter one controls the indicators and the longer one headlamp dipping and flashing. A stalk on the right operates the two-speed windscreen wipers, and the washers by pulling it towards the driver. The key-operated ignition/starter switch, incorporating a steering lock, is on the lower facia to the right of the steering column shroud.

The dashboard of chassis number 10077, with highly polished teak veneer finish complementing the wooden rim of the elegant Nardi three-spoke steering wheel. The three central auxiliary dials in the pods on the dashboard top edge are angled towards the driver.

Immediately in front of the driver are two large pods housing the speedometer and rev counter. The speedometer incorporates an odometer and trip recorder, with warning lights for turn indicators and sidelamps. The rev counter dial contains warning lights for choke, main beam and the electric fuel pump. The instrument lighting rheostat and trip recorder reset knobs are positioned on the facia between the two main dials. In the top centre of the main facia panel is a bank of three smaller auxiliary dial pods for oil temperature, oil pressure and water temperature. Below them is a radio, with an ammeter to one side and the petrol gauge, with low-fuel warning light, on the other. All gauges have white digits on a black background.

The main bank of five switches, with circular black plastic levers, is in a raised section of the centre console below the radio. These switches control the lights, electric fuel pump, left and right blower fans and interior lights. Below the switches are two circular vents with knurled central control knobs. At each extremity of the facia is a vertical sliding lever, which channels air to either the windscreen demister slot or footwell for that side of the car; a matching lever on the facia alongside the inner edge of the glovebox controls the heater output. The choke knob is on the facia between the steering column and door pillar, with the bonnet release lever sited below the facia on the driver's side near the door post.

Luggage Compartment

The boot contains the twin aluminium fuel tanks, spray-coated with glass-fibre, mounted in the floor and wings to form the sides to the spare wheel well; a balance pipe connects the two tanks. Fuel capacity is 112 litres (24.6 Imperial/29.5 US gallons). The fuel filler is beneath a flap on the left rear wing, irrespective of whether the car is right- or left-hand drive, and is released by a lever in the left-side rear trim panel, with an emergency release in the boot. The spare wheel is fixed flat in a well in the boot floor; the well also contains the tool roll and is covered with a black-painted plywood panel. The boot floor and sides are lined with black carpet and all plain metal surfaces are painted satin black. Access to the boot is via a lockable lever alongside the fuel filler release. The boot lid is supported by a manually positioned sprung support rod on the left side.

Engine

The 4390cc (267.9cu in) 60° V12 engine is a wet-sump unit with a single overhead camshaft per bank and two mounting points. The bore and stroke are 81x71mm (3.19x2.79in) and the power output is a factory-quoted 320bhp (DIN) at

ENGINE

Type	60° V12
Type number	217B
Cubic capacity	4390cc (267.9cu in)
Bore and stroke	81x71mm (3.19x2.79in)
Compression ratio	8.8:1
Maximum power	320bhp (DIN) at 6600rpm
Maximum torque	37kgm (267lb ft) at 5000rpm
Carburettors	3 Weber 40DFI/4

TIMING DATA

Inlet valves open	13°15' BTDC
Inlet valves close	59° ABDC
Exhaust valves open	59° BBDC
Exhaust valves close	13°15' ATDC
Firing order	1-7-5-11-3-9-6-12-2-8-4-10

Valve clearances with a cold engine should be 0.2mm (0.0079in) for inlets and 0.25mm (0.0098in) for exhausts, measured between the valve pads and rocker arms.

SYSTEM CAPACITIES

Fuel tank	112 litres (24.6 Imperial/29.5 US gallons)		
	Litres	**Imp Pints**	**US Pints**
Cooling System	13.0	22.9	27.5
Washer bottle	1.0	1.8	2.1
Engine oil	10.75	18.9	22.7
Gearbox oil	5.0	8.8	10.6
Differential oil	2.5	4.4	5.3

The 4390cc engine is dominated by the large central air filter box, with the twin oil filters forward of it, and the brake and clutch fluid reservoirs plus brake booster visible in the rear corner of the bay.

6600rpm, with maximum torque of 37kgm (267lb ft) developed at 5000rpm. The engine, factory type number 217B, is a bored-out version of that fitted in the second series 330 GT 2+2 and 330 GTC/S, and construction materials, operation and component layout are generally very similar to these engines.

The triple Weber 40DCI/4 carburettors are fitted on individual manifolds, the rear one with a tapping for the vacuum feed to the brake servo. Fuel is supplied by a Fispa diaphragm mechanical pump, with a Fispa electric booster pump operated by a facia switch. The twin 12-volt Marelli S85A distributors are of the 15° type, each with a Marelli 12v BZR201A coil. The water pump has a by-pass valve to maintain a constant system pressure and is driven by the triplex timing chain. A three-blade fan in front of the radiator is electrically driven and thermostatically controlled.

Each bank of cylinders has a pair of triple-branch free-flow steel manifolds, with a heat shield fitted above them. The manifolds are flanged to twin collector pipes that siamese into one large-bore pipe for each bank. Each pipe then feeds into its own silencer box assembly, suspended below the cabin floor, from which twin pipes exit. These loop to clear the rear suspension and emerge as a pair of chrome-plated tailpipes on either side, suspended from rubber hangers.

The standard air filter box is of black-painted pressed steel, with the top panel retained by three knurled nuts. Within the casing, which is rectangular with curved ends, are three separate circular elements, one around each carburettor intake. Air is drawn into the box via a pair of rectangular nozzles, which protrude over the cam covers on each side of the casing.

The normal oil pressure with an oil temperature of 100°C should be 5.5kg/cm^2 (78psi) at 6500rpm, with a minimum value of 4kg/cm^2 (57psi) under the same conditions. The minimum slow running pressure (at 700-800rpm) should be 1.0-1.5kg/cm^2 (14-21psi).

Transmission

The 365 California is fitted with the same gearbox and transmission arrangement as the second series 330 GT 2+2 models (see page 56). The all-

GEAR RATIOS

	Gearbox	Overall
First	2.536:1	10.778:1
Second	1.77:1	7.522:1
Third	1.256:1	5.338:1
Fourth	1.000:1	4.250:1
Fifth	0.796:1	3.383:1
Reverse	3.218:1	13.676:1
Final drive		4.250:1 (8:34)

synchromesh five-speed gearbox is located conventionally and connected by a propshaft to the live rear axle with limited slip differential. The gearbox and final drive ratios are also identical on both models, as is the hydraulically-operated Borg & Beck clutch.

Electrical Equipment & Lights

The electrical system is 12-volt, served from a 60amp/hour battery, which is sited in the rear corner of the engine bay on the opposite side to the driver. A Marelli GCA-101/B alternator is mounted on the front of the engine and driven by a vee-belt off the crankshaft pulley. The starter motor is mounted on the lower right section of the flywheel bellhousing, integral with its solenoid suspended below it. Twin air horns, mounted in the nose forward of the radiator, are actuated by the horn push in the centre of the steering wheel. Specifications for the major electrical components are given in the panel on the next page.

The lighting equipment, all of Carello manufacture, remained constant throughout the production run, although there are a number of detail variations to the rear light assemblies. Left-hand dipping headlamps are provided for right-hand-drive cars, but no cars were sold new in France, so the question of yellow headlamp bulbs does not arise. The headlamps are single 7in (178mm) diameter combined dip/main beam units in a deep recess in each front wing. They are fitted with Perspex covers, normally without any trim ring, and retained by three chrome-plated screws. Retractable driving lights are provided beneath body-coloured circular panels on most examples, but chassis 10327 had them omitted by the first owner and chassis 09631 lost them when a new nose was fitted during a factory restoration in the late 1970s. Beneath each front quarter-bumper is a rectangular white-lensed side/turn indicator lamp in a chrome-plated body. Apart from the original Pininfarina show car (chassis 08347), teardrop-shaped orange turn indicator lights are fitted in the front wing sides virtually in line with the headlamp centre.

The standard front light arrangement, with head-lamp under a clear plastic cover, rectangular side/turn indicator light below the quarter bumper, and retractable driving light beneath the circular panel in the top of the nose.

Variations on the rear light theme: colours of lenses and surrounds vary to a surprising degree for such a small-scale production run.

Major Electrical Equipment

Battery	12-volt SAFA 65SNS, 74amp/hour
Alternator	Marelli 50.35.014.1
Starter motor	Marelli MT21T-1.8/12D9
Ignition	Twin 12v Marelli S85A 15° distributors, each with a 12v Marelli BZR201/A 15° coil
Sparking plugs	Champion N6Y

Suspension Settings

Front toe-out	0 to +1.5mm (0.059in)
Front camber	1° (fixed)
Rear toe-in	None
Rear camber	0°
Castor angle	2°30′
Dampers: front	Koni 82H1321
rear	Koni 82N1322

At the rear there is a pair of combined stop/tail/turn/reversing light units on the inset tail panel; these have the same circular lenses as the 500 Superfast. The outline of these light units follows the shape of the extremities of the tail panel, with a horizontal split. There is a reflector in the top half and three circular light units in the bottom half. There are a number of variations on the reflector and lens surround colours: a white reflector with chrome lens surround, a combined red/orange reflector with a red lens surround, a red reflector with a red surround, or an orange reflector with a red surround. The Pininfarina show car originally had flat lenses but was fitted with a triple circular arrangement before being sold. Chassis 09631, the one restored at the factory in the late 1970s, had three larger circular units, which appear to be from the 365 GT4 2+2, fitted directly onto the tail panel. The 'standard' original arrangement is a concave outer orange turn indicator, next to which is the concave red stop/tail light, with a white reversing light at the inner end of the assembly, in the centre of which is a circular red reflector. The number plate illumination lamps are mounted in the inner ends of the rear quarter-bumpers – except for the Pininfarina show car, which had vertically-mounted chromed rectangular units on either side of the number plate support bracket.

Suspension & Steering

Front and rear suspension systems are virtually identical to those of the 330 GT 2+2 models (see page 57), as are the steering system and turning circle, except that hydraulic power-assisted steering was standard on the 365 California. The independent front suspension uses unequal length upper and lower wishbones, joined by the hub carrier at the outer end and mounted to the chassis via rubber bushes at the inner end, with a coil spring between the wishbones. A telescopic damper is mounted between the top wishbone and a chassis bracket, and there is an anti-roll bar.

The rear suspension is by semi-elliptic leaf springs attached to a bracket on the half-shaft tube at the lower end and a chassis bracket at the upper end, with twin parallel radius arms to each side of the axle to prevent longitudinal movement. Supplementary coil springs have hydraulic dampers mounted co-axially within them. Left- or right-hand drive was available despite the very limited production run, but only two right-hand-drive cars were built.

Brakes

As with the 330 GT 2+2 models, Dunlop disc brakes are provided to all four wheels. The system is virtually identical to that fitted to the second series models, with a Dunlop vacuum servo.

Wheels & Tyres

Standard equipment is Borrani wire wheels with chrome-plated spokes and polished aluminium 7Lx15in rims with 205-15in tyres. The splined hubs have a triple-eared centre nut. The spare wheel is mounted horizontally in a well, under a removable panel in the boot floor.

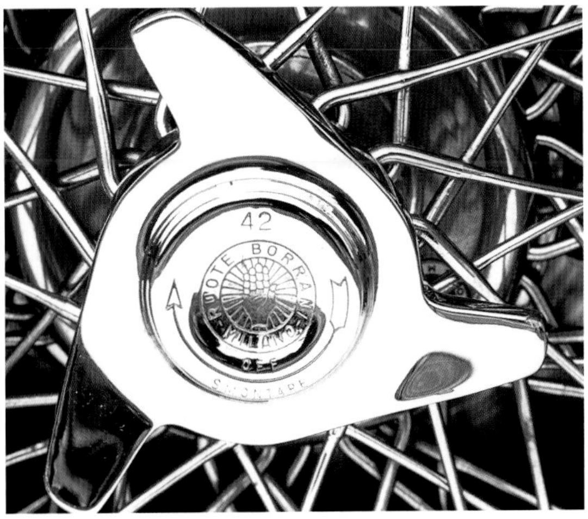

The triple-ear hub nut, here with Borrani 'hand' logo, common to the series.

Wheels & Tyres

Wheels, front & rear	7Lx15in Borrani wire wheels with alloy rims, type RW3812
Tyres, front & rear	Dunlop 205-15in or Pirelli 210HR-15in

The engine bay identification plate giving model and engine type, plus chassis number, with lubrication plate alongside.

Production

During 1966 and 1967. Chassis numbers: 08347, 09127, 09447, 09615, 09631, 09801, 09849, 09889, 09935, 09985, 10077, 10105, 10327, 10369. Only two cars (09985 and 10369) were right-hand drive. Total production 14.

Identification & Colours

For Identification Plates, Body Colours, Leather Upholstery Colours and Carpet Colours see the tables in the *275 GT Berlinetta* chapter.

Factory Literature

1967
The 1967 model range brochure contains two pages on the 365 California with photograph and specifications in Italian/French/English; factory reference 11/66.

Chapter 3

275 GT Berlinetta

The 275 GTB was the direct replacement for the 250 GT Lusso berlinetta in the Ferrari range and was introduced at the 1964 Paris Salon together with the open version, the 275 GTS. The first prototype, built on chassis 05161GT in 1963, was fitted with a 250 GT engine and so really should be called a 250 GTB. The overall shape had a strong family resemblance to the 250 GTO, although the front was more blunt and the curves fuller, and as a road car it was much better equipped. This was the first Ferrari road car to feature independent rear suspension, a five-speed transaxle and cast aluminium wheels, although the Borrani wire wheels that had been *de rigueur* over the years were still available as an option.

The standard bodyshell was steel, with aluminium bonnet, boot and door panels, but for almost all of the production run an all-aluminium body was optional. Some cars have been partly or wholly rebodied in non-original material, making proof of a particular car's provenance a minefield for these models. Apart from the few competition 365 GTB/4s, this problem does not occur with the other series production models of the period. As with all series production V12 Ferraris of the time, the body was designed by Pininfarina and, apart from the prototypes, was constructed at the Scaglietti works in Modena.

The short nose was found to create front-end lift at high speed, so a revised model was displayed at the 1965 Paris Salon. It featured a longer and slimmer nose panel that is even more evocative of the 250 GTO. At the same time the rear window was enlarged and the boot lid hinges became external chrome-plated parts. A small series of competition cars was built for private customers between 1964 and 1966; details can be found in the *Competition Derivatives* chapter.

A year later, again at the Paris Salon, the original 3.3-litre two-camshaft engine was succeeded by a four-camshaft version and the model designation became 275 GTB/4A, this being the first Ferrari road car to have a four-camshaft engine. Visually, the only body difference was a central bulge on the bonnet of the four-camshaft version, although some owners of two-camshaft models have subsequently added this feature for aesthetic reasons. It has become common practice to refer to a two-camshaft car as a 275 GTB/2 to differentiate between the two models but this is not an official designation, purely a latter-day convenience. The 'A' in the 275 GTB/4A model title stood for *Alberi Distribuzione*, Italian for camshaft, but was soon dropped and factory literature refers to the model purely as a 275 GTB/4.

In February 1967 a spider version of the 275

A 'short-nose' two-cam 275 GTB in silver, a colour that suits the full curves of the 275 Berlinettas. This example features the standard 'starburst' alloy wheels that were unique to this model.

DIMENSIONS & WEIGHTS

	275 GTB ('short-nose')		275 GTB ('long-nose')		275 GTB/4 ('long-nose')	
	mm	in	mm	in	mm	in
Overall length	4325	170.28	4410	173.62	4410	173.62
Overall width	1725	67.91	1725	67.91	1725	67.91
Overall height	1200	47.24	1200	47.24	1200	47.24
Wheelbase	2400	94.49	2400	94.49	2400	94.49
Front track						
6½ x14in rim	1377[1]	54.21	1401	55.16	1401	55.16
7x14in rim	1409	55.47	1409	55.47	1409	55.47
7x15in rim	1377	54.21	1377	54.21	1377	54.21
Rear track						
6½x14in rim	1393[1]	54.84	1417	55.79	1417	55.79
7x14in, 7x15in, or						
7½x15in rims	1426	56.14	1426	56.14	1426	56.14
Weight (dry)	1100kg	2425lb	1100kg	2425lb	1100kg	2425lb

[1] As 'long-nose' 275 GTB if second type of aluminium wheels fitted

A 'short-nose' 275 GTB wearing optional Borrani wire wheels. The bonnet has the wide central raised section normally found on two-cam cars with the optional six-carburettor set-up.

GTB/4 was announced. It was constructed at the behest of the American importer, Luigi Chinetti, and was called the 275 GTS/4 NART Spider. This model is included here, rather than with the 275 GTS models, as it has nothing in common with that car but uses the mechanicals of the 275 GTB/4, and is basically a soft-top version of that model. In fact, some factory invoices for the model listed a charge for conversion from berlinetta to spider. Ten examples were constructed during 1967 and early 1968. One of these, chassis 09437, was raced in the 1967 Sebring 12 Hours by Denise McCluggage and Pinkie Rollo,

coming 17th overall and second in class. It was road tested by *Road & Track* magazine and also appeared in the film *The Thomas Crown Affair*, featuring Steve McQueen and Faye Dunaway. Steve McQueen was a car fanatic and, after his affair with the 275 GTS/4 NART Spider in the film, he bought one (chassis 10249) for his personal use. Over the years the 275 GTS/4 NART Spider has become one of the most sought-after, and valuable, of the Ferrari road cars. All were originally destined for the USA, but the final example built, chassis 11057, resided in Europe from new until quite recently, when it too crossed the Atlantic. Like the berlinetta, the spider was constructed at the Scaglietti works in Modena.

Production of the 275 GTB/4 ceased in 1968, with a total of 330 cars built. It was replaced by the 4.4-litre 365 GTB/4, the early prototypes of which had a very 275 GTB-like nose profile.

Body & Chassis

Chassis construction of the 275 GTB, which had a 2400mm (94.49in) wheelbase, followed familiar Ferrari practice. There were two longitudinal oval steel tubes, joined by a large rectangular front cross-member and with a smaller section tubular front bulkhead to support the firewall, steering column, pedal box and facia. Central cross-bracing under the cabin floor and outriggers to

An identifying feature of a 'short-nose' 275 GTB is the absence of external boot hinges.

A 'long-nose' two-cam 275 GTB fitted with optional Borrani wire wheels. Two-cam cars with the standard three-carburettor set-up have a completely flat bonnet.

support the body sides were developed directly from those used on preceding 250 GT berlinettas. To this main structure was welded a series of small cross-section circular and square steel tubes, to provide what might best be described as a space-frame to support and secure the body panels.

This new chassis, type 563, differed from those of the 250 GT series in that the main longitudinal tubes tapered inwards towards the rear to support the transaxle and to provide pick-up points for the independent rear suspension – two features not previously seen on a roadgoing

Ferrari. With this chassis the engine had four mounting points, one either side of the flywheel housing and one on each side of the block virtually in line with the second bank of cylinders (from the front of the engine). The transaxle had three mounting points, one on either side at the lower front and one on top of the casing at the centre rear.

In early 1966 the chassis was modified to become the type 563/66, the reason being a change in the driveline to eliminate alignment problems between the engine and transaxle. This

Views of a four-cam car illustrate the lines – beautifully balanced with a touch of aggression – that make the 275 GTB one of Pininfarina's classic design triumphs. The front view shows the only body difference between 'long-nose' two-cam and four-cam models – the slim central bonnet bulge of the four-cam model. In the rear view the external boot hinges are apparent.

alignment has to be very precise as the driveshaft runs at engine speed. The answer was to mount the engine and transaxle on more compliant mountings and to attach one to the other with a rigid torque tube, thus making them virtually one unit. The engine block and transaxle casing castings were modified to provide a pair of support points on each. Those on the engine were almost central on each side of the block and those on the transaxle also moved to a central position on the lower sides of the casing. The same configuration continued for the 275 GTB/4 without further

modification, although the chassis type number changed to 596. Thus the major differences between the early and late types of chassis are the location and number of engine/transaxle mounting points – seven and four respectively. The paint finish of either type of chassis is satin black, as used in the engine bay and boot.

The family resemblance to the body style of the 250 GTO can be seen clearly, with the general overall shape of the 1962 model integrated with the 1964 version's deeply-curved windscreen profile. Pininfarina had refined the shape created

One of the rarest and most sought-after of all Ferrari road cars is the 275 GTS/4 NART Spider, of which only ten examples were built. From the windscreen forward it is identical to the Berlinetta, and, as can be seen, the balance of line is not lost.

Even with the soft-top in place the lines are very tight and graceful. The flat boot lid features exposed hinges and this example, chassis number 10621, is fitted with optional Borrani wire wheels.

by the factory racing department and its own 1964 interpretation into a habitable street model. Its powerful, aggressive curves emulated the lines of the most successful GT racing car of all time.

The first series of cars with the two-camshaft engine had what is called today the short nose, which has a deep radiator intake with quarter-bumpers mounted just below the lower corners. Other identifying features of this model are the size of the rear screen, internal boot hinges and the rain channel above the doors finishing at the rear corner of the glass. Depending upon the number of carburettors (three or six) and the type of air filter fitted, the front-hinged bonnet on two-camshaft cars was either flat or had a wide shallow raised section, deepening towards the rear edge.

The 'long-nose' version, with its shallower and more elliptical radiator opening, was introduced in late 1965. Its slimmer quarter-bumpers ran into the extremities of the radiator opening, the rear screen was larger, external boot hinges were used and the rain channel above the doors extended into the rear quarter panel.

Thus there are both 'short-nose' and 'long-

nose' two-camshaft models on the type 563 chassis, 'long-nose' two-camshaft models on the type 563/66 chassis and 275 GTB/4s on the type 596 chassis. The second 'long-nose' body config-uration was carried through into the 275 GTB/4 model, the only differentiating feature being the provision of a long central bonnet bulge to clear the carburettor air cleaner.

The standard body construction for all models was welded steel panels, with aluminium doors, bonnet and boot lid on steel frames, although an all-aluminium body was available. All-aluminium cars retained steel inner and outer sill panels, to which the aluminium body was fastened with solid rivets. Other parts of the aluminium panels were fixed to the steel support frame by the same method. To permit flexing, the aluminium bodies had joint lines at the top and bottom of the screen pillars, between the rear quarter panel and roof and at the sill joint. The original double-skinned pressed steel floor panels with glass-fibre quilt infill were replaced around the middle of 1965 with glass-fibre mouldings, together with the fire-wall incorporating the pedal boxes.

The exposed boot hinge found on all 'long-nose' models.

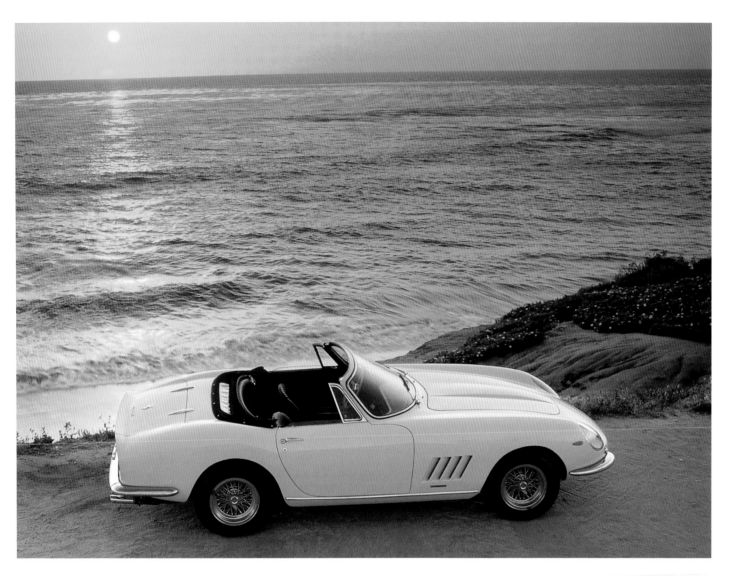

This 275 GTS/4 NART Spider, chassis number 09437, is the first car built. It raced in the Sebring 12 Hours in 1967, but is seen here with the top down in the quieter setting of the California coastline. Note the enamel NART badge on the tail panel.

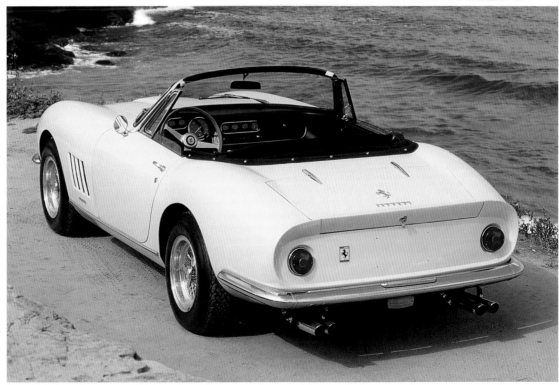

A number of 'short-nose' models have been rebodied to 'long-nose' configuration; some are period changes, perhaps after an accident, and others more recent alterations desired by the owners. Similarly, some two-camshaft models have been fitted with 'four-camshaft' bonnets and both two- and four-camshaft examples have been decapitated to replicate 275 GTS/4 NART Spiders. Only ten examples of this version were produced, thus making it extremely rare and desirable. It is built on the same 596 chassis and uses the same construction materials as the berlinettas, but has a folding canvas soft-top and a different boot profile.

Body Trim & Fittings

Adornment of the lines of the body is minimal on all models in the series. The two-camshaft 'short-nose' cars feature a relatively deep, almost rectangular, radiator opening with rounded corners angled forwards towards the top edge. The opening has a slim aluminium surround and a slightly recessed aluminium egg-crate grille with a chromed *Cavallino Rampante* mounted in the centre. The 'long-nose' examples have a more pronounced roll-over curve to a shallower, more elliptical grille opening. The deeply-recessed egg-crate grille carries no emblem. On both 'long-nose' and 'short-nose' examples, an enamel Ferrari badge is fitted in a shallow recess on the upper nose panel, roughly midway between the nose and the leading edge of the bonnet. There is a rectangular Pininfarina badge on each front wing side below the line of the four louvres, and a Ferrari script badge on the tail panel above the number plate on 'short-nose' models. The script badge is on the boot lid of 'long-nose' cars, sometimes surmounted by a chrome-plated *Cavallino Rampante*.

The steel front quarter-bumpers are chrome-plated. These are deep bumpers that finish at the lower corner of the grille on the 'short-nose' cars and slim bumpers running into the grille extremities on 'long-nose' cars. The steel rear bumper is a three-piece chrome-plated item, which wraps around the rear wings almost to the trailing edges of the rear wheelarches. A triangular aluminium strip, mounted on the upper sill section immediately below the door, adorns the body between the front and rear wheelarches. Further brightwork is confined to the chrome-plated front and rear screen surrounds, rain channel cover strip, headlamp cover surrounds, door glass frames, screen wiper arms and blade frames, boot push-button lock (on the rear lip of the lid) and door handles with push-buttons in the trailing end. These contain the keylock in the push-button on early cars, but by the time the 'long-nose' examples appeared a chrome-plated circular keylock in the door panel (below the push-button) had been substituted. The 'long-nose' examples also feature chrome-plated cast zinc external boot hinges, which are not aesthetically pleasing but do release more luggage space.

Three vertical louvres on the rear quarter panels, matching the profile of the four on the front wing but in a smaller size, provide cockpit air extraction via a sliding panel on the inner face. Obviously the 275 GTS/4 Spider does not have these louvres. Its soft-top features a rectangular clear plastic panel in the rear face and is retained by two over-centre catches on the screen rail. The standard fuel filler location is within the boot, but customers could opt for an aluminium quick-release filler inset into the rear wing. Some examples have had this option added at a later date as, apart from giving more of a racing appearance, it stops fuel being spilled in the boot if somebody is careless while refuelling.

Plain glass is fitted all round and the windscreen is laminated. The self-parking two-speed wipers normally park on the left for left-hand drive and on the right for right-hand drive, but there seem to be exceptions. The door windows are provided with swivelling quarterlights with a chrome-plated retaining catch at the front lower edge. In April 1966 a heated rear window, controlled by a facia switch, became standard.

PAINT COLOURS

Amaranto 19.374 lt./20.153
Argento Auteuil 106.E.1
Azzuro La Plata 20.A.167
Azzurro Met 19.278M/
    20.336/1.443.648
Blu 19.343
Blu 20.444
Blu Chiaro 20.295
Blu Chiaro Met 2.443.604
Blu Notte 20.454
Blu Porpora 66.426
Blu Sera 20.264
Blu Sera Met 20.100M/
    106.A.18/2.443.603
Blu Scuro 20.448/95C-6159
Blu Turchese 23.132
Bianco 20.414
Bianco Polo Park l20.W.152
Celeste Met 20.411
Celeste Chiaro 106.A.26
Giallo
Grigio Argento 20.265/
    25.090
Grigio Ferro 106.E.8
Grigio Fumo 20.294
Grigio Notte 106.E.28
Marrone 2.662.378
Nero
Nocciola 20.451
Nocciola Met 106.M.27
Oro Chiaro Met 19.410M
Rosso 19.374
Rosso Chiaro 20.R.190
Rosso Chiaro 20.R.191
Rosso Cina 20.456
Rosso Cordoba Met 106.R.7
Rosso Rubino Met 20.481
Verde 20.449
Verde Pino 20.453/106.G.30

The colours above apply to 500 Superfast, 365 California, 275 GTB, 275 GTB/4 and 275 GTS/4 models. They were also used for the 330 GTC, 330 GTS, 365 GTC and 365 GT 2+2 up to mid-1969. In addition to this range of body colours, customers could order any specific colour to suit their requirements.

The four engine bay exhaust air vents on the front wings have a Pininfarina script badge below them. Their design is replicated by the triple cabin exhaust air louvres on the sail panels. Both features are common to all 275 Berlinettas.

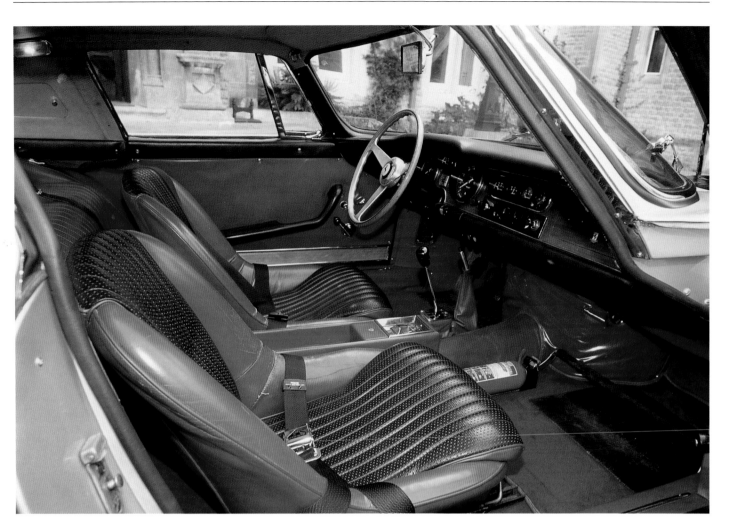

The interior of a 'short-nose' two-cam model, featuring the weave-effect vinyl centre sections to the seat cushions and backrests. The fire extinguisher in the passenger footwell is a modern safety addition, while the Ferrari club badge on the lid of the glovebox and small shield on the centre console have been added by the owner. Door trim design did not change during the production run of the series.

Paintwork

A truly vast range of colours was available for Ferraris at this time and customers could also chose special colours, so it is fair to say that there was no such thing as a standard colour range. Principally, Scaglietti-built cars, such as the 275 GTB series in this chapter, were delivered with paint manufactured by Glidden & Salchi, whereas those built by Pininfarina had paint manufactured by either PPG or Duco, the latter only being in solid (non-metallic) colours. Inevitably there was a crossover to meet specific customer requirements, so one cannot say that a Scaglietti-built example is non-

original if it is finished in a PPG or Duco paint, or equally that a Pininfarina-built car is non-original if it has Glidden & Salchi paint.

The panel on page 30 lists all known colours available during the period in question; where a code number is not listed, this is because the manufacturer did not issue one.

The chassis, engine bay, boot interior, unseen inner surfaces, underwing areas and underside were always painted in a satin black finish.

Interior Trim & Fittings

On the two-cam cars there were four variations available for the upholstery of the bucket seats: cord cloth and vinyl, cord cloth and leather, weave effect vinyl or full leather – the last being the most popular choice. The colour of the cord cloth was normally black, blue, grey or tan, to match the vinyl or leather surrounds. The standard upholstery on the four-cam models was full leather, although cloth could still be specified.

The pair of bucket seats had well-bolstered sides for good lateral support and the centre sections featured ten longitudinally-stitched panels, with a single row of cross-stitching on both the cushion and backrest. Leather was provided by the

British firm of Connolly Bros, long-time suppliers to Ferrari, and the range of colours available is shown in the panel on page 33. The seats were mounted on runners with adjustment via a lever under the front edge of the cushion. There was no height or backrest angle adjustment.

The door pulls incorporated armrests, with a chrome-plated opening lever forward of the pull section and the window winder below it. On four-cam models electric windows became available as an option, with control switches in the centre console behind the ashtray. An emergency window winder was provided, with plugged circular holes in the door trim to insert it. The base of the door trim featured a polished aluminium kick strip, as did the shut face of the sill panel. Adjustable vertical rectangular fresh air ventilation inlets were provided on the outer face of each footwell, drawing air from under the front wings.

The floor and rear parcels shelf were normally carpeted, the footwells incorporating ribbed black rubber heelmats for both driver and passenger, with an additional one on the vertical face of the footwell on the passenger's side. The passenger footwell was also fitted with a footbrace bar with a black covering of ribbed rubber. The range of carpet colours is given in the accompanying table. At the customer's request the carpet could be replaced by a bubble-surfaced black vinyl covering. The centre section of the firewall, transmission tunnel, front and rear inner wheelarches, door panels, facia top and rear bulkhead were trimmed in vinyl as standard. The rear bulkhead

was lightly padded with vertical fluting. The rear shelf on berlinettas had a pair of leather luggage straps with chromed support brackets.

The roof lining was perforated ivory-coloured vinyl, suspended on a sprung steel frame and retained by matching vinyl-covered cant rails. The similarly-covered rear quarter panels incorporated a sliding ventilation flap with a round knob, beneath which was a diamond-mesh grille. Rigid aluminium sun visors, covered with matching ivory vinyl, were provided and the dipping interior mirror was positioned between them. The passenger-side visor incorporated a vanity mirror.

The chrome gear lever with black plastic knob was in an open chrome-plated gate, located to the left of the transmission tunnel on all models, regardless of steering wheel position. Immediately behind the gear lever, but central on the tunnel, was an ashtray with a chrome-plated sliding lid; on the four-cam models it had a red illuminating light on the forward edge. Behind the ashtray were the electric window switches, if fitted, and then an oddments tray. On two-cam cars the tray had a veneered base to match the facia but on four-cam cars it was upholstered in the same material as the surrounding tunnel. The vinyl-gaitered handbrake projected from the floor alongside the front of the transmission tunnel, on the driver's side. Two rectangular interior lights were provided, one on each cant rail to the rear of the door, actuated by door switches or a master switch on the facia. Forward of each interior light was a chrome-plated coat hook.

A full leather interior in a 275 GTB/4, showing the dashboard layout. The differences between this dashboard and that of the two-cam model on page 31 can be seen.

CARPET COLOURS

Beige
Black
Green
Grey
Red

The colours above apply to 500 Superfast, 365 California, 275 GTB, 275 GTB/4 and 275 GTS/4 models. They were also used for the 330 GTC, 330 GTS, 365 GTC and 365 GT 2+2 up to mid-1969. Specific colours to a customer's requirements were also available.

LEATHER COLOURS

Beige VM846
Beige VM3218
Beige VM3309
Black VM8500
Blue VM3015
Blue VM3087
Dark Red VM893
Grey VM3230
Light Blue VM3469
Red VM3171
White VM3323

The colours above apply to
500 Superfast, 365 California,
275 GTB, 275 GTB/4 and 275
GTS/4 models. They were also
used for the 330 GTC, 330
GTS, 365 GTC and 365 GT
2+2 up to mid-1969.
Ferrari used Connolly
leather and the numbers
given above are therefore
Connolly's codes for its
Vaumol leather. This is now
available under the name of
Connolly Classic. As with the
external colours, customers
could order a specific colour
to their requirements.

The main instrument
display, as seen in the
separate binnacle style of
'long-nose' cars.

Facia & Instruments

At a quick glance, the facias of the 'short-nose' and 'long-nose' models appear identical, but they are slightly different. The 'short-nose' model's facia has a one-piece top section trimmed in black vinyl, with a shallow hump over the instruments in front of the steering column. The 'long-nose' model's facia has a separate and deeper main instrument nacelle cut into the facia top, also trimmed in black vinyl, and twin slim demister slots with black plastic surrounds are cut into the facia top close to the windscreen. The 'short-nose' model's facia is teak veneered, whereas that of the 'long-nose' model is trimmed in black vinyl or leather. Along the lower edge, both models have a padded roll covered with black vinyl. While these are the standard specifications, inevitably there are cars that do not conform because of a customer's particular wishes. It is also probable that some early 'long-nose' cars had the old style of facia – there is nothing to confirm categorically when the change in layout took place.

Immediately in front of the driver is the elegant aluminium three-spoked wood-rim steering wheel with aluminium boss. The horn push at its centre bears the *Cavallino Rampante* on a yellow background. Two slender stalks projecting from the left of the steering column control the direction indicators and the headlamp main/dip beam functions on all models. On 'long-nose' models there is an additional stalk on the right of the column to actuate the windscreen wiper speed control, and the washers by pulling it towards the driver. On 'short-nose' models the washers are operated by a floor-mounted push-button switch sited by the driver's footrest, close to the bonnet release catch. The key-operated ignition/starter switch, incorporating a steering lock, is mounted on the lower right of the steering column.

On the 'short-nose' models the speedometer and rev counter are immediately in front of the driver, with a small black plastic binnacle between their upper sections containing oil temperature and pressure gauges. Below this is the horizontal slide-action choke lever. The speedometer incorporates a trip recorder and odometer, together with a green 'lights on' warning lamp and a pair of red direction indicator warning lamps. The rev counter incorporates a further three warning lights: amber to indicate use of the rear demister blower, violet to show that the electric fuel pumps are in operation and blue for headlamp main beam. A further central instrument binnacle on the facia, above a bank of switches, contains a water temperature gauge, ammeter, fuel gauge (with reserve warning light) and clock. All instruments feature black dials with white characters. On the facia to the driver's side of this binnacle are an instrument panel light switch and the sliding heating and ventilation controls. The switch panel below the centre binnacle contains rocker switches for the windscreen wipers, lights, fuel pump, left-side electric fan switch, right-side and demist electric fan switch, main interior light switch, a spare switch (used for the heated rear screen after April 1966) and a cigar lighter. A small lidded glovebox is provided in the facia panel on the passenger's side. This sometimes had a lock, but normally just a retaining catch. The facia has a narrow polished aluminium trim around the perimeter. The fuse and relay board is mounted under the passenger's side of the facia.

The 'long-nose' model's facia features a virtually identical instrument and switch layout, but the group in front of the driver is within a separate nacelle set into the main facia panel and faced with black vinyl. The base of this nacelle meets the steering column shroud and incorporates the ignition switch.

Luggage Compartment

On cars with the type 563 chassis the single riveted-aluminium fuel tank is beneath the boot floor and has a capacity of 94 litres (20.7 Imperial/37.0 US gallons). The filler pipe and cap are in the right rear corner inside the boot. A shaped foam rubber seal on the underside of the boot lid closes onto the filler surround to prevent ingress of petrol fumes. In these models the spare wheel is fixed flat on the boot floor close to the passenger compartment bulkhead. The boot area is lined with a black carpet lightly flecked with grey and all plain metal surfaces are painted satin black. A light, on the boot ceiling between the hinges, is actuated by a switch plate on the lid when the boot is opened. The tool kit roll is stowed in one the rear wing recesses.

The boot of a 'short-nose' two-cam car, identifiable by the internal hinges and the spare wheel position on the boot floor. The boot area of later models is virtually identical, apart from the spare wheel being mounted in a well below a removable floor panel. The standard fuel filler location is in the right corner of the lid opening as shown here. This example has had a red carpet added to match the interior trim colour.

Cars with the type 569 chassis have twin aluminium tanks, one in each rear wing, coated with glass-fibre and connected by a balance pipe. This arrangement freed space in the centre of the boot floor, which was extended downwards to incorporate a spare wheel well. Total tank capacity and fuel filler location remained the same, as did the carpet, paint finish and illumination. The tool kit roll is housed in the spare wheel recess.

In both instances the boot lid, with a push-button key-operated lock, is supported by a self-locking telescopic stay on the right side.

Engine

Two-camshaft, Type 213

The two-camshaft engine is a 3286cc (200.5cu in) 60° V12 producing 280bhp (DIN) at 7600rpm and with maximum torque of 30kgm (216lb ft) at 5500rpm. The factory type number is 213, whether it has two or four mounting points, and it is a direct descendant of the 250/275 LM units, types 210 and 211 respectively. The cylinder bore is 77mm (3.03in) and the 58.8mm (2.31in) stroke is identical to that of the preceding 250 GT units, with which it also shares the same arrangement of a single overhead camshaft per bank.

The block, cylinder heads, bellhousing, sump, cam covers and all other cover plates are cast from Silumin alloy to the normal high standards that have come to be expected from the Ferrari foundry at Maranello. Steel push-fit cylinder liners are fitted. The camshaft on each head runs between the inlet and exhaust valves, beneath a crackle-black finished rocker cover bearing the Ferrari script. Each camshaft is supported in six carriers, which also house the rocker arm assemblies, and has a gearwheel bolted to the forward end. The camshaft drive is via a triplex chain from the crankshaft, and the chain has a tension adjustment on the lower right side of its casing. The valves are actuated via steel rocker arms, with screw adjustment of the valve clearances.

The inlet valves are on the inside of each head and fed via cast alloy manifolds in the vee. Mounted on the manifolds is either the standard triple twin-choke downdraught Weber 40DCZ/6 or 40DFI/1 carburettor assembly, or the optional set-up of six Weber 40DCN3 carburettors. The petrol feed pipe runs on the left of the carburettor assembly and the throttle linkage rod assembly, running in roller bearings, is on the right – irrespective of whether the car is right- or left-hand drive. The difference comes on the cable crank arms, plus the length, route and bracketing of the cable, which is 800mm (31.5in) long on left-hand-drive cars and 900mm (35.4in) long on right-hand-drive examples. Fuel is fed to the carburettors via a Fispa Sup 150 mechanical pump with gauze filter and a back-up Fispa PBE10 electric pump is also provided, controlled by a facia switch. The exhaust valves are on the outside of the vee and, like the inlet valves, have sintered bronze seats shrunk into the cylinder head, twin springs and run in bronze guides. From the end of 1965 a modified type of guide was fitted to both inlet and exhaust valves, incorporating a Teflon ring seal to provide better oil control.

From the exhaust valves the gasses pass into a pair of triple-branch free-flow steel manifolds for each bank of cylinders, with a heat shield fitted above them. The manifolds feed into a twin collector pipe that is siamesed into one large-bore pipe for each bank. Each pipe then feeds into its own triple silencer box assembly, suspended below the cabin floor, from which twin pipes exit. These loop to clear the rear suspension and emerge as a pair of chrome-plated tailpipes, suspended from rubber hangers, on either side at the rear.

The standard air filter box is black-painted pressed steel, with the top panel retained by three knurled nuts. The air filter was produced in two varieties, one shallower than the other. The early deep version has three separate circular elements, one around each carburettor intake, within the casing, which is rectangular with curved ends, while the later shallow version has a single element that extends around the perimeter of the similar-sized case. Air is drawn into the box on each side via a pair of rectangular nozzles, which protrude over the cam covers. Sometimes a pancake-type filter, as described on page 47 in the *275 GT Spider* chapter, was fitted to early cars, but this is more usually found on the 275 GTS model.

A vertically-mounted Marelli S85A-12v-15° or S85E distributor is provided for each bank of cylinders, driven off the rear end of the respective camshaft and fed by its own Marelli 12-volt BZR201A coil. From the distributors, the high tension leads run through a pressed steel shroud, bolted to the appropriate cam cover, to serve the individual Marchal 34HF or Champion N6Y sparking plugs via an insulated snap-connector cap. The cylinder firing order is given on a horizontal plate riveted to the top face of the timing chain casing.

TOOL KIT

Scissor-type jack with ratchet handle
Rear extractor screws
Front hub extractor
Rear hub extractor
Generator belt type 60475
Phillips screwdriver for screws up to 4mm (0.16in)
Phillips screwdriver for screws 5-6mm (0.20-0.24in)
Phillips screwdriver for screws 7-9mm (0.27-0.35in)
125mm (4.9in) long flat-bladed screwdriver
150mm (5.9in) long flat-bladed screwdriver
Grease gun
Fiamm oil for horn compressor
Weber carburettor key type 510/a
Sparking plug spanner
500g (1.1lb) hammer
1kg (2.2lb) lead mallet
Universal pliers
Set of seven 8-22mm open-ended spanners

The crankshaft is machined from a single billet of forged steel and runs in seven main bearings, with the forged steel connecting rods for opposing cylinders paired on a single journal. The main, big end and small end bearings are white metal. A splined triple sprocket is attached to the front end of the crankshaft, just forward of the oil pump drive gear, to drive the triple timing chain. The steel flywheel, with its starter ring gear, is bolted to a flange on the rear end of the crankshaft. The connecting rod big end bolts are specially shaped to prevent rotation. The light alloy pistons are flat-topped with cut-outs for valve clearance and are fitted with three rings, the lowest for oil control. Below the rings, the piston skirt is cut away on each side around the gudgeon pin.

The ribbed Silumin alloy sump has a boss for the oil temperature gauge sensor on the rear face and internal baffles are cast into the removable base plate with drain plug. The oil pump, gear-driven from the crankshaft, is at the front of the sump and has a gauze filter on its inlet. Oil is then pumped to the primary filter, mounted vertically at the front of the engine on the top right, with adjacent oil pressure relief valve. A secondary filter is mounted on the top left of the engine at the front. The aluminium-handled dipstick projects from a tube on the left side of the crankcase, while twin aluminium-capped oil filler/breather pipes are adjacent to the filters at the top front of the engine. The normal oil pressure with an oil temperature of 100°C should be 5.5kg/cm^2 (78psi) at 7000rpm, with a minimum value of 4kg/cm^2 (57psi) under the same conditions. The minimum slow running pressure (at 700-800rpm) should be 1.0-1.5kg/cm^2 (14-21psi).

The engine is water cooled by a front-mounted radiator, with circulation by a mechanical pump sited in the top centre of the timing chain casing, driven directly by the timing chain. A thermostatic valve is fitted in the rear face of the radiator top header section, at the water inlet pipe connection, to control the flow of water dependent upon engine temperature. An expansion tank with system pressure control valve, to maintain a pressure of 0.9kg/cm^2 (12.8psi), is sited on the left side forward of the radiator, which is cooled by a thermostatically-controlled electric fan that cuts in at 84°C and cuts out when temperature falls below 75°C. The engine's maximum operating temperature is 110°C. Two small rubber tubes, from the main cooling circuit adjacent to the radiator, serve the interior heater/demister matrix in the control box behind the facia. The recommended anti-freeze solution depends upon the external temperatures to be encountered. For temperatures down to −10°C a 22 per cent anti-freeze mixture is recommended, increasing to 28 per cent at −15°C, 34 per cent at −20°C and 44 per cent at −30°C. Cooling system drain plugs are provided at the base of the radiator and on the sides of the block in line with the second cylinder from the rear.

Four-camshaft, Type 226

The basic structure and materials of the four-camshaft unit, type 226, are virtually identical to those of the two-camshaft design but this engine is more powerful, producing 300bhp (DIN) at 8000rpm and maximum torque of 32kgm (231lb ft) at 6050rpm. The main differences are in the cylinder head layout and the provision of dry-sump lubrication, which necessitate changes to some other components. The cylinder block of the four-cam engine always has two mountings, which are located on the side of the block roughly in line with the third cylinder from the front.

The camshafts on each head run above the inlet and exhaust valves respectively, each under a slim crackle-black finished rocker cover bearing the Ferrari script. Each camshaft runs in white metal bearings and is supported by front, rear and five intermediate carriers. On each cylinder bank, one camshaft operates the inlet valves and the other the exhausts. A gearwheel is bolted to the front of each camshaft and is driven via an intermediate gearwheel on a shaft with a cog drive from

ENGINE

Type	275 GTB (2 cam)	275 GTB/4
Type	60° V12	60° V12
Type number	213	226
Cubic capacity	3285.722cc (200.5cu in)	3285.722cc (200.5cu in)
Bore and stroke	77x58.8mm (3.03x2.31in)	77x58.8mm (3.03x2.31in)
Compression ratio	9.2:1	9.2:1
Maximum power	280bhp (DIN) at 7600rpm	300bhp (DIN) at 8000rpm
Maximum torque	30kgm (216lb ft) at 5500rpm	32kgm (231lb ft) at 6050rpm
Carburettors	3 Weber 40DCZ/6 or 40DFI/1 6 Weber 40DCN3 optional	6 Weber 40DCN9, 17 or 18

TIMING DATA

	275 GTB (2 cam)	275 GTB/4
Inlet valves open	18° BTDC	45° BTDC
Inlet valves close	56° ABDC	65° ABDC
Exhaust valves open	56° BBDC	60° BBDC
Exhaust valves close	18° ATDC	41° ATDC
Firing order (2 & 4 cam)	1-7-5-11-3-9-6-12-2-8-4-10	

The two-camshaft engine timing figures should be measured with a valve clearance of 0.5mm (0.0197in) between the valve pads and rocker arms. Valve clearances for the two- and four-camshaft engines when cold, should be 0.2mm (0.0079in) for inlet valves and 0.25mm (0.0098in) for exhaust valves. On the two-cam engine exhaust clearances are measured between the valve pad and rocker arm, and on the four-cam unit between the valve pad and camshaft.

SYSTEM CAPACITIES

	275 GTB (2 cam)			275 GTB/4		
Fuel tank [1]	94 litres (20.7 Imperial/24.8 US gallons)			94 litres (20.7 Imperial/24.8 US gallons)		
	Litres	Imp pints	US pints	Litres	Imp pints	US pints
Cooling System	10	17.6	21.1	12	21.1	25.4
Washer bottle	0.5	0.9	1.1	0.5	0.9	1.1
Engine oil	10	17.6	21.1	14	24.7	29.6
Gearbox/Differential oil	4.4	7.8	9.3	4.4	7.8	9.3

[1] Option of 140-litre (30.8 Imperial/37.0 US gallon) tank for competition use

the duplex timing chain. This chain is driven from the crankshaft and has a tension adjustment on the lower right side of its casing.

The valves are actuated via steel bucket followers that bear directly onto the camshaft lobes, with shims to alter the valve clearances. On early cars the shims were located within the bucket, bearing on the valve stem, but this arrangement was very time-consuming when adjusting valve clearances, as the camshaft had to be removed to alter them. To reduce the time taken to set clearances, the arrangement was changed to one with a recess in the head of the bucket. The camshaft then bore on the shims, which could be removed by compressing the valve with a special tool without the necessity of removing the camshaft. A drawback of this arrangement is that it has been known for the shims to become dislodged if the recommended maximum rev limit is exceeded – with dire consequences wherever they happen to be thrown or become lodged!

The inlet valves are on the inside of each head and are fed via cast alloy manifolds in the vee. Mounted on the manifolds are six Weber 40DCN9, 17 or 18 carburettors, the last type used from chassis number 10345. The 40DCN18 carburettors had a starter choke and so the choke lever on the facia nacelle was omitted when these

were fitted. Few owners ever use the choke on any Ferrari, preferring to let the electric pumps get the fuel to the carburettors and then give a few hefty pumps on the accelerator to prime them. If everything is in order, the engine then fires. The petrol feed pipe runs on the right of the carburettor assembly and the throttle linkage rod assembly on the left, irrespective of whether the car is right- or left-hand drive. Early cars have a linkage incorporating a throttle cable, which was replaced by a full rod system. The fuel feed system is very similar in layout to that of the twin-tank two-cam cars, but a return pipe to the fuel tank is provided on cars from chassis number 10201.

The exhaust valves are on the outside of the vee and the gasses pass into a pair of triple-branch free-flow steel manifolds, with a heat shield above them, on each cylinder bank. Each manifold is flanged to the triple-feed inlets of the front silencer box. From there a pair of pipes run into the main twin-box silencer below the cabin and the tail pipes, suspended on rubber hangers, follow a similar path to those of the two-cam cars.

The standard air filter box is black-painted pressed steel, with the top panel retained by three knurled nuts. A single filter element extends around the inner perimeter of the casing, which is similar in design to the later two-cam type.

The engine bay of a 'short-nose' two-cam model fitted with three carburettors and a pancake air filter, which gives a clearer view of the engine bay than the more common pressed steel filter arrangement. The cylinder firing order plate can be seen on the top of the timing chain casing at the front of the engine.

The four-cam engine bay is dominated by the large black-painted air filter box, which hides almost everything. The cylinder firing order plate is fixed to the top rear of the filter casing, with a lubrication plate at the front, while the right-side camshaft covers can be seen beneath the filter intake nozzles.

A Marelli S85A-12v-15° or S85E distributor (from chassis 10031), mounted at an angle towards the centre of the car, is provided for each bank of cylinders. It is driven off the rear end of the exhaust camshaft and fed by its own Marelli 12vBZR201A coil. From the distributors, the high-tension leads run in a pressed steel shroud, bolted to the inlet cam cover, to the Champion N6Y sparking plugs. These are located centrally between the cam covers and have insulated snap-connector caps.

The internal reciprocating parts of the engine (crankshaft, pistons, connecting rods and fly-wheel) are all very similar in design and materials to the two-cam model. However, the sump is of a completely different design due to the dry-sump lubrication system. As with the two-cam model, the oil pump drive is directly off a gearwheel at the front end of the crankshaft, just behind the timing chain drive sprockets. However, as it is a dry-sump system, there are two pumps in tandem: one is the pressure pump for lubrication and the second is the scavenge pump to collect oil from the sump and return it to the catch tank. This is mounted in the rear part of the front wing below the battery, with a filler neck and cap incorporating the oil level dipstick. From here the pressure pump supplies the oil, via twin filters and a pres-

sure relief valve high on the front right of the engine, to the oilways. Initially an oil cooler, mounted in front of the water radiator in the nose of the car, was included in the circuit. However, high oil temperature proved not to be a problem, so the cooler was dispensed with from chassis 09993. A tapping for the oil temperature gauge is provided on the oil entry pipe to the sump. The normal oil pressure with an oil temperature of 120°C should be 6.0-6.5kg/cm^2 (85-92psi) at 8000rpm, with a minimum value of 4.5-5.0kg/cm^2 (64-71psi) under the same conditions.

The water pump is driven directly off the timing chain, as on the two-cam model, but its location is in the left side of the timing chain casing. The general cooling arrangement is very similar to the two-cam model, but the return piping arrangement from the cylinder heads to the radiator is different. A solid aluminium tube runs from a connection at the rear of each head, between the cam covers and above the sparking plugs, via a flexible joint to a collector pipe and thence via another flexible connection to the radiator thermostat boss. This has a tapping for the water temperature gauge sensor. Twin cooling fans with thermostatic control are provided. Their operating parameters and suggested anti-freeze percentage mixtures are as for the two-cam model.

Transmission

The 275 series featured the first use by Ferrari of a transaxle on a road model, although the factory had plenty of experience with this type of unit on its competition cars. Translating racing car technology to acceptable levels of reliability and comfort for road car use took a little sorting out, mainly relating to the coupling shaft between the engine and transaxle.

Initially, to make the assembly as rigid as possible, the engine block had four mounting points, one at each corner, and was attached to the chassis via thin rubber bushes. The transaxle is similarly rigidly fixed to the chassis via three mounting points, one on either side of the lower front of the casing and one at the top rear centre. A 16.5mm (0.65in) diameter steel shaft, splined at each end into a rigid bolted flange and running at engine speed, couples the two together. There is a central support bearing in a bracket attached to the chassis. The shaft was designed to have a degree of flex in it to take up any misalignment between the engine and transaxle, but the arrangement proved difficult to set up and maintain accurately, due to the engine and transaxle imposing conflicting loads on the shaft. This caused rapid wear on the central bearing, allowing the shaft to flex more than desired, and resulted in unpleasant vibration problems. Late in 1965 the problem was addressed by providing an 18.5mm (0.73in) diameter driveshaft, splined into universal joints at either end, which were flanged to the engine and transaxle shafts. This allowed greater disparity between the conflicting forces, resulting in much smoother running for infinitely longer periods.

In April 1966 Ferrari announced the third and final variation to the driveshaft system in its *Technical Circular Letter 36*. For this new arrangement the engine block was modified to have only two supports, one on either side approximately in line with the third cylinder from the front, using more flexible rubber mounts. The transaxle support was also modified to twin mountings, which were sited approximately mid-way along each side of the

casing, again with more flexible rubber mounts. The steel driveshaft ran through a rigid torque tube, flanged at either end, which joined the engine and transaxle in one long solid assembly. This finally eliminated the previous vibration problems and the drive remained in this form to the end of 275 GTB/4 production.

The flywheel-mounted clutch was initially a Fichtel & Sachs single dry-plate unit with three-spoke spring diaphragm and hydraulic operation. At the end of 1965, at the same time as the adoption of universal joints at either end of the driveshaft, this was replaced by a multi-spring diaphragm plate Borg & Beck unit giving smoother and more progressive operation. This unit was then used until the end of 275 GTB/4 production. The hydraulic fluid reservoir is mounted in tandem with the brake reservoirs, above the pedal box at the rear of the engine bay, on the driver's side. The pedal has a height adjustment facility by means of three semi-circular cut-outs on its pad pin, where the position of the fixing bolt to the lever arm can be changed.

The five-speed transaxle has a Silumin alloy casing and, as previously mentioned, has either three-point mounting on early two-cam models, or two-point mounting on late two-cam and all four-cam models. Early three-point mounting casings have the filler plug on the left-side casing plate, on the boss where the gear selector shaft enters. This was modified early in the production run to locate the filler plug in the bottom rear corner of the plate, immediately above the drain plug. A gear-driven oil pump with gauze filter is provided within the casing.

The driveshaft from the engine is connected to a flange on the end of the primary shaft, which runs in roller bearings in the base of the gearbox section of the transaxle. There is an oil-seal ring at the point of entry to the casing. The primary shaft is in two halves, splined at the centre, with an intermediate support bearing and carries fourth and fifth gearwheels, plus transfer gears for first, reverse and second/third gears. The secondary shaft runs immediately above the primary one and carries transfer gears for fourth and fifth gears, together with (from front to back) the third, second, first and reverse gearwheels. The forward gears are helical with Porsche-designed synchromesh rings, while reverse gear is straight cut. From chassis 09947, the synchromesh rings were provided with a molybdenum coating to increase longevity and provide a smoother gearchange.

At the rear of the secondary shaft is the axle drive pinion, which meshes directly into the crown wheel of the peg-type limited slip differential, with universal couplings at each end of the splined sliding half-shafts. This was changed to a ZF limited slip type, with modified half-shafts to

The normal rear light arrangement, although some later cars had horizontal rectangular reflectors and all US-market models had full red lenses.

GEAR RATIOS

| | Standard ratios | | Optional |
	Gearbox	Overall	Gearbox ratios
First	3.075:1	10.931:1	2.468:1
Second	2.12:1	7.536:1	1.84:1
Third	1.572:1	5.588:1	1.454:1
Fourth	1.25:1	4.444:1	1.2:1
Fifth	1.104:1	3.925:1	1.104:1
Reverse	2.67:1	9.492:1	2.67:1
Final drive	3.555:1 (9:32)		Options as below

Optional final drive ratios: 4.571:1 (7:32), 4.375:1 (8:35), 4.250:1 (8:34), 4.125:1 (8:33), 4.000:1 (8:32), 3.889:1 (9:35), 3.778:1 (9:34), 3.667:1 (9:33), 3.444:1 (9:31), 3.300:1 (10:33), and 3.182:1 (11:35).

Front lighting arrangement, with circular side/turn indicator light below the headlamp, and semi-recessed orange teardrop repeater light on the wing side. The 'long-nose' model (centre) differs from the 'short-nose' (left) in having the side/turn indicator more deeply recessed because of the change in shape of the nose. One 275 GTB/4, chassis number 09551 (right), was manufactured with uncovered headlamps: the appearance is a question of personal taste but at least misted-up covers are not a problem.

suit the new assembly, concurrent with the main driveshaft and clutch changes at the end of 1965.

The gear lever moves in an open gate to the left side of the transmission tunnel, with first gear in a dog-leg to the left rear corner. Reverse is immediately opposite, with second to fifth gear forming an H pattern to their right. From the base of the lever a solid rod runs alongside the main driveshaft to enter the gearbox through a raised boss on the left sideplate, where a lever actuates the fourth/fifth, second/third and first/reverse selector fork rods. These are mounted one above the other in that order. A speedometer cable connection is sited on the top right side of the gearbox front cover plate.

Electrical Equipment & Lights

The electrical system is 12-volt, served from a 60 or 74amp/hour battery, sited in the rear of the front wing on the opposite side to the driver. The battery is fed by a Bosch alternator mounted on the front of the engine and driven by a vee-belt off a pulley on the water pump on two-cam models or from a dedicated central pulley on four-cam models. On all cars the starter motor is mounted on the lower right section of the flywheel bell-housing, integral with its solenoid suspended below it. Twin air horns, actuated by the horn push in the centre of the steering wheel, are mounted in the engine compartment of 'short-nose' cars and in the nose in front of the radiator in 'long-nose' cars.

The lighting equipment is all of Carello man-

ufacture and remained constant through the production run from 'short-nose' two-cam cars to the 275 GTB/4. The only significant variations were left-hand dipping headlamps for right-hand-drive cars (type 08.410.000 instead of 07.410.000) with 40/45watt bulbs, and yellow headlamp bulbs for the French market. The headlamps are mounted in the front wings under clear Perspex covers, with chrome-plated surround rings retained by screws. The covers tend to mist up in damp conditions and this dramatically reduces the performance of the lights. At least one customer, who still owns his car, decided that he preferred the car without Perspex covers, so chassis 09551, a 275 GTB/4, never had them fitted and there are not even any fixing holes provided in the body. Recessed into the forward edge of the wings below the headlamps are side/turn indicator lamps with white lenses; the location is slightly different on 'short-nose' and 'long-nose' examples. In the front wing sides, virtually in line with the headlamp centres, are teardrop-shaped orange indicator repeater lights. At the rear is a pair of circular combined stop/tail/turn/reflector lamp units on the tail panel, virtually identical to those used on the 250 GT Lusso model. A small central circular reflector (some late-series cars have a horizontal rectangular one) is bounded by an upper orange lens and a lower red one. The number plate lamps are two small rectangular units in a slim chrome-plated housing mounted on the top face of the bumper. Immediately below the number plate lamp, fixed to the lower face of the bumper, is a small rectangular reversing lamp, which is actuated by a switch on the gearchange tower when reverse is engaged.

Suspension & Steering

The 275 GTB was Ferrari's first road car with fully independent suspension. The layout remained basically unaltered throughout the life of the model, apart from some changes necessary to incorporate the ZF differential at the end of 1965 and a concurrent strengthening of the upper rear wishbones to provide increased rear-end rigidity.

Major Electrical Equipment

	275 GTB (2 cam)	275 GTB/4
Battery	12-volt Marelli 6AC11, 60amp/hour or SAFA 6SNS5, 74amp/hour	12-volt SAFA 6SNS5, 74amp/hour
Alternator	Marelli GCA-101/B	Marelli GCA-101/B
Starter motor	Marelli MT21T-1.8/12D9	Marelli MT21T-1.8/12D9
Ignition	Two Marelli S85A-12v-15° distributors, each with a Marelli 12v BZR201A coil	Two Marelli S85A-12v-15° or S85E distributors, each with a Marelli 12v BZR201A coil
Sparking plugs	Marchal 34HF, Champion N4 or N6Y	Champion N6Y

Much of the suspension development was entrusted to English engineer and racing driver Mike Parkes, who worked and drove for Ferrari in the mid-1960s. His input and fine-tuning of the layout is probably one of the main reasons why the handling received wide praise at the time. The set-up combines fairly light steering (for a heavy front-engined car) with taut, relatively neutral high-speed handling – although the firm suspension was less of a joy on poor surfaces at low speed.

Unequal-length pressed steel upper and lower wishbones are used all round, joined by the hub carriers at the outer end and mounted to the chassis via rubber bushes at the inner end. Each wheel has its own coil spring and damper assembly, while anti-roll bars are fitted front and rear. Two chassis-mounted conical rubber bump stops are provided for each suspension unit.

The dampers are co-axially mounted within the coil springs. At the front they are positioned between the wishbones but at the rear the half-shafts prevent this so the springs and dampers are fixed above the top wishbones, between these and mounting brackets on the chassis.

The front hub carriers are machined forged steel, carrying a stub axle on which the brake disc and splined hub assembly run on roller bearings. The rear hub carriers are machined cast steel, with a central hole through which the driveshaft passes, and are retained by a bolt to the splined hub and brake disc, both of which run in roller bearings. The splined front and rear hubs are attached to the brake discs by an eight-bolt flange, with tappings in the disc for the retaining bolts.

Steering is unassisted with a worm and roller steering box, mounted on the front chassis cross-member at the lower end of the universally-jointed steering column. The box has a screw and lock-nut facility for adjustment of any play on the upper face, and track adjustment is provided on the track rods. The steering ball joints are non-adjustable and require no lubrication. The steering has 3.25 turns lock to lock, with a turning circle of 14.07 metres (46ft 2in). All models were available with either left- or right-hand drive, except for the 275 GTS/4 NART Spider which was left-hand drive only.

Brakes

As with the preceding 250 GT series, Dunlop disc brakes were provided to all four wheels, with separate hydraulic circuits for the front and rear wheels with their own master cylinders. The vacuum servo, supplied from the inlet manifold, was initially a Dunlop C48, then a Girling and from December 1966 a Bonaldi unit. A floor-mounted cable-operated handbrake works rather inefficiently on its own set of pads on each rear wheel and has automatic wear adjustment. The cable length is adjusted by screws where the twin cables join the lever arm. The pedal box arrangement and pedal lever shape were changed at the end of 1965, but still retained pedal height adjustment as described in the Transmission section.

The Dunlop discs, 279.4mm (11.0in) in diameter by 12.7mm (0.5in) thick at the front and 274.6mm (10.81in) in diameter by 12.7mm (0.5in) thick at the rear, are solid cast iron, as are the calipers. Such dimensions would appear marginal today on any bread-and-butter 'repmobile', never mind on a vehicle weighing over a ton and capable of over 150mph, but at the time these discs were about the best available. The recommended brake pads for normal touring conditions were Mintex VBO-5201/N2 (M33) at the front and Mintex VBO-5138/N2 (M33) at the rear.

The brakes provide generally acceptable performance under touring conditions, so long as the vacuum servo is charged. However, one high-speed stop can exhaust the servo unit; the driver then finds that superhuman force is needed to bring the car to a stop immediately afterwards, even from a low speed. The high-speed braking problem is exacerbated by a tendency for the cast iron calipers to spread under heavy load and the associated high temperature build-up, thus reducing the braking efficiency and giving a soft feel to the pedal. The servo problem becomes more acute with the six-carburettor set-up, as these models have a higher speed potential and the vacuum take-off is from the manifold of only one carburettor. As there is no inlet manifold balance pipe, the degree of vacuum assistance – and hence braking capability – is drastically reduced. Some cars have had modifications in this area, either by providing a balance pipe and/or a vacuum reservoir tank discreetly hidden in the wing.

Wheels & Tyres

The first series of 6.5x14in light alloy wheels are unique to the 275 GTB 'short-nose' model. Manufactured by Campagnolo, they are sometimes referred to as the 'starburst' pattern. Like all alloy wheels on this series of cars, they are retained by a straight triple-eared chrome-plated hub nut.

FACTORY LITERATURE

1964
• Owner's handbook in Italian/French/English, black-and-white cover, for the 275 GTB/S models. Reprinted by the factory firstly with a black-and-white cover and then twice more with green covers. All carried factory reference 01/65. The first item in a numbering system that continues today.

1965
• Sales folder with yellow cover in Italian/French/English, tyre size in specifications 205-14. A second version was produced with the tyre size changed to 195/205-14 and a third example with tyre size 195/205-14 and the addition of an automatically-operated thermostatic radiator fan.
• Mechanical spare parts catalogue for the 275 GTB/S models; factory reference 03/65.

1966
• The 1966 model range brochure includes two pages on the 275 GTB, with photograph and specifications in Italian/French/English; factory reference 07/66.
• Mechanical spare parts catalogue for the 275 GTB/S models, with factory reference 10/63 (the 63 is a misprint and should be 65 or 66). This has been reprinted at least four times over the years by the factory, with different colour covers, the original cover being grey, yellow and blue. The last two printings had no print reference.

1967
• The 1967 model range brochure contains two pages on the 275 GTB/4, with photograph and specifications in Italian/French/English; factory reference 11/66.
• Sales brochure for the 275 GTB/4 model; factory print reference 13/66. This brochure was reprinted in 1967 using print reference 13/67.
• Mechanical spare parts catalogue for the 275 GTB/4 model; factory print reference 17/67. Produced with three different-coloured covers.

SUSPENSION SETTINGS

	275 GTB (2 cam)	275 GTB/4
Front toe-in	−3 to −5mm (−0.118 to −0.197in)	−5mm max (−0.197in)
Front camber	+0°	+0°20'
Rear toe-in	−4 to −6mm (−0157 to −0.236in)	−6mm max (−0.236in)
Rear camber	−0°50'	−1°35'
Castor angle	2°30'	2°30'
Dampers: front	Koni 82N-1349	Koni 82N-1349
rear	Koni 82N-1350	Koni 82N-1350

A second type of light alloy wheel, increased to 7in (178mm) width, features a much simpler design of a series of small rectangular holes around the hub circumference, reflecting the design used on Ferrari competition cars of the period. This simpler style is used on the 'long-nose' and 275 GTB/4 cars. Both types of wheel have a satin silver paint finish under clear lacquer. Tyres offered as standard are listed in the table.

As an option Borrani wire wheels with 72 chrome-plated spokes and polished aluminium rims were offered, with 6.5x14in as standard. Various competition-orientated options were available also, as detailed in the table. The hub spinners for the Borrani wheels normally have triple angled ears, as opposed to the straight-eared variety used on the alloy wheels. These more open wheels undoubtedly provide better brake cooling and heat dissipation but, because of the loads imposed on them, need regular checks for spoke tightness and rim alignment.

The spare wheel was mounted horizontally on the boot floor in the 'short-nose' models. When the single under-floor fuel tank was replaced by a pair in the rear wings on 'long-nose' cars, the spare wheel moved to a well in the boot floor, with an access panel forming the base of the luggage area.

WHEELS & TYRES

Two-camshaft Models

Wheels, front & rear	6.50x14in cast light alloy (1st pattern) 7.00x14in cast light alloy (2nd pattern) Optional Borrani wire wheels with alloy rims 6½x14 type RW3874, 7x14 type RW4039
Tyres, front & rear	Pirelli HS 210-14 or Dunlop SP 205HR-14

Note: 7x14in and 7x15in front and rear wheels were homologated for this model, together with 7½x15in rear wheels, principally for competition use.

Four-camshaft Models

Wheels, front & rear	700Lx14in cast light alloy, optional Borrani wire wheels with alloy rims.
Tyres, front & rear	Michelin 205-14in and 205VR-14 X

The two designs of standard alloy wheel: the 'sunburst' pattern of 'short-nose' cars (right) and the ten-hole version for 'long-nose' models (far right).

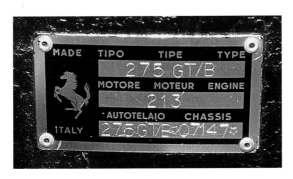

Identification plate (right) fixed to inner wing panel gives model type, engine type and chassis number. Model type and chassis number stamped on front crossmember (far right).

Engine number stamped on lower right rear side of block, close to bellhousing.

IDENTIFICATION PLATES

1. General vehicle data plate giving model type with engine and chassis numbers on engine bay valance panel.
2. Chassis number stamped in frame close to front suspension mounting point.
3. Engine number stamped in block on right rear side close to bellhousing.

Chapter 4
275 GT Spider

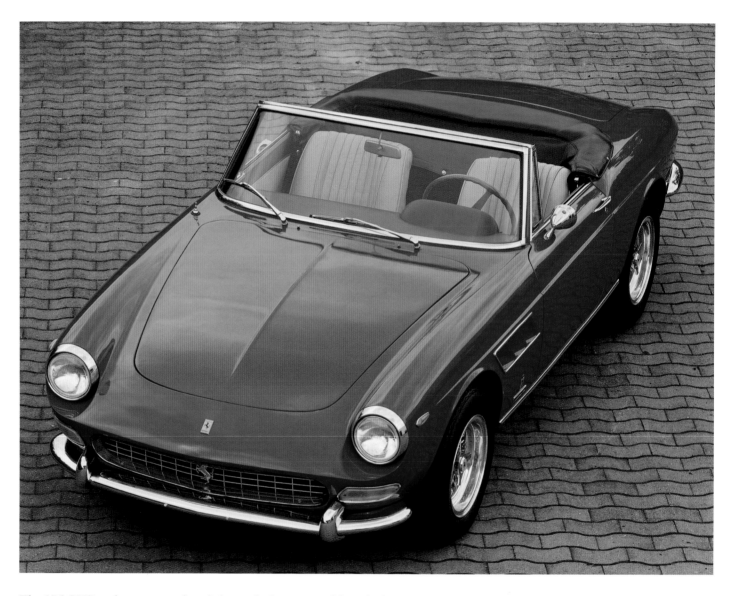

The 275 GTS spider was introduced alongside the 275 GT Berlinetta at the 1964 Paris Salon, but featured a completely different body style that had nothing in common with the fixed-head model. It had an air of chic elegance in its tight and restrained, almost delicate, lines rather than the stronger statement of power exuded by the full curves of the berlinetta. This was the replacement in the Ferrari range for the 250 GT Cabriolet and 250 GT California Spider models that had ceased production in 1962 and 1963 respectively.

Although the 275 GTB wore cast aluminium wheels as standard, the 275 GTS was only offered with Borrani wire wheels, which the factory and/or Pininfarina probably considered more harmonious with the lines of the car. The first Pininfarina press photographs showed a car – almost certainly prototype chassis 06001 – with a 'twin' passenger seat (ostensibly wide enough to accommodate two people), but it is believed that very few cars, perhaps six at most, ever received this treatment as homologation was turned down in

From high level the compact, beautifully balanced lines of the 275 GTS can be appreciated to the full, and the central bonnet ridge can also be clearly seen.

These views of chassis number 07989, a US-market car, show all the main body features of the 275 GTS, including the full-width front bumper (with plain overriders) and rear quarter bumpers (with rubber-faced overriders). Front wing exhaust air outlets with triple louvres indicate a late series model. The red pinstriping is non-standard, but it is subtle and does not look out of place.

DIMENSIONS & WEIGHT

	mm	in
Overall length	4350	171.26
Overall width	1675	65.94
Overall height	1250	49.21
Wheelbase	2400	94.49
Front track	1377	54.21
Rear track	1393	54.84
Weight (dry)	1150kg	2535lb

numerous European countries on safety grounds.

Like its berlinetta cousin, the 275 GTS was designed by Pininfarina, but while the berlinetta was constructed at the Scaglietti works in Modena, the 275 GTS spider was built in-house at Pininfarina and then shipped to Ferrari to receive its mechanical components.

Mechanically the 275 GTS was a virtually identical package to the 275 GTB, although the factory literature quoted maximum power output of 260bhp (DIN) at 7000rpm instead of 280bhp

(DIN) at 7600rpm. Production continued until early 1966, when the model was superseded by the 330 GTS, which was virtually identical bodily from the windscreen rearward.

Body & Chassis

The 275 GTS chassis is type number 563 and is thus identical to that of the 'short-nose' and early 'long-nose' 275 GTBs. The solid coupling of the engine to the transaxle – via a torque tube and ZF

From high level all the major interior features can be seen. Note the handbrake position, on the driver's side of the transmission tunnel.

limited slip differential – was never used on this model as its replacement, the 330 GTS, arrived around the time that they were incorporated into the 275 GTB.

The body, designed and built by Pininfarina, shares no common panels with the 275 GTB, although the materials used are the same – steel with aluminium doors, bonnet and boot lid. No production examples of the 275 GTS are known to have been fitted with all-alloy bodies. Whereas the 275 GTB has front quarter bumpers and a full-width wrap-around rear unit, the 275 GTS is exactly the opposite with a full-width front bumper and rear quarter units, all featuring overriders. The convertible roof is heavyweight canvas, with a rectangular clear Perspex panel, on

a folding steel frame. It is secured to the screen rail by two over-centre fasteners when erected and folds into a recess behind the seats, where it is provided with a protective vinyl cover retained by chromed press-studs. Pininfarina press photographs of the period show two styles of hard-top available for the model, but it is believed that very few cars were provided with this option.

During the 275 GTS production run there was only one minor change to the body details, when the 11-slot front wing vents were replaced by a three-slot arrangement, which would continue on the succeeding 330 GTS. It is possible that the very last examples of the 275 GTS were fitted with the nose of the 330 GTS. Certainly the prototype of the 330 GTS's coupé cousin, 330 GTC chassis

When electric windows are fitted, a circular plug replaces the manual winder. In the passenger footwell is a folding aluminium foot brace with ribbed rubber sheath.

Dashboard views show the main instrument and switch locations, although on late series cars there are variations to switch positions as noted in the text.

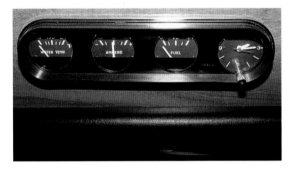

number 06431GT, was built on a 275 GTS chassis and its 4-litre engine had four mounting points as on the 275 series at that time.

Body Trim & Fittings

The front of the 275 GTS features a shallow rectangular radiator opening with rounded corners and an aluminium trim surround. The inset aluminium egg-crate grille has a polished aluminium *Cavallino Rampante* at its centre. A one-piece chrome-plated steel bumper, with plain chromed overriders, is fixed to the chassis via tubular supports projecting through the lower nose panel. At the rear, wrap-around quarter bumpers are provided and have black rubber-faced overriders at their inner ends. A rectangular enamel Ferrari badge is fitted on the upper nose panel between the grille and leading edge of the bonnet, and a chromed Ferrari script badge, with a '275' badge beneath it, is mounted centrally close to the trailing edge of the boot lid. Slim horizontal rectangular Pininfarina badges, with Pininfarina enamel shields above them, are fitted to the lower sides of the front wings.

The front-hinged bonnet has a raised central rib, but is free of any adornment. The body sides feature a waist crease line, below which are the front wing louvres. On early cars in the series this

was an 11-louvre pattern – also used on the 250 GT 2+2, 330 GT 2+2 and 500 Superfast – painted in the body colour. Early in 1965 this arrangement was altered to a triple-louvre assembly, with a slim polished aluminium trim surround to the front, top and bottom edges.

A triangular aluminium strip adorns the body side between the front and rear wheelarches, mounted on the upper sill section immediately below the base of the door. Further brightwork is confined to the chrome-plated windscreen surround, headlamp rims, quarterlight frames, door glasses, screen wiper arms and blade frames, plus the push-button locks on the boot and in the door handles and the circular keylock on the doors.

Plain glass is fitted and the windscreen is laminated. The two-speed self-parking wipers normally park on the right on left-hand-drive cars and on the left on right-hand-drive examples. The door windows are provided with swivelling quarterlights with a chrome-plated retaining catch in the lower front corner. During the production run electric windows became available, actuated by switches alongside the cigar lighter in the front face of the central glove tray.

Paintwork

As mentioned in the chapter on the companion 275 GTB models, a truly vast range of colours was available for Ferrari cars at this time and the same comments there apply to the 275 GTS. As the 275 GTS was built by Pininfarina, it should have a paint colour from either PPG or Duco but one cannot say that a Pininfarina-built car is non-original if it is finished in a paint from the Glidden & Salchi range. The table on page 30 in the *275 GT Berlinetta* chapter lists the colours available.

Interior Trim & Fittings

The standard seat upholstery material is full leather. The seats are less overtly sporting than those in the berlinetta, with shallower side bolsters and deeper padding. As with the 275 GTB, the leather was supplied by the British firm of Connolly Bros and the range of colours available is shown in the table on page 33 in the *275 GT Berlinetta* chapter. The seats are mounted on runners, with adjustment via a lever under the front edge of the cushion. A lever on the outer lower edge of the squab alters its rake. The door pulls incorporate armrests, with a chrome-plated door handle at the forward end and the window winder forward of the pull section. When electric windows are fitted, the winder is replaced by a circular plug or a rectangular chrome plate with a central hole to accept the emergency winder. The base of the door trim features a pair of polished aluminium strips, and an aluminium kick plate is provided on the shut face of the sill.

Normally the floor, centre section of the firewall, transmission tunnel and rear shelf are carpeted, with ribbed black rubber heelmats incorporated in the footwell carpets for both driver and passenger. There is additional ribbed black rubber on the vertical face of the footwell and the footrest bar on the passenger's side. Black 'bobble' vinyl covering was available as an option for the floor, tunnel and rear shelf. The range of carpet colours is listed in the table on page 32 in the *275 GT Berlinetta* chapter. Door panels and front and rear inner wheelarches are trimmed in vinyl of upholstery colour, and the facia top and bottom rolls are trimmed in black vinyl.

Sun visors are vinyl-covered, the passenger's incorporating a vanity mirror, and the dipping rear view mirror is positioned between them. Also mounted on the upper screen rail, at the outer extremities, are the soft-top fixings.

A black plastic knob tops the chrome gear lever, which is in an open chrome-plated gate. On all models, whether right- or left-hand drive, the gate is on the left side of the transmission tunnel at the front of the centre console. On the right is a chromed lidded ashtray, with a cigar lighter in the front face of the glove tray behind it. The handbrake projects from the floor in a vinyl gaiter and is positioned alongside the front of the transmission tunnel, on the driver's side. An interior light is provided beneath the centre of the facia. When electric windows are fitted the switches are mounted alongside the cigar lighter.

Facia & Instruments

At a glance the facias of the spider and berlinetta models appear very similar and indeed they share the basic instrument layout, but there are numerous differences. Compared with the 'short-nose' berlinettas, the 275 GTS facia has a separate and deeper main instrument nacelle cut into the facia top, and a shallower section extending across the cabin. The instrument nacelle surround, facia top and bottom padded roll section are all covered with black vinyl. The nacelle and facia panels have a teak veneer finish on early examples and a black vinyl covering on late cars. The facia top has twin slim demister slots, with black plastic surrounds, close to the windscreen.

The steering wheel and horn push are identical to those on the berlinetta. Two slender stalks project from the left of the steering column, the shorter one controlling direction indicators, the longer one sidelamps/headlamps. Headlamp dip beam is controlled by a facia switch. On later models an additional stalk on the right of the column actuates the windscreen wiper speed

control, and the washers by pulling it towards the driver. The key-operated ignition/starter switch, incorporating a steering lock, is mounted on the lower right of the steering column shroud. A floor-mounted push-button for the windscreen washers is sited by the driver's footrest, close to the bonnet release catch on early models.

The layout of the gauges (with white characters on a black background) and the functions that they indicate is identical to the berlinetta, but the switch arrangement is different. On early cars a small panel on the lower edge of the facia, between the steering column and door pillar, contains switches for the instrument panel lights, headlamps, two-speed wipers and ventilation fan. A further switch on the opposite side of the column is for the electric fuel pump. Later cars adopted a rocker switch assembly in the centre of the facia, similar in layout to that of the berlinetta. On the facia outboard of the main binnacle are two vertical slide levers, the furthest from the binnacle controlling the driver's side fresh air intake and the one closest to it actuating the central air/demister control flap. A matching slider control on the facia alongside the inner edge of the binnacle controls heater output, while another outboard on the passenger's side controls that side's fresh air intake. On late series cars, the heater control lever is mounted horizontally below the central instrument binnacle, with the rocker switches in a cut-out in the lower facia roll below it. Immediately in front of the passenger is a radio

ENGINE

Type	60° V12
Type number	213
Cubic capacity	3285.722cc (200.5cu in)
Bore and stroke	77x58.8mm (3.03x2.31in)
Compression ratio	9.2:1
Maximum power	260bhp (DIN) at 7000rpm
Maximum torque	30kgm (216lb ft) at 5000rpm
Carburettors	3 Weber 40DCZ/6 or 40DFI/1

TIMING DATA

Inlet valves open	18° BTDC
Inlet valves close	56° ABDC
Exhaust valves open	56° BBDC
Exhaust valves close	18° ATDC
Firing order	1-7-5-11-3-9-6-12-2-6-4-10

The above timing figures should be measured with a valve clearance of 0.5mm (0.0197in) between the valve pads and rocker arms. Valve clearances with a cold engine should be 0.2mm (0.0079in) for inlets and 0.25mm (0.0098in) for exhausts, measured between the valve pads and rocker arms.

SYSTEM CAPACITIES

Fuel tank	86 litres (18.9 Imperial/22.7 US gallons)		
	Litres	**Imp Pints**	**US Pints**
Cooling System	12.0	21.1	25.4
Washer bottle	0.5	0.9	1.1
Engine oil	10.0	17.6	21.1
Gearbox & differential oil	4.4	7.8	9.3

FACTORY LITERATURE

1964
• Owner's handbook in Italian/French/English, with black-and-white cover, for the 275 GTB/S models. Reprinted by the factory firstly with a black-and-white cover and then twice more with green covers. All carried factory reference 01/65. The first item in a literature numbering system that continues today.

1965
• Sales folder with blue cover in Italian/French/ English, tyre size in specifications 205x14. A second version was produced with the tyre size changed to 195/205-14 and a third example with tyre size 195/205-14 and the addition of an automatically-operated thermostatic radiator fan.
• Mechanical spare parts catalogue for the 275 GTB/S models; factory reference 03/65.

1966
• The 1966 model range brochure includes two pages on the 275 GTS model, with photograph and specifications in Italian/French/English; factory reference 07/66.
• Mechanical spare parts catalogue for the 275 GTB/S models, with factory reference 10/63 (the 63 is obviously a misprint and should read 65 or 66). This has been reprinted at least four times over the years by the factory, with different coloured covers, the original cover being grey, yellow and blue. The last two printings carried no factory reference.

The engine bay, showing the pancake-type air filter over the triple-carburettor assembly that was normal wear on the 275 GTS. Twin air horns can just be seen in front of the radiator, while the black panel forward of the battery covers the fuse and relay board.

The gear lever in an open gate, with the chrome-lidded ashtray featuring crossed Ferrari and Pininfarina flags alongside, and the cigar lighter in the forward face of the central glove tray. The gear lever remained on the left even with right-hand drive.

blanking plate, carrying a rectangular aluminium Pininfarina badge, with a small lockable glovebox under the padded roll below it.

Luggage Compartment

The push-button for the lockable boot is mounted on the centre tail panel just below the lid. The location of this, together with the shape of the luggage compartment and the slightly smaller fuel tank of 86 litres (18.9 Imperial/22.7 US gallons), are the only specification differences between the 275 GTS and the details given in the 275 GT Berlinetta chapter for the 'short-nose' berlinetta.

Engine

The 275 GTS's two-camshaft engine, factory type number 213, is identical to that in the concurrently produced berlinettas, including the location of the components, but has a factory-quoted power output of 260bhp (DIN) at 7000rpm instead of 280bhp (DIN) at 7600rpm. Maximum torque on the GTS is identical at 30kgm (216lb ft) but is developed at 5000rpm, 500rpm lower.

A six-carburettor assembly could be ordered for the berlinetta but this was not offered on the spider, although some cars have been modified subsequently to this set-up. According to factory literature, the carburettor air filter for both berlinetta and spider models is identical. However, a number of spiders have a long pancake filter containing three separate circular elements, with the intake ports of the standard pressed steel unit replaced by a slotted chrome grille around the vertical perimeter. As this assembly also features on some berlinettas, it was probably a case of fitting what was available at any given time. Spiders and berlinettas share the same exhaust system layout, but the tailpipe brackets on the spider are closer to the end of the pipes and thus the systems have different part numbers.

Transmission

The transmission of the 275 GTS is identical to that of the 275 GT Berlinetta, apart from a standard final drive ratio of 3.30:1 (10:33) instead of the standard 3.555:1 (9:32) of the latter. The 275 GTS has four engine mounting points and three transaxle ones. The modification to the main driveshaft to incorporate universal joints at either end was also carried through into the spider variant. None of the 275 GTS models ever received the final torque tube driveshaft and ZF differential assembly.

GEAR RATIOS

	Gearbox	Overall
First	3.075:1	10.147:1
Second	2.12:1	6.996:1
Third	1.572:1	5.187:1
Fourth	1.25:1	4.125:1
Fifth	1.104:1	3.643:1
Reverse	2.67:1	8.811:1
Final drive	3.30:1 (10:33)	

MAJOR ELECTRICAL EQUIPMENT

Battery	12-volt Marelli 6AC11, 60amp/hour
Dynamo	Marelli GCA-101/B
Starter motor	Marelli MT21T-1.8/12D9
Ignition	Twin Marelli S85A-12v-15° distributors, each with a Marelli 12v BZR201A coil
Sparking plugs	Marchal 34HF

Electrical Equipment & Lights

The main components of the electrical system and their layout are generally the same as those provided on the two-cam berlinetta. Specifications for the major components are provided in the panels in the 275 GT Berlinetta chapter. The battery is mounted in the rear corner of the engine compartment, on the opposite side to the driver, with the fuse and relay board on the inner wing panel immediately in front of it.

As with the berlinetta, the lighting equipment is all of Carello manufacture. The open headlamps are mounted in shallow recesses at the leading edge of the front wings, with elliptical surface-mounted side/turn indicator lights below them. These either had plain white lenses or combined orange/white lenses, depending on the market destination. Teardrop-shaped orange turn indicator lights are mounted on the front wing sides virtually in line with the headlamp centres and just behind their rims, at the start of the body crease line. At the rear there is a pair of elliptical stop/tail/turn/ lamp units on the tail panel; the orange indicator section curves around on to the rear wing. Units with full red lenses are found on US-market cars. Separate recessed circular reflectors are mounted inboard of the lamps in chrome-plated sleeves. The number plate lamps are two small vertical chrome-plated rectangular units, on either side of the number plate carrier. When a reversing light is fitted, it is mounted below the left quarter bumper alongside the overrider and actuated by a switch on the gearchange tower when reverse is selected.

SUSPENSION SETTINGS

Front toe-in	−3 to −5mm (−0.118 to −0.197in)
Front camber	+0° to 0°20′
Rear toe-in	−4 to −6mm (−0.157 to −0.236in)
Rear camber	−0°30′ to −1°10′
Castor angle	2°30′
Dampers: front	Koni 82 N-1349
rear	Koni 82 N-1350

Suspension & Steering

The suspension and steering arrangements are virtually identical to those of the 'short-nose'

berlinettas, except for the provision of slightly softer road springs, to give a more comfortable ride in keeping with the less sporting nature of the open version. As with the berlinettas, left- or right-hand drive was available.

Brakes

All components and dimensions are identical to those of the 'short-nose' berlinettas, apart from minor differences to the pedal box.

Wheels & Tyres

Borrani wire wheels with 72 chrome-plated spokes and polished aluminium 6.5x14in rims, with a single centre-nut fixing on a splined hub, are standard equipment on the 275 GTS. The hub spinners for the Borrani wheels normally have triple angled ears, as opposed to the straight-eared variety used on the alloy wheels of the berlinettas. The spare wheel is mounted horizontally on the boot floor, against the cabin bulkhead. The berlinetta's aluminium wheels were not normally offered as an option, but there is no reason why they could not be fitted as the hubs are identical. At least one car, chassis 07681, had them retrofitted by the factory when returned for various modifications in 1966, although it now wears the familiar Borrani wheels.

WHEELS & TYRES

Wheels, front & rear	6.50x14in Borrani wire wheels with alloy rims type RW3874
Tyres, front & rear	Pirelli HS 210-14 or Dunlop SP 205HR-14

IDENTIFICATION PLATES

1. General vehicle data plate giving model type with engine and chassis numbers on engine bay valance panel.
2. Chassis number stamped in frame close to front suspension mounting point.
3. Engine number stamped in block on right rear side close to bellhousing.

Depending on market, the turn portion of the front side/indicator light unit would have a white or orange lens. The rear light unit, here in full red US-market specification, has a recessed circular reflector alongside.

PRODUCTION

Between 1964 and 1966, chassis numbers 06315-08653. Total production 200.

A detail of the 'bent' triple-ear hub nut with the *Cavallino Rampante* at its centre. Occasionally the Borrani logo replaces the Ferrari one.

Identification plate fixed to inner wing panel gives model type, engine type and chassis number.

Chapter 5

330 GT 2+2

A right-hand drive 330 GT 2+2 illustrates the main features of the Series I model: twin headlamps, 11-louvre wing vents, Borrani wire wheels and no bumper overriders.

Although there had been 4-litre cars, called 330 Americas, produced in 1963 using the 250 GT 2+2 bodyshell, the definitive 330 GT 2+2 was not announced until the normal pre-season Ferrari Press Conference in January 1964. The new model made its public debut at the Brussels Salon at the end of that month. The paired headlamp arrangement was the most prominent feature of its relatively conservative and smooth lines. Incorporation of this feature is attributed to the English

DIMENSIONS & WEIGHT

	mm	in
Overall length	4840	190.55
Overall width	1715	67.52
Overall height	1360	53.54
Wheelbase	2650	104.33
Front track	1397	55.00
Rear track	1389	54.68
Weight (dry)	1380kg	3042lb

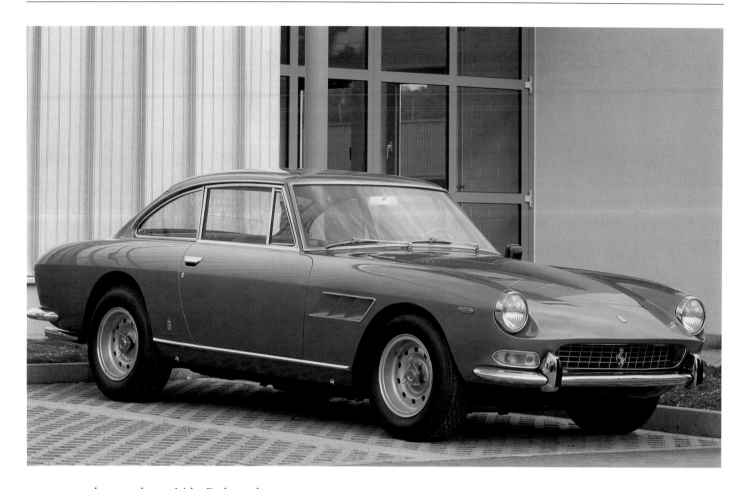

engineer and racing driver, Mike Parkes, who was working for Ferrari at the time. The model provided reasonable 2+2 seating in an airy cabin that featured slim pillars and a generous glass area. Initially the model was fitted with a four-speed plus overdrive gearbox, but this gave way to a five-speed 'box during 1965. On these twin-headlamp cars, Borrani wire wheels with knock-off spinners, as worn by contemporary Ferraris, were fitted.

In the middle of 1965 the front end of the car was redesigned, to provide a nose with a smoother, more homogeneous single-headlamp style, virtually identical to that of the 275 GTS. At the same time cast alloy disc wheels replaced the wire wheels, modernising the appearance still further, but the knock-off hub fixing was retained. Concurrently the 11-slot front wing vents were replaced by a three-slot arrangement, as they had been on the 275 GTS model earlier in the year. Under the skin, the four-speed with overdrive gearbox was replaced by a five-speed unit. This updated model gave rise to twin-headlamp cars being known as series I, and the single-headlamp examples being known as series II. Production continued into 1967, when some late-series examples were fitted with 4.4-litre engines and some also with automatic gearboxes – as prototypes for the yet to be announced 365 GT 2+2 model. These amendments were unpublicised and it is not known exactly how many cars were involved.

Body & Chassis

The 330 GT 2+2 chassis, type 571, has a 2650mm (104.33in) wheelbase and is constructed along familiar Ferrari lines for the period. Two main longitudinal oval steel tubes run either side of the engine, under the cabin and rise in an arc over the rear axle, incorporating brackets for the rearward spring hanger attachment; the forward spring hanger attachment points are on the main rear cabin cross-tube. At the front, the main oval tubes are joined by a large shallow U-section cross-member, to the front of which is welded a tubular support frame of smaller section for the front body and bumper. Another small-section tubular support frame, with a welded sheet metal infill

In Series II form the 330 GT 2+2 has single headlamps, triple-louvre wing vents, cast aluminium wheels and bumpers with overriders. Metallic paint finishes suit these larger models.

Another Series II, this time with the rarely fitted optional Borrani wire wheels.

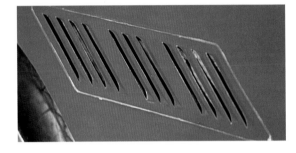

Details of engine bay exhaust vents on the front wings in 11-louvre Series I and triple-louvre Series II forms.

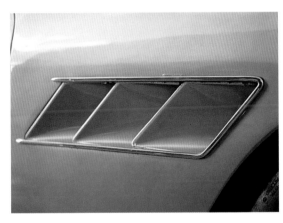

This door handle design is common to both Series I and II versions of the 330 GT 2+2, as well as the 500 Superfast.

panel, forms the front bulkhead, firewall, steering column, pedal box and facia support. Braced tubes run forward from this frame to the front cross-member to support the front wings. On series II cars the floorpan, plus sections of the firewall and the pedal boxes, are glass-fibre mouldings bonded to the chassis. Beneath the cabin is a longitudinal and lateral square-section tubular frame attached to the two main oval tubes, with the sheet metal rear section of the transmission tunnel welded to them. Further small-section tubes are provided, welded to the main frame, to support other elements of the bodywork, which is welded to the tubular structure. The standard finish of the chassis is satin black paint.

The body bears no resemblance to the preced-ing 250 GT 2+2 model, being a much more rounded – some might even say heavier looking – design from Pininfarina, with an attributed influ-ence by Michael Parkes for the twin-headlamp arrangement. The bodies of both series I and II models are constructed of welded steel panels, with an aluminium bonnet and boot lid on steel frames. Series I cars were produced up to the middle of 1965 and feature the twin headlamps with circular side/turn indicator lamps below them, an 11-louvre vent on the side of each front wing and plain chrome-plated steel bumpers front and rear. The series II body differs in having single headlamps with elliptical side/turn indicator lamps below them, triple-louvre vents with pol-ished aluminium trim surround on the front wings, rubber-faced vertical overriders on the bumpers and a slightly more rounded end profile to the radiator grille. The body features from the cabin rearward are identical on both models.

Body Trim & Fittings

The front of the 330 GT 2+2 features a shallow rectangular radiator opening with rounded corners, the curve being more pronounced on series II models, with a polished aluminium trim surround. An inset aluminium egg-crate grille carries a *Cavallino Rampante* at its centre. Below the grille is a one-piece chrome-plated steel bumper, which is plain on series I cars but has vertical rubber-faced chromed steel overriders mounted at the grille extremities on series II cars. The bumper is fixed to the chassis via tubular sup-ports projecting through the lower nose panel. At the rear there is a one-piece wrap-around chrome-plated bumper; series II models have overriders to match those at the front. A rectangular enamel Ferrari badge is fitted on the upper nose panel between the grille and leading edge of the bonnet

Both series of 330 GT 2+2 have a Pininfarina shield and script badge on each rear wing, and Ferrari script on the boot lid.

and a chromed Ferrari script badge is mounted centrally just above the chrome-plated circular keylock on the boot lid. Slim horizontal rectangular Pininfarina badges, with Pininfarina enamel shield badges above them, are fitted low down on the rear wings, between the trailing edge of the door and the rear wheelarch. On some very early examples these badges were fitted low down on the front wings.

The flat bonnet is front hinged and has a manually-positioned sprung support stay near the left forward edge. A triangular aluminium strip runs along the upper sill immediately below the door. Further brightwork is confined to chrome-plated front and rear screen surrounds, quarterlight frames, door glasses, screen wiper arms and blade frames, headlamp bezel surrounds on series I cars, headlamp rims on series II cars, polished aluminium front wing louvre surrounds on series II cars, chrome-plated jacking point plugs at the front and rear of each sill, lift-and-pull chrome-plated cast zinc door handles, circular keylocks, and a chrome trim ring to the fuel filler flap. The flap has a circular chrome-plated centre badge with a black *Cavallino Rampante* emblem.

Plain glass is fitted all round and the windscreen is laminated. There are two-speed self-parking wipers, which normally park on the right on left-hand-drive cars and on the left on right-hand-drive examples. The door windows are provided with swivelling quarterlights, operated by a catch at the lower front corner on series I cars and by a black plastic knurled knob on the door of series II cars. The opening rear quarter windows are hinged at the forward end, with an over-centre retaining catch in the lower rear corner.

Paintwork

As mentioned in the chapter on the 275 GTB models, a vast range of colours was available for Ferraris at this time and the same comments made there apply to the 330 GT 2+2. As this model was built by Pininfarina it should have a paint colour manufactured by either PPG or Duco. The most popular period colour choice seems to have been either silver or one of the various shades of metallic blue. The table on page 30 lists the range.

Interior Trim & Fittings

Standard seat upholstery material is full Connolly leather and the range of colours available is shown in the table on page 33 in the *275 GT Berlinetta* chapter. The front seats are mounted on runners permitting linear adjustment via a lever under the front edge of the cushion, while a lever on the outer lower edge of the squab alters its rake. Elasticated map pockets are provided on the rear of the front seat squabs, which tilt forwards for access to the rear seats. Although the doors are wide, access is made easier by moving the front seats forward on their runners. There are individual rear seats, joined by a one-piece padded backrest, on either side of the transmission tunnel, over which is a central armrest with a chrome-lidded ashtray in the forward face.

Incorporated in each armrest is a door pull, above which is a chrome-plated door handle in its escutcheon plate. The window winder is in the door panel below the armrest pull. On series II models electric windows became available as an option, with the control switches on the centre console forward of the gear lever. The base of the door trim is fitted with a polished aluminium kick strip, as is the shut face of the sill panel.

The floor is carpeted, with ribbed black rubber heelmats for both driver and passenger. The range of carpet colours is provided in the table on page 32 in the *275 GT Berlinetta* chapter. The centre console, transmission tunnel, front and rear inner wheelarches, door panels and rear parcels shelf are trimmed in leather and vinyl to match the seat colour. Black vinyl is standard on the bottom roll, facia and door cappings. The headlining is plain ivory-coloured vinyl, suspended on a sprung steel frame, and is retained by matching vinyl-covered cant rails and rear quarter panel trims.

Vinyl-covered sun visors are provided, the passenger's incorporating a vanity mirror. Between them, also mounted on the upper screen rail, is the dipping interior mirror. Two roof-mounted interior lights are operated automatically by door switches, or manually by a facia switch.

The chrome gear lever is mounted centrally on the transmission tunnel and is topped by a black plastic knob; the gaiter is the same colour as the

Quarterlight opening changed from an over-centre catch on Series I cars (top) to a plastic knurled knob for the Series II (above).

PAINT & TRIM COLOURS

For Paint Colours, Leather Upholstery Colours and Carpet Colours see the tables in the *275 GT Berlinetta* chapter.

Interior comparison of Series I (right) and Series II (below) models shows that the main difference on the later version is the provision of a centre console, on which some of the switches were relocated. This Series I has a non-standard steering wheel and gear lever knob, although they are period items.

interior trim on series II cars. To the rear of this is a chromed-lidded ashtray. The handbrake projects from the floor in an upholstery-coloured vinyl gaiter and is positioned alongside the front of the transmission tunnel, on the driver's side.

Facia & Instruments

The facia panel has a teak veneer finish as standard, although customers could specify an alternative finish if required. One British customer specified black Formica on his left-hand-drive example (chassis 08663). The facia has a long raised section over the instrument cluster and the top surface is black vinyl with a padded rolled edge, repeated at the base. The facia top has two

slim demister slots, with black plastic surrounds, close to the windscreen. A lidded glove compartment, with push-button catch and interior light, is provided on the passenger's side.

The wood-rim steering wheel has plain aluminium spokes and an aluminium boss. The central yellow horn button features the *Cavallino Rampante* emblem and has a black plastic rim. Two slender chrome-plated stalks, with black plastic finger pads, project from the left of the steering column to control the direction indicators and the headlamp main/dipped beam and flashers. On series I cars a right-hand stalk operates the overdrive, and a floor-mounted push-button for the windscreen washers is sited by the driver's footrest. Wipers and washers on series II cars are controlled by a right-hand column stalk, with the washers actuated by pulling it towards the driver.

The general layout of the individual gauges, with white characters on a black background, and the functions that they indicate are similar to those on the 275 models. The speedometer and rev counter are directly in front of the driver on either side of the steering column, with the oil temperature and pressure gauges between them. The water temperature and fuel gauges, ammeter and clock are grouped in the centre of the facia. This arrangement is common to both series I and II models, but the switch layout is different.

Series I cars have a central rocker switch panel in the lower edge of the facia. This panel contains the key-operated turn and push ignition switch, plus switches for the sidelamps, electric fuel pump, left and right blower fans, rear window demister fan and interior light, plus a cigar lighter. Between this bank of switches and the four ancillary gauges are a pair of swivelling circular fresh air outlets, with a regulating slide lever in a vertical slot between them. The instrument lighting switch/rheostat is alongside the passenger's side vent and the two-speed windscreen wiper switch alongside the driver's side vent. At the extremities of the facia are vertical slide levers to open the air supply to each demister slot; an additional slide lever on the driver's side regulates the heater output. Below the facia on either side of the car are manually-operated air intakes, so that air can be provided to either side independently. The bonnet release catch and choke lever are below the facia inboard of the steering column, with an electrical socket on the outer side. The fuse and relay board is mounted under the facia on the passenger's side.

On series II cars a centre console runs up into the lower edge of the facia and the main toggle switches are mounted on its upper face. Below the switches is a blanking plate for the optional radio, with a crossed flag Ferrari/Pininfarina badge under it. Three swivelling circular vents are provided in the centre of the facia, each with a central knurled plastic knob to control airflow. The interior and sidelamp switches are mounted in a recess in the lower facia roll on the outside of the steering column, with the ignition switch/steering lock mounted alongside them in an extension from the column shroud. The sliding levers controlling heating and demisting are as on the series I model.

Luggage Compartment

The boot contains the fuel tank, which is a rectangular vertical unit mounted behind the rear seats. Fuel capacity is 90 litres (19.8 Imperial/23.75 US gallons). The filler is under a cover flap on the wing, adjacent to the front corner of the boot lid; on series I cars it is on the right wing and on series II models on the left. The spare wheel is fixed flat in a well in the boot floor, along with the tool kit roll. The well is covered with a black-painted plywood panel, and the boot floor and sides are lined with black carpet. All plain metal surfaces are painted satin black. Two lights, mounted on the boot ceiling, are actuated by individual switch plates on the lid when the boot is opened. Access to the boot is via a key-operated lock on the lid, which is supported by a telescopic ratchet stay when open.

Engine

The 3967cc (242.1cu in) 60° V12 wet-sump engine, type 209, has a single overhead camshaft per cylinder bank and produces 300bhp (DIN) at 6600rpm, with maximum torque of 33.2kgm (240lb ft) at 5000rpm. The cylinder bore is the same as the 275 series at 77mm (3.03in), the

increased capacity coming from a longer stroke of 71mm (2.80in). The construction materials, operation and component layout, are generally very similar to the 275 series two-cam engine with four mounting points (described in the *275 GT Berlinetta* chapter on page 34) with only relatively small specification differences as detailed here. From chassis number 08729, the engine block was provided with only two mounting points and the engine type number became 209/66.

Central dashboard section on a Series I. For the Series II the rocker switches within the lower crash roll were replaced by a bank of toggle switches on the centre console, there were three air vents instead of two, and the ventilation control levers were repositioned.

ENGINE

Type	60° V12
Type number	209
Cubic capacity	3967cc (242.1cu in)
Bore & stroke	77x71mm (3.03x2.80in)
Compression ratio	8.8:1
Maximum power	300bhp (DIN) at 6600rpm
Maximum torque	33.2kgm (240lb ft) at 5000rpm
Carburettors	3 Weber 40DCZ/6 or 40DFI

TIMING DATA

Inlet valves open	27° BTDC
Inlet valves close	65° ABDC
Exhaust valves open	74° BBDC
Exhaust valves close	16° ATDC
Firing order	1-7-5-11-3-9-6-12-2-8-4-10

Valve clearances with a cold engine should be 0.15mm (0.0059in) for inlet valves and 0.2mm (0.0079in) for exhaust valves, measured between the valve pads and rocker arm.

SYSTEM CAPACITIES

Fuel tank	90 litres (19.8 Imperial/23.7 US gallons)		
	Litres	**Imp Pints**	**US Pints**
Cooling system	13.0	22.9	27.5
Washer bottle	0.5	0.9	1.1
Engine oil	10.0	17.6	21.1
Gearbox oil:			
4-Speed + O/d	3.25	5.7	6.9
5-Speed	5.0	8.8	10.6
Differential oil:			
4-speed + O/d	1.8	3.2	3.8
5-speed + limited slip	2.5	4.4	5.3

TOOL KIT

Pillar-type jack with integral handle
Weber carburettor spanner
Universal pliers
Large flat-bladed screwdriver
Medium flat-bladed screwdriver
Grease gun
Lead mallet
Hammer
Sparking plug spanner
Hub extractor
Oil filter wrench
Generator belt
Set of seven 8-22mm open-ended spanners

The triple Weber 40DCZ/6 or 40DFI carburettors are fitted on individual manifolds, the rear one with a tapping for the vacuum feed to the brake servos. Fuel is supplied by a Fispa Sup 150 diaphragm mechanical fuel pump, with a Fispa PBE10 electric booster pump operated by a facia switch. The distributors are twin Marelli S85A-12v-15° types, each with a Marelli 12-volt BZR201A coil. On series I cars the water pump is mounted on the same shaft as the six-blade cooling fan and driven by a vee-belt from the crankshaft pulley; sometimes there is an auxiliary thermostatically-controlled electric fan in front of the radiator. On series II cars the mechanically-driven fan is omitted, with cooling initially via a

Engine bay of a Series I fitted with a pancake air filter of the type more normally seen on the 275 GTS – but it does provide a clearer view of the V12. Orange cases of the twin oil filters are at the front, twin distributors to the rear. Twin air horns and compressor can be seen on the far inner wing.

A Series II fitted with the standard air filter box, with intake nozzles over the crackle-finish camshaft covers.

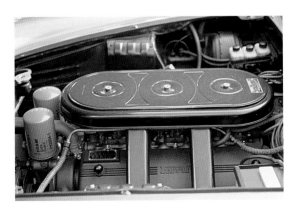

three-blade thermostatically-controlled electric fan in front of the radiator, but from chassis 09509 by twin three-blade electric fans . The water pump has a by-pass valve to maintain constant system pressure and is driven by the triplex timing chain.

Each bank of cylinders has a pair of triple-branch free-flow steel manifolds, with a heat shield fitted above them. The manifolds are flanged to twin collector pipes that siamese into one large-bore pipe for each bank. Each pipe then feeds into its own silencer box assembly suspended below the cabin floor, from which twin pipes exit. These loop to clear the rear suspension and enter two supplementary expansion boxes, emerging as a pair of chrome-plated tailpipes, suspended from rubber hangers, on either side at the rear.

The standard air filter box is black-painted pressed steel, with the top panel retained by three knurled nuts. Within the rectangular casing (with curved ends) are three separate circular elements, one around each carburettor intake. Air is drawn into the box via a pair of rectangular nozzles, which protrude over the cam covers on each side of the casing. Some examples are fitted with a long pancake filter arrangement, containing a separate filter element around each carburettor intake.

The normal oil pressure with an oil temperature of 100°C should be 5.5kg/cm² (78psi) at

6600rpm, with a minimum value of 4kg/cm² (57psi) under the same conditions. The minimum slow running pressure (at 700-800rpm) should be 1.0-1.5kg/cm² (14-21psi).

Transmission

While the contemporary 275 series and later 330 GTC/S models have a five-speed transaxle, the 330 GT 2+2, in both series I and II form, has a conventional gearbox at the rear of the clutch bellhousing with a propshaft to a live rear axle.

Series I cars are fitted with an all-synchromesh four-speed gearbox, with an electrically-operated overdrive mounted on the rear of the gearbox and a mechanically-operated Fichtel & Sachs clutch. This single-plate unit is mounted on the flywheel in the bellhousing. The spring-diaphragm clutch pressure plate is actuated mechanically by a rod linkage, incorporating a sprung load-reduction lever, from the clutch pedal. The gearbox casing is in two halves, which are bolted together. The front contains the main and secondary gear shafts running in roller bearings, plus the reverse gear transfer shaft, with the filler/level plug on the left side and a removable top cover. The rear contains the selector mechanism from the lever linkage, which is in a separate turret casing bolted to the top of it, and the gearbox oil pump, with mesh filter screen, in the lower part. The pump is driven off an extension from the secondary shaft in the front of the casing. A pressure relief valve is provided in the top face of the casing.

The gear lever turret has a tapping for the reversing light switch, so that the lamps illuminate when reverse gear is engaged. The gearchange is to the conventional 'H' pattern, with reverse outside the 'H', to the right and forward alongside third. The electric solenoid-operated overdrive is bolted to the end of the gearbox casing. Two rubber-bushed support brackets at the rear end are bolted to a plate attached to the chassis, and the unit has its own oil filler plug. The overdrive is for use at speeds in excess of 100kph (62.1mph) in fourth gear and is actuated by a lever on the right of the steering column. Disengagement is manual via the same lever or automatic if a lower gear is selected, via a switch on the front top of the gearbox cover.

Some late series I cars and all series II cars have a normal five-speed gearbox without overdrive and are fitted with a Borg & Beck hydraulically-operated clutch. The fluid reservoir is mounted in tandem with those for the brake circuits and the pedal assembly is changed to a suspended type. The gear lever positions for first to fourth gears are the same as on the four-speed gearbox, while fifth is where reverse is in the four-speed box and reverse is opposite fifth.

Gear Ratios

| | Gearbox ratios | | Overall ratios | |
	4-speed O/d	5-speed	4-speed O/d	5-speed
First	2.536:1	2.536:1	10.778:1	10.778:1
Second	1.77:1	1.77:1	7.522:1	7.522:1
Third	1.256:1	1.256:1	5.338:1	5.338:1
Fourth	1.000:1	1.000:1	4.250:1	4.250:1
Fifth (O/d on Series I)	0.778:1	0.796:1	3.306:1	3.383:1
Reverse	3.218:1	3.218:1	13.676:1	13.676:1
Final drive (standard)	4.25:1 (8:34)	4.25:1 (8:34)		
Final drive (optional)	4.00:1 (8:32) or 3.778:1 (9:34)			

Drive is carried from the output shaft via a flanged rubber 'doughnut' coupling to the tubular propeller shaft, which has a sliding splined coupling and universal joint at its connection to the differential. Grease nipples are provided to lubricate the front bearing, sliding joint and universal joint. Series II cars are provided with a ZF-type limited slip differential. The differential casing has an oil filler plug on the left side forward of the half-shaft tube and a drain plug on the rear face. Half-shaft tubes are bolted to the differential casing, to form a rigid rear axle assembly containing a splined half-shaft to each rear wheel. The axle is supported on the rear springs, with twin tie rods in rubber bushes attached to the chassis frame on each side to prevent longitudinal movement.

Tail light treatment: the reflector on the red Series I is mounted in the more usual vertical fashion, but a horizontal position as on the blue Series II is sometimes seen.

Front lighting of Series I (left) and Series II (below left). Differences on the earlier car are twin headlamps in a chromed surround and a circular side/turn indicator light unit. Orange teardrop repeater on the wing side did not change.

Electrical Equipment & Lights

The electrical system is 12-volt, served from a 60, 65, or 74amp/hour battery, sited in the rear corner of the engine compartment on the opposite side to the driver. The Marelli GCA-101/B alternator, mounted on the front of the engine, is driven by a vee-belt off a crankshaft pulley that also serves the water pump on series I models, and directly off the crankshaft pulley on series II cars. On both models the starter motor is mounted on the lower right of the flywheel bellhousing, integral with its solenoid suspended below it. Twin air horns, actuated by the horn push in the centre of the steering wheel, are mounted on the engine bay's inner wing panel. The overdrive unit is manufactured by Bianchi and fitted with a Lucas 7615F actuating solenoid. The fuse and relay board is mounted on the firewall in the engine bay. Specifications for the major electrical components are provided in the accompanying table.

The headlamps on both series I and II models were manufactured by Marchal until mid-1966 and Carello thereafter. All other lighting is by Carello and, apart from the headlamp and sidelamp arrangement, remained constant throughout the production run. The only variations were left-hand dipping headlamps for right-hand-drive cars and the provision of yellow headlamp bulbs for French-market cars. The series I cars have a pair of headlamps, an outer 7in (178mm) dipped-beam unit and an inner 5in (127mm) main-beam unit. They are mounted in an elliptical chrome-plated bezel, retained by screws, at the front of the wings. Series II cars have a single 7in (178mm) headlamp, with a chrome-plated trim ring, fitted in a shallow recess in each front wing. On series I cars there is a circular white-lensed side/turn indicator in each front wing below the headlamps. On series II cars an elliptical side/turn indicator is fitted, with either a plain white lens or a combined orange and white lens, depending on market. Teardrop-shaped orange repeater indicators are positioned on the sides of the front wings, virtually in line with the headlamp centres.

On the tail panel a pair of horizontal rectangular combined stop/tail/turn lamps curve around the edge of the rear wing and inboard of these are two separate rectangular reflectors, normally mounted vertically but sometimes horizontally. The number-plate lamps are in two slim chrome-plated trapezoidal housings, mounted on the top face of the rear bumper. Two small rectangular reversing lamps, actuated by a switch on the gear-change turret when reverse gear is engaged, are fixed to the lower face of the bumper.

Suspension & Steering

The front suspension is independent, with unequal-length forged steel upper and lower wishbones. These are joined by the hub carrier at the outer end and mounted to the chassis via rubber bushes at the inner end, with a coil spring between the wishbones. A telescopic damper is mounted between the top wishbone and a chassis bracket and an anti-roll bar links the two front suspension units via brackets on the lower spring-retaining buckets. Each suspension unit has a pair of chassis-mounted rubber bump stops.

The rear suspension is by semi-elliptic leaf springs, which have six leaves with polyethylene inserts between them. Supplementary coil springs have hydraulic dampers mounted co-axially within them, attached to a bracket on the half-shaft tube at the lower end and a chassis bracket at the upper end. Twin parallel radius arms on each side of the axle prevent longitudinal movement. These are fixed to brackets on the half-shaft tubes and run forwards to chassis brackets, with Silentbloc bushes all round. A rubber bump stop, with height-adjusting shims, is mounted on a bracket on the side of each main rear chassis rail, close to the rear end of the spring.

The front hub carriers are machined forged steel, carrying a stub axle on which the brake disc and a splined hub assembly run on roller bearings. The rear hub carriers are machined cast steel, with a central oil seal through which the half-shaft passes, running in roller bearings and retained to the splined hub and brake disc by a castellated nut with split pin. The splined front and rear hubs are attached to the brake discs by an eight-bolt flange.

Steering is unassisted with a worm and roller steering box, mounted on the front chassis cross-member at the lower end of the universally-jointed steering column. The box has a screw and lock-nut for adjustment of any play on the upper

MAJOR ELECTRICAL EQUIPMENT

Battery	12-volt Baroclem M11AS88, 65amp/hour or 12-volt Marelli 6AC11OR, 60amp/hour or 12-volt SAFA 6SNS5, 74amp/hour
Alternator	Marelli GCA-101/B
Starter motor	Marelli MT21T-1.8/12D9
Ignition	Twin Marelli S85A-12v-15° distributors Twin Marelli 12V BZR201A coils
Sparking plugs	Marchal 34HF

SUSPENSION SETTINGS

Front toe-out	+0 to +1.5mm (+0 to +0.059in)
Front camber	1° fixed
Rear toe-in	None
Rear camber	0°
Castor angle	2°30'
Front dampers	Koni 82H1321 or RIV 474226
Rear dampers	Koni 82N1322 or RIV 474257

face, together with an oil filler plug. Track adjustment is provided on the track rods. The steering ball joints are non-adjustable and require no lubrication. The steering has a turning circle of 13.78 metres (45ft 2in). Both series I and II models were available in either left-or right-hand drive. ZF power-assisted steering was optional from chassis 08599, but could not be retro-fitted to earlier cars.

Brakes

As with the preceding 250 GT 2+2 series, Dunlop disc brakes are fitted to all four wheels. On the 330 GT 2+2 series I completely separate front and rear systems are provided. There are even duplicate Bonaldi vacuum servo units, served from the rear carburettor inlet manifold. On the series II this over-elaborate set-up was rationalised to a single Dunlop C84 vacuum servo unit serving both circuits and then, from chassis 09083, to a Bonaldi VAC type. For the series II the fluid reservoirs were altered from metal to plastic and mounted in tandem with the clutch fluid reservoir. A floor-mounted cable-operated handbrake works on its own set of pads on each rear wheel caliper. There are adjuster screws on the housing and cable-adjustment screws where the twin cables join the lever arm below the cabin.

With the introduction of the series II model, the floor-mounted pedal box was changed to a suspended arrangement. The recommended brake pads for normal touring conditions are Mintex VBO-5201/N2 (M33) at the front and Mintex VBO-5138/N2 (M33) at the rear.

Wheels & Tyres

Borrani RW3801W wire wheels with 72 chrome-plated spokes and polished aluminium 6.5x15in rims are standard on the series I 330 GT 2+2. They have a single centre-nut fixing on a splined hub. The series II model has ten-hole light alloy wheels as standard but the Borrani wire wheels are optional. The hub spinners for the Borrani wheels normally have triple angled ears, as opposed to the straight-eared kind used on the alloy wheels. The spare wheel is mounted horizontally in a well, under a removable panel in the boot floor.

Standard wheels were Borrani wires for the Series I, ten-hole alloys for the Series II.

PRODUCTION

Series I: (twin headlamp) during 1964 and 1965, chassis numbers 04963-07533. Total production 625.

Series II: (single headlamp) between 1965 and 1967, chassis numbers 07537-10193. Total production 474.

IDENTIFICATION PLATES

1. General vehicle data plate giving model type with engine and chassis numbers on engine bay firewall panel.
2. Chassis number stamped in frame close to front suspension mounting point.
3. Engine number and type stamped in block on right rear side close to bellhousing.

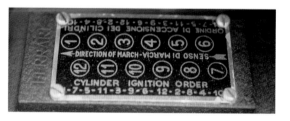

Cylinder firing order plate at the forward end of the left camshaft cover.

WHEELS & TYRES

Wheels, front & rear:	
Series I	6.50Lx15 Borrani wire wheels with alloy rims, RW3801W
Series II	7Lx15 Borrani cast light alloy, RW3812
Tyres, front & rear:	
Series I	Dunlop 205-15in, Michelin X 205VR-15 or Pirelli 210HR-15
Series II	Dunlop 205-15in or Pirelli 210HR-15

Identification plate fixed to the firewall gives model type, engine type and chassis number.

Chapter 6
330 GTC/S & 365 GTC/S

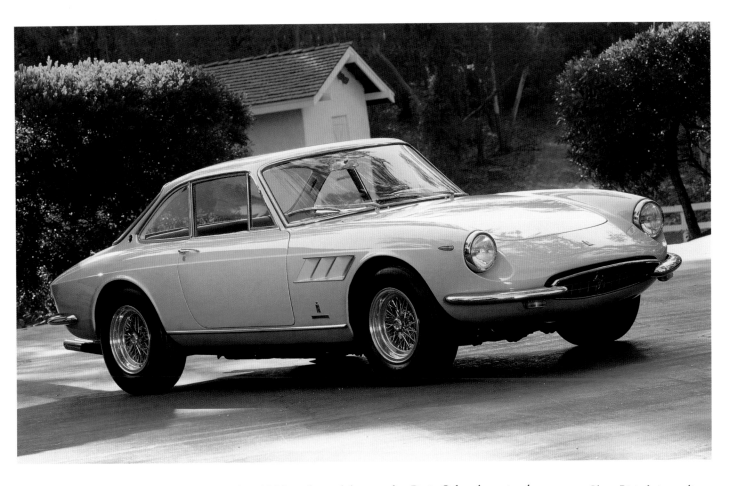

Introduced into the Ferrari range at the 1966 Geneva Salon, the 330 GTC featured a 4-litre twin-cam V12 engine virtually identical in configuration to that used in the 330 GT 2+2 model. However, instead of an engine-mounted gearbox driving through a propeller shaft to a conventional live rear axle, there was a five-speed transaxle with an enclosed torque tube driveshaft. The 330 GTC was an addition to the Ferrari range, not a replacement for an outgoing model, although some people view it more as the true successor to the 250 GT Lusso than the 275 GTB. It may seem strange that the company should produce another two-seater model alongside the 275 GTB in what was – and still is – a very limited and exclusive market.

The coupé was followed by an open version, the 330 GTS, which became available prior to its

show debut at the Paris Salon later in the year. The frontal treatment, with its shallow oval grille, was reminiscent of the 500 Superfast, while the tail replicated that of the 275 GTS model. The only visual difference between the coupé and spider models was in the cabin area, the coupé having a fixed head with elegant slim pillars and a panoramic glass area, while the spider had a folding soft-top retained by two clips on the screen rail. As with the 275 GTB, cast aluminium wheels were standard, with Borrani wire wheels optional. A special 330 GTC was built for Leopoldo Pirelli on chassis number 10581. It was fitted with the type 245/C engine as used in the 365 GTC and featured a specially cast set of 15in Campagnolo five-spoke alloy wheels – a design that would appear on the 365 GTB/4 and which in stylised form is still a key feature of Ferraris today.

Clean Pininfarina styling of the 330 GTC works well even in bright yellow. Triple-louvre wing vents distinguish 330 models from later 365 versions. An after-market nudge bar has been added to provide some protection to the nose of this US-market car.

A right-hand drive 330 GTC fitted with optional Borrani wire wheels. From any angle, the marriage of 500 Superfast front styling with the tail section of the 275 GTS works well, providing tightly flowing lines.

Production of both models ceased in late 1968, when the replacement 365 GTC and 365 GTS were announced. As history now shows, the 365 GTC/S models would be the last Ferrari road cars to be fitted with a single overhead camshaft per bank V12 engine, all subsequent engines having twin camshafts per bank. The 365 GTC and 365 GTS models are visually very similar to their predecessors, the only external difference being the replacement of the front wing vents by small matt-black louvred vent panels near the corners of the trailing edge of the bonnet. Inside there are further detail differences, the most obvious being the addition of two circular adjustable ventilation outlets in the centre of the facia top. As with the 330 GTC/S models, Borrani wire wheels were available as an option. The production period lasted only until 1970, so relatively few were produced – particularly of the spider version which

was not made beyond 1969. This makes them one of the rarer production models of the period. Sales probably suffered from the arrival of the more aggressively styled and powerful 365 GTB/4 (featured in the Ferrari catalogue at the same time with a price tag only about ten per cent higher) and from increasingly strict US legislation, which meant that these models could no longer be sold

DIMENSIONS & WEIGHTS

	330 GTC		330 GTS		365 GTC		365 GTS	
	mm	in	mm	in	mm	in	mm	in
Overall length	4470	176.00	4430	174.41	4470	176.00	4430	174.41
Overall width	1675	65.94	1675	65.94	1675	65.94	1675	65.94
Overall height	1300	51.18	1250	49.21	1300	51.18	1250	49.21
Wheelbase	2400	94.49	2400	94.49	2400	94.49	2400	94.49
Front track	1401	55.16	1401	55.16	1410	55.51	1410	55.51
Rear track	1417	55.79	1417	55.79	1414	55.67	1414	55.67
Weight (dry)	1300kg	2866lb	1200kg	2646lb	1350kg	2976lb	1250kg	2756lb

The styling works just as well in convertible form. This left-hand drive 330 GTS is also fitted with the popular alternative Borrani wire wheels.

in that market without major modification. Obviously, Ferrari was not willing to spend money for this purpose on a model nearing its sell-by date.

It would probably be fair to say that these coupés and spiders were aimed at a different clientele from that buying the concurrent 275 and 365 berlinettas. They were not as overtly sporting, more conservative in appearance and had a less aggressive stance. They suited customers who required a supremely elegant, fast, easier-to-drive and less ostentatious form of Ferrari motoring.

Body & Chassis

The 2400mm (94.49in) wheelbase chassis of the 330 GTC/S is type 592, while the 365 GTC/S is type 592/C – the difference in title relating to the engine mounting point locations for the larger capacity engine. The 330 GTC was the first model

to use the two-point mounting on both engine and transaxle with the solid torque tube connection. That proved to be a success in eliminating balancing and alignment problems, and was introduced on the 275 GTB in April 1966. The general chassis construction principles are very similar to those used on the 275 series, with a cross-braced centre section and ladder-type outriggers. The different type numbers mainly relate to the variations in minor tube location due to the different body style and shape. The firewall, footwell boxes and floor panels are glass-fibre mouldings.

The steel bodies, which have aluminium bonnets and boot lids, were designed and built by Pininfarina. They share the rear section of the 275 GTS model, coupled to a front section that is very similar in profile to the 500 Superfast. The slim-pillared cabin area on the coupés is unique to the 330 and 365 GTCs, while the spider version's

Two examples of the 365 GTC, one wearing standard ten-hole alloy wheels, the other optional Borrani wire wheels. For the 365 versions the front wing vents were replaced by black exhaust louvres on the bonnet, just visible in the front view.

cabin profile echoes that of the 275 GTS. The only differentiating body feature between the 330 and 365 models is the engine bay air vent system. The 330 GTC/S models have triple louvres on the front wing sides, as featured on late-series 275 GTS, 500 Superfast and 330 GT 2+2 models, whereas the 365 GTC/S models have trapezoidal black plastic louvres cut into the rear corners of the bonnet, with plain wing sides. Chrome-plated quarter bumpers are provided all round, those at the rear being fitted with rubber-faced overriders.

The convertible roof of the GTS models is of heavyweight canvas, with a rectangular clear Perspex panel in the rear, on a folding steel frame.

There is an external chrome-plated lateral strip on the frame above the rear window. The soft-top is secured to the screen rail by two over-centre fasteners and folds into a recess behind the seats, where it is provided with a protective vinyl cover retained by chromed press-studs. A hard-top was available but rarely supplied.

Body Trim & Fittings

These models feature a shallow, projecting elliptical radiator opening, with an aluminium trim surround to the inner lip. The inset aluminium egg-crate grille carries a chrome-plated *Cavallino*

PAINT & TRIM COLOURS

For Paint Colours, Leather Upholstery Colours and Carpet Colours see the *275 GT Berlinetta* chapter for cars up to mid-1969 and the *365 GTB/4* chapter for cars from mid-1969.

Only 20 examples of the 365 GTS were built, all left-hand drive. These two are fitted respectively with standard ten-hole alloy wheels and optional Borrani wires.

Unlike 365 models, the 330 versions displayed their designation beneath the Ferrari script on the boot lid.

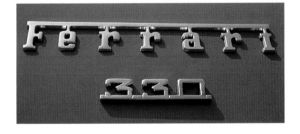

Rampante at its centre. The slim wrap-around chrome-plated front quarter bumpers run into the grille extremities. At the rear, the wrap-around quarter bumpers are fitted with black rubber-faced overriders at their inner ends. A rectangular enamel Ferrari badge is fitted on the upper nose panel between the grille and leading edge of the bonnet, and a chromed Ferrari script badge is mounted centrally close to the trailing edge of the boot lid. The 330 GTC/S models also have a '330' badge below the Ferrari badge on the boot lid. Slim horizontal rectangular Pininfarina badges, with Pininfarina enamel shields above them, are fitted to the front wing lower sides on all models.

The front-hinged bonnet is plain on the 330 GTC/S, but, as mentioned earlier, the 365 GTC/S models have trapezoidal black plastic louvres at the rear corners. The bonnet is supported by a manually-positioned sprung rod on the front left

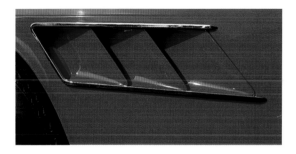

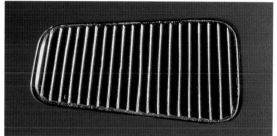

Hot air escapes from the engine bay through triple-louvre vents in the front wings on 330 models or two black louvred panels in the bonnet on 365 versions.

side when open. The body sides feature a waist-line crease, below which are the engine bay air louvres on the front wings of the 330 GTC/S. These have a slim polished aluminium surround to the front, top and bottom edges.

A triangular aluminium strip on the upper sill runs between the front and rear wheelarches and there are chrome-plated screen and window surrounds. Other brightwork is confined to headlamp rims, windscreen wiper arms and blade frames, boot push-button lock on the GTS (central on the rear panel just below the boot lid), fuel filler flap trim identical to the 330 GT 2+2 on coupés (the spider's fuel filler is within the boot), plus push-button door handles and circular keylock below. Boot access on GTCs is via a chrome-plated lever (with keylock) on the inner left door shut, with a concealed emergency release alongside.

Plain glass and a laminated windscreen are fitted. The two-speed self-parking wipers park on the right for left-hand drive and on the left for right-hand drive. The door windows are provided with swivelling quarterlights, operated by a circular knurled black plastic knob on the upper door panel below the quarterlight on coupés and by a chrome quarter-turn catch in the front corner of the quarterlight on spiders. On the coupés the rear screen is heated, with a switch on the centre console and a warning light in the rev counter.

Paintwork

A vast range of colours was available for Ferraris at this time, as listed in the *275 GT Berlinetta* and *365 GTB/4* chapters (see pages 30 and 86), and the comments made there also apply to the 330 GTC/S and 365 GTC/S. As these cars were built by Pininfarina they should have a paint colour manufactured by either PPG or Duco.

Interior Trim & Fittings

The standard seat upholstery material is full leather and the colours available for the 330 GTC/S and 365 GTC/S models are shown in the tables in the *275 GT Berlinetta* and the *365 GTB/4* chapters respectively (see pages 33 and 89). The seats are mounted on runners, with adjustment via a lever under the front edge of the

Elegant fuel filler cap of GTC models is released by a small lever on the rear parcel shelf.

Three different door trim layouts: 330 GTC (top) has a straight armrest with quarterlight knob within the door panel; 330 GTS (centre) armrest has an upturned front section and the quarterlight catch is on the window frame; 365 GTC (bottom) armrest differs again but coupé style of quarterlight knob is retained; 365 GTS (not shown) trim is virtually identical to that of the 330 GTS. All cars had electric windows, but this 330 GTS appears to have been retrimmed without the plug for the emergency winder.

Each rear pillar on coupés contains a sliding lever to open and close the ventilation outlet.

The interior of a 330 GTS: the design is generally the same for all 330 and 365 models in the series apart from differences to ventilation layout and door armrests.

cushion. A circular knurled black plastic knob on the outer lower edge of the squab alters its rake. The backrest can be tilted forward for access to the carpeted luggage platform, where coupés are fitted with leather luggage-retaining straps.

The front of the armrests incorporate door pulls – horizontal on the 330 GTC but angled upwards on the 330 GTS and 365 GTC/S – with a chrome-plated door-opening trigger at the front of the armrest. The armrest is normally trimmed in black vinyl to match the door capping, but could be ordered in upholstery colour to match the rest of the door trim. A circular plug in the door panel forward of the armrest can be removed to insert the emergency winder for the electric windows, in case of motor failure. The control switches for the windows are in the centre console behind the ashtray. A polished aluminium kick

strip is attached along the shut face of the sills.

The floor and rear luggage platform were normally carpeted, with black rubber heelmats incorporated for both driver and passenger. The range of carpet colours is provided in the tables in the *275 GT Berlinetta* and the *365 GTB/4* chapters (see pages 32 and 89), which are applicable to the 330 GTC/S and 365 GTC/S models respectively. The centre section of the firewall, transmission tunnel, front inner wheelarches, facia top and bottom roll are trimmed as standard in black vinyl, although the centre console could be in the upholstery colour. The coupé's headlining is plain ivory-coloured vinyl with longitudinal fluting, surrounded and retained by deep cant rails upholstered in the same material, as are the rear screen pillars. The coupé's rear parcels shelf is normally trimmed in black vinyl. There are vinyl-covered sun visors, the passenger's incorporating a vanity mirror, with a dipping interior mirror between them. At the outer extremities of the upper screen rail are the GTS model's soft-top fixings.

The chrome gear lever, topped by a black plastic knob, is in an open chrome-plated gate on the left of the transmission tunnel at the front of the centre console on all models, whether right- or left-hand drive. The knob on 365 models has the gearchange pattern engraved in white on its top face. To the right of the gate is a chrome ashtray, featuring a crossed Ferrari and Pininfarina flag badge on the lid. A cigar lighter is housed centrally in the front face of the glove tray, behind

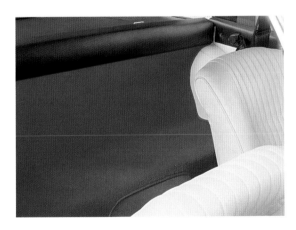

The carpeted rear luggage platform found on coupés, with chrome-plated retainers for luggage straps visible on the forward edge of the parcel shelf.

the ashtray and between the electric window switches. Under the facia are the umbrella-type handbrake (between steering column and centre console) and bonnet release lever (at the outer end) with an emergency pull-ring alongside. On 365 GTC/S models, the choke lever is also suspended below the facia, outboard of the steering column. The release lever for the fuel filler flap on the coupés is positioned on the rear parcels shelf. An interior light is provided, suspended beneath the facia on spider models. Coupés have a pair of slim rectangular interior lights mounted on the cant rail above the rear side windows, with a small chrome-plated coat hook to their rear. A sliding lever in each rear screen pillar on the coupés opens a flap to extract air from the cabin through a small chrome-rimmed circular outlet on the outside base of each pillar.

Facia & Instruments

At a glance the facias and centre consoles of the 330 GTC/S and 365 GTC/S models appear very similar, and are in the basic instrument layout, but there are various differences, mainly in the layout of ventilation controls. Both feature a separate main oval instrument nacelle in front of the driver containing the speedometer and rev counter. Between them are the oil temperature and pressure gauges in the upper part and the water temperature gauge centrally below, forming a triangular arrangement. Below and to either side of the water temperature gauge are the reset button for the trip odometer and the instrument lights rheostat. The speedometer dial contains an odometer with trip, plus red turn indicator and green sidelamp warning lights. The rev counter dial has warning lights for choke (365 GTC/S only), heated rear window, main beam and electric fuel pump. Central on the facia are three auxiliary dials – a fuel gauge (with low level warning light), a clock and an ammeter. All gauges have white digits on a black background. A lockable glovebox with interior light is provided on the passenger's side of the facia. On all models, a pair of vertical sliding levers at the outer extremities of the facia control air distribution to that side of the car. On the 330 GTC/S models a single vertical sliding lever in the centre of the facia, between the auxiliary gauges and glovebox, regulates the heater. The 365 GTC/S models have a pair of sliding levers in this location, allowing separate heater control for each side of the car.

The instrument nacelle surround, facia top and bottom padded roll section are all covered in black vinyl. The nacelle and facia panels have a teak veneer finish, with an aluminium trim strip along the lower edge of the facia. The 330 GTC/S facia top has slim demister slots below the wind-

Seen on a 330 GTS, the main instrument layout ahead of the driver is essentially the same for all models.

Centre console and dashboard section differs between 330 and 365 models. The large view shows a 330 GTS, while the detail – from a 365 GTC – highlights the main changes: two vertical slide levers instead of one, and two ventilation outlets on top of the dashboard instead of three on the centre console.

screen, whereas the 365 GTC/S has two central directionally-adjustable circular demister outlets on the facia top, with matching outlets on either side of the forward sides of the centre console. Air is directed to the screen and/or the footwells via the sliding levers at the ends of the facia.

Luggage Compartment

Below the boot floor are the twin aluminium fuel tanks, spray-coated with glass-fibre, which form the sides of the spare wheel well. Fuel capacity is 90 litres (19.8 Imperial/23.7 US gallons). The combined filler cap and cover flap is on the left rear wing of the coupés and in the right rear corner of the boot lid opening on the spider variants, exactly as on the 275 GTS model. The boot floor and sides are lined with black carpet and all plain metal surfaces are painted satin black. A light, mounted on the ceiling of the boot, is actuated by a switch plate on the lid when the boot is opened. Boot access is via a key-operated lever lock in the left-side door shut on coupés and a key-operated lock on the tail panel on spiders; the lid is supported by a right-side telescopic ratchet stay.

Engine

The 330 GTC/S has a 3967cc (242.1cu in) 60° V12 wet-sump engine with a single overhead camshaft per cylinder bank, producing 300bhp (DIN) at 6600rpm and with maximum torque of 33.2kgm (240lb ft) at 5000rpm. The factory type number is 209/66, the latter part of the type number referring to the twin engine-mount configuration, also adopted on the 330 GT 2+2 model in 1966. The construction materials, operation and component layout are identical to the 330 GT 2+2 engine with two mounting points, with only the small differences detailed below.

Triple Weber carburettors are either 40DCZ/6 (as on the 330 GT 2+2) or 40DFI/2 on individual manifolds, fed by a Fispa Sup 150 diaphragm mechanical fuel pump, with either a Fispa PBE10 or Bendix model 467087 electric booster pump controlled by a facia switch. A crankcase purging system, which provides hose connections from the cam covers to the inlet manifolds and air filter casing, is fitted so that oil fumes are burned in the engine rather than discharged to atmosphere. Radiator cooling is via a pair of thermostatically-controlled, three-blade electric fans in front of the radiator. If the optional air conditioning is fitted, the pump is mounted on the lower right front of the timing chain casing, with its own twin drive belt direct off the crankshaft pulley and a condenser coil mounted on a bracket forward of the radiator. The evaporator coil is mounted behind the centre console vents, which have the operating switches in their centres.

Each bank of cylinders has a pair of triple-branch free-flow steel manifolds, with a heat shield fitted above them. The manifolds are flanged to twin collector pipes, which then feed the gases via slip joint connections into twin silencer boxes, with separate heat shields above

On spider versions – this is a 330 GTS – the fuel filler is in the lower right corner of the boot opening, as on the 275 GTS. On all models in the series the spare wheel is housed in a recess beneath a panel in the boot floor.

The wood-rim steering wheel has an aluminium boss and plain aluminium spokes featuring an engraved pattern. The central horn push is a yellow button, with black plastic rim, featuring the *Cavallino Rampante* emblem. A pair of slender chrome-plated stalks, with black plastic finger pads, project from the left of the steering column. One works the direction indicators, the other the headlamp main/dipped beam and flasher functions (and sidelamps as well on the 365 GTC/S). A stalk on the right operates the two-speed windscreen wipers, and the washers by pulling it towards the driver. The key-operated ignition/starter switch, incorporating a steering lock, is mounted on the lower facia roll, to the right of the steering column shroud, irrespective of whether the car is right- or left-hand drive.

The face of the centre console carries a bank of six switches, with circular black plastic levers, along the upper edge. These control sidelamps (on the 330 GTC/S) or hazard warning lights (on right-hand-drive 365 GTC/S cars, spare on left-hand drive), electric fuel pump, left-side ventilation fan, right-side ventilation fan, rear window demister element and interior light. Below the switches are three circular ventilation outlets for the optional air conditioning system, and below these a radio blanking plate featuring a rectangular aluminium Pininfarina badge.

TOOL KIT

Scissor-type jack with ratchet
  handle
Rear hub extractor screws
Rear hub extractor
Front hub extractor
Hammer
Lead mallet
Pliers
Phillips screwdriver for screws
  up to 4mm (0.16in)
Phillips screwdriver for screws
  5-6mm (0.20-0.24in)
Phillips screwdriver for screws
  7-9mm (0.27-0.35in)
120mm (4.7in) long flat-
  bladed screwdriver
150mm (5.9in) long flat-
  bladed screwdriver
Generator belt SV574 Pirelli
  type 60645
Weber carburettor spanner
  type 510/a
Grease gun
Grease gun extension nozzle
Sparking plug spanner
Oil filter cartridge wrench
Set of seven 8-22mm open
  ended spanners

them, below the cabin floor. The twin pipes that exit loop to clear the rear suspension and emerge as a pair of chrome-plated tailpipes, suspended from rubber hangers, on either side at the rear.

On cars below chassis number 09893 a single oil cooler was fitted in the nose in front of the water radiator's electric fans; subsequently twin oil-cooler radiators were used in the same location. Earlier cars may have been retro-fitted with this duplex assembly if a customer complained of excessive oil temperature. The normal oil pressure with an oil temperature of 120°C should be 5.5kg/cm^2 (78psi) at 7000rpm, with a minimum value of 4kg/cm^2 (57psi) under the same conditions. Minimum slow running pressure (at 700-800rpm) should be 1.0-1.5kg/cm^2 (14-21psi).

A modified fuel delivery system was incorporated from chassis number 09989, due to fuel in the lines getting too hot and vaporising. The alteration involved re-routing the fuel feed pipe from the tank to run more centrally under the car, away from the right-side exhaust system, and modifying the connection between the fuel suction pipe and tank. Again, earlier examples may have had this modification carried out if a customer experienced problems.

The 365 GTC/S has a 4390cc (267.9cu in) wet-sump 60° V12 engine, with a single overhead camshaft per cylinder bank, producing 320bhp (DIN) at 6600rpm, with 37kgm (267lb ft) of torque at 5000rpm. The factory type number is 245/C. The unit's construction materials, operation and component layout are identical to the 330 GTC/S engine, apart from the larger 81mm (3.19in) cylinder bore with push-fit rather than pressed-in cylinder liners and the small specification differences detailed below.

The triple Weber carburettors are 40DFI/5 or 40DFI/7, on individual manifolds. The chassis numbers of the 47 cars fitted with the latter type are: 365 GTC – 12439, 12441, 12443, 12447, 12449, 12461, 12471, 12487, 12499, 12503, 12519, 12541, 12543, 12551, 12557, 12571, 12595, 12601, 12645, 12649, 12655, 12657, 12673, 12677, 12707, 12709, 12713, 12715, 12721, 12725, 12729, 12737, 12739, 12747, 12773, 12785 and 12795; 365 GTS – 12453, 12455, 12457, 12459, 12463, 12465, 12473, 12477, 12489 and 12493. Twin Bendix electric fuel pumps are fitted close to the tank at the rear of the car. Each bank of cylinders has a pair of triple-branch free-flow steel manifolds, with a heat shield fitted above them. The manifolds siamese to twin collector pipes that then feed via slip joint connections into twin silencer boxes suspended below the cabin floor.

The normal oil pressure with an oil temperature of 120°C should be 4.5kg/cm^2 (64psi) at 6600rpm, with a minimum value of 4kg/cm^2

As with most Ferraris of the period, the 330 GTC engine bay is dominated by a large air cleaner assembly over the carburettors, hiding most other components from view.

This 365 GTC view shows the standard grey sound-deadening quilt with diamond pattern, and the internal shrouds around the bonnet air outlets.

(57psi) under the same conditions. The minimum slow running pressure (at 700-800rpm) should be 1.0-1.5kg/cm^2 (14-21psi). The oil cooler radiator is integral with the water radiator, rather than a separate unit. As with the 330 GTC/S models, air conditioning was optional and the component arrangement is the same as for those models.

Transmission

The transmission on 330 and 365 GTC/S models is virtually identical to that of the post-April 1966 275 GT Berlinettas (see page 38), apart from different fifth gear ratios and a standard final drive ratio of 3.444:1 (9:31) instead of 3.20:1 (10:32). All 330 and 365 GTC/S models have two engine

ENGINE

	330 GTC/S	365 GTC/S
Type	60° V12	60° V12
Type number	209/66	245/C
Cubic capacity	3967.44cc (242.1cu in)	4390.358cc (267.9cu in)
Bore & stroke	77x71mm (3.03x2.80in)	81x71mm (3.19x2.80in)
Compression ratio	8.8:1	8.8:1
Maximum power	300bhp (DIN) at 7000rpm	320bhp (DIN) at 6600rpm
Maximum torque	33.2kgm (240lb ft)	37kgm (267lb ft)
	at 5000rpm	at 5000rpm
Carburettors	3 Weber 40DCZ/6, or 40DFI/2	3 Weber 40DFI/5, or 40DFI/7

TIMING DATA

	330 GTC/S	365 GTC/S
Inlet valves open	27° BTDC	13°15' BTDC
Inlet valves close	65° ABDC	59° ABDC
Exhaust valves open	74° BBDC	59° BBDC
Exhaust valves close	16° ATDC	13°15' ATDC
Firing order	1-7-5-11-3-9-6-12-2-8-4-10	

330 GTC/S – Valve clearances with a cold engine should be 0.15mm (0.0059in) for inlets and 0.2mm (0.0079in) for exhausts, measured between the valve pads and rocker arms.
365 GTC/S – Valve clearances with a cold engine should be 0.2mm (0.0079in) for inlets and 0.25mm (0.0098in) for exhausts, measured between the valve pads and rocker arms.

SYSTEM CAPACITIES

	330 GTC/S			365 GTC/S		
Fuel tank	90 litres			90 litres		
	(19.8 Imperial/23.7 US gallons)			(19.8 Imperial/23.7 US gallons)		
	Litres	Imp pints	US pints	Litres	Imp pints	US pints
Cooling System	12.5	22.0	26.4	13.0	22.9	27.5
Washer bottle	1.0	1.8	2.1	1.0	1.8	2.1
Engine oil	10.0	17.6	21.1	11.0	19.4	23.3
Gearbox/differential oil	4.4	7.8	9.3	4.4	7.8	9.3

GEAR RATIOS

	330 GTC/S		365 GTC/S	
	Gearbox	Overall	Gearbox	Overall
First	3.075:1	10.592:1	3.075:1	10.592:1
Second	2.12:1	7.302:1	2.12:1	7.302:1
Third	1.572:1	5.415:1	1.572:1	5.415:1
Fourth	1.25:1	4.305:1	1.25:1	4.305:1
Fifth	0.964:1	3.320:1	0.96:1	3.307:1
Reverse	2.67:1	9.197:1	2.67:1	9.197:1
Final drive	3.444:1 (9:31)		3.444:1 (9:31)	

PRODUCTION

330 GTC between 1966 and 1968, chassis numbers 08329-11577. Total production 598.

330 GTS between 1966 and 1968, chassis numbers 08899-11713. Total production 100.

365 GTC between 1968 and 1970, chassis numbers 11589-12785. Total production 168.

365 GTS during 1969, chassis numbers 12163-12493. Total production 20.

MAJOR ELECTRICAL EQUIPMENT

330 GTC/S & 365 GTC/S

Battery	12-volt SAFA 6SNS-5, 74amp/hour or
	12-volt Fiamm 6B5, 75amp/hour
Alternator	Lucas 11AC-N.542-162-50
Starter motor	Marelli MT21T-1.8/12D9
Ignition	Twin Marelli S85A-12V-15°
	Twin Marelli 12v BZR201A coils
Sparking plugs	Champion N6Y

and two transaxle mounting points, with a rigid torque tube connection between. From chassis 09939, molybdenum-sprayed synchromesh rings were fitted, for easier gearchanging and longevity. The 365 GTC/S models were fitted with one-piece half-shafts with Lobro-type homokinetic universal joints.

Electrical Equipment & Lights

The electrical system is 12-volt, negative earth, served from a 74 or 75amp/hour battery sited in the rear corner of the engine bay on the opposite side to the driver. A Lucas alternator, mounted on the front of the engine, is driven by a vee-belt directly off the crankshaft pulley. The starter motor is mounted on the lower right section of the flywheel bellhousing, integral with its solenoid suspended below it, on both models. Twin air horns are mounted in the nose, forward of the radiator and electric fans, and actuated by the horn push in the centre of the steering wheel. The fuse and relay boards are positioned under the bonnet on the firewall, close to the battery. Specifications for the major electrical components are provided in the panel.

The headlamps were manufactured by Marchal until mid-1966, Carello thereafter. Other lighting is all by Carello and remained constant throughout the production run of both series. The only variations were left-hand dipping headlamps for right-hand-drive cars and the provision of yellow headlamp bulbs for France. The front side/turn indicator lamps, with clear lenses, are in small rectangular chrome-plated casings, suspended below and towards the inner end of each quarter bumper. In the front wing sides, virtually in line with the headlamp centres, are teardrop-shaped orange indicator repeaters.

At the rear there is a pair of elliptical stop/tail/turn indicator lamp units on the tail panel, the orange indicator section curving around the wing extremity. Units with full red lenses are provided on US-market cars. Separate recessed circular reflectors are mounted inboard of them in chrome-plated sleeves. The number plate lamps are two small vertically-mounted chrome-plated rectangular units, on either side of the number plate. A pair of reversing lights is fitted, mounted below the quarter bumper alongside the overrider on each side and actuated by a switch on the gearchange tower upon engagement of reverse.

Small circular red warning lamps, illuminated when a door is open, are fitted in the trailing edge of the door frames on 365 GTC/S models.

Suspension & Steering

The front and rear suspension design is the same as the 275 series cars, with pressed steel unequal length wishbones, coil springs and telescopic dampers to each wheel – only the individual components vary in their detail and settings. Similarly, worm-and-roller unassisted steering is employed, giving a turning circle of 13.95 metres (45ft 9in).

Suspension Settings

	330 GTC/S	365 GTC/S
Front toe-in	−4 to −5mm	−4 to −5mm
	(−0.157 to −0.197in)	(−0.157 to −0.197in)
Front camber	0° to +0°20'	0° to +0°20'
Rear toe-in	5mm (0.197in)	2-3mm (0.079-0.118in)
Rear camber	−0°50' to −1°15'	−2°
Castor angle	2°18'15"	2°18'15"
Dampers: front	Koni 82P1451	Koni 82P1451
rear	Koni 82N1452	Koni 82N1452

Left- or right-hand drive was available on all models, although the 365 GTS was only ever manufactured with left-hand drive.

Brakes

On the 330 GTC/S models, Girling disc brakes are provided to all four wheels, with a vacuum-operated servo fed from the rear carburettor inlet manifold. A tandem master cylinder with twin reservoirs supplies separate front and rear brake circuits. The servo was initially a Dunlop C84 unit, but this was succeeded by an additional Bonaldi type 18172 unit in December 1966 and then, from chassis 09829 in May 1967, a Bonaldi Master Vac 14-18943. An umbrella-type cable-operated handbrake, mounted under the facia, works on its own set of pads in separate calipers on each rear disc with automatic adjustment on the housings. There are cable adjustment screws where the twin cables join the lever arm to the cable beneath the cabin. The recommended brake pads for normal touring conditions are Ferodo DS11, with VBO-type 8073/R handbrake pads.

The 365 GTC/S models have a very similar brake system layout, except that they are fitted with ATE type L38KN calipers and discs with Texstar Y1431G pads. There are a Bonaldi Z3-5 servo, a rear circuit pressure-limiting valve and a drum handbrake arrangement using Energit 338 shoes, operating in the bell of the rear discs.

The pedal box provides suspended pedal arrangements on both series, with a facility on the pedal pad pins for height adjustment as on the 275 series models.

Wheels & Tyres

Borrani ten-hole 7Lx14in light alloy wheels, finished in silver with a clear lacquer coat, are the standard equipment on both series. The wheels have a single centre-nut fixing on a splined hub and are identical to those fitted to late 275 GTB and 275 GTB/4 models. Borrani wire wheels with polished aluminium rims in the same size were optional. The hub spinners for the Borrani wire wheels normally have triple angled ears with a

Factory Literature

1966
• The 1966 model range brochure includes two pages on the 330 GTC, with photograph and specifications in Italian/French/English; factory reference 07/66.
• Owner's handbook for the 330 GTC, with factory reference 09/66, initially with yellow cover, then reprinted with a beige/black/red cover.
• Workshop manual for the 330 GTC in Italian.
• Sales brochure for the 330 GTC; factory reference 12/66.
• Sales brochure for the 330 GTS; factory reference 14/66.

1967
• The 1967 model range brochure includes two pages on the 330 GTC and two pages on the 330 GTS, with photographs and specifications in Italian/French/English; factory reference 11/66.
• Sales brochure for the 330 GTC; factory reference 12/67.
• Sales brochure for the 330 GTS; factory reference 14/67.
• Mechanical spare parts catalogue for the 330 GTC, with factory print reference 16/67 and beige/red/blue cover. Reprinted twice more with different colour covers; once with reference 16/67 and once without.

1968
• Sales brochure for 365 GTC; factory reference 28/68.

1969
• The 1969 model range brochure includes two pages on the 365 GTC and two pages on the 365 GTS, with photographs and specifications in Italian/French/English; factory reference 27/68.
• Owner's handbook for the 330 GTC/S and 365 GTC/S, factory reference 32/69, with yellow/red/blue cover, containing 12-page supplement on the 365 GTC/S variations.

Although most Borrani wire wheels fitted to Ferraris carry the *Cavallino Rampante* logo on the spinner, some have the Borrani 'hand' logo as on this 330 GTC wheel.

Borrani crest in the centre, as opposed to the straight-eared variety with a *Cavallino Rampante* emblem used on the alloy wheels. The spare wheel is mounted horizontally in a well between the twin fuel tanks, under a removable panel. The standard tyres are listed in the panel.

Identification plates for a 330 GTS and 365 GTC: they are fixed to the inner wing panel and give model type, engine type and chassis number.

Wheels & Tyres

Wheels, front & rear	7Lx14in cast light alloy Optional Borrani wire wheels with aluminium rims type RW4039
Tyres, front & rear	
330 GTC/S	Pirelli HS 210-14 or Dunlop SP 205HR-14
365 GTC/S	Firestone Cavallino 205VR-14

Identification Plates

1. General vehicle data plate giving model type with engine and chassis numbers on engine bay valance panel, with engine lubrication plate below – on right on 330 GTC/S and on left on 365 GTC/S.
2. Chassis number stamped in frame close to front suspension mounting point.
3. Engine number stamped in block on right rear side close to bellhousing.

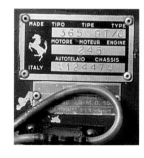

Chapter 7
365 GT 2+2

At the 1967 Paris Salon, the 365 GT 2+2 was introduced as a replacement for the 330 GT 2+2. As with the 330 GT 2+2, it was constructed at Pininfarina's factory in Turin and then shipped to Ferrari in Maranello for installation of mechanical components. Although the two cars shared the same wheelbase of 2650mm (104.33in), the new 365 GT 2+2 was wider, with increases of 90mm (3.54in) and 69mm (2.72in) in the front and rear track respectively, and with greater front and rear overhangs it was 134mm (5.28in) longer. The sheer size of the car, relative to its period stablemates, led to the nickname 'Queen Mary' among English-speaking Ferrari enthusiasts.

Although the contemporary models in the Ferrari range featured combined gearbox/differential transaxles, the 365 GT 2+2 retained a conventional five-speed gearbox mated to the engine, with a propeller shaft rigidly mounted to the differential. It did have independent rear suspension, rather than the live rear axle of its predecessor.

The overall lines were similar to those of the 500 Superfast, but with a larger cabin and virtually a three-box configuration, which did not have the harmony of line that the roof flowing into the

neat Kamm tail gave the 500 Superfast. There were two firsts for Ferrari on this model: the introduction of power-assisted steering as standard equipment and the adoption of hydraulic self-levelling rear suspension to give a constant ride height whatever the load. With these features allied to electrically-operated door and quarter light windows, a fitted radio with electric aerial, and optional air conditioning, it can be seen that the 365 GT 2+2 was the most luxuriously appointed car that Ferrari had hitherto built.

The standard road wheels were cast alloy, initially of the small square-hole design used on the concurrent 275 GTB/4 and 365 GTC/S models, but of 15in (381mm) diameter with knock-off hubs. Later in the production run they changed to the five-spoke 'star' pattern, which had been introduced on the 365 GTB/4 in 1968. Borrani aluminium-rimmed wire wheels remained an option throughout production, which ended in early 1971, leaving Ferrari without a feasible 2+2 in the range until the 365 GT4 2+2 arrived in late 1972. It is believed that four examples were fitted with the automatic transmission, originally tested on the 330 GT 2+2 for special customers to eval-

In profile it can be seen why the 365 GT 2+2 earned the nickname 'Queen Mary'. Although it has low, smooth lines, it is a very long car at a fraction under five metres. This US-market example (note the all-orange front side/turn indicator light units) rides on optional Borrani wire wheels. Later US-market models also had small orange side marker lights on the rear wings.

Nose shape is similar to the 500 Superfast, but the 365 GT 2+2 has heavier quarter bumpers incorporating large side/turn indicator lights that are vulnerable to knocks. Profile of cabin and tail was developed from the Pininfarina 330 GTC 'Speciale' (pictured on page 116), although the rear screen follows the buttress line rather than being recessed.

uate. However, automatic transmission would not become generally available as a Ferrari option until the introduction of the 400 series in 1976.

Body & Chassis

The 365 GT 2+2 chassis, type 591, has a 2650mm (104.33in) wheelbase and is constructed along the familiar Ferrari lines for the period. The chassis was developed from that of the preceding 330 GT 2+2, albeit with a modified rear section to incorporate independent suspension, with two main longitudinal oval steel tubes with substructures welded to them, plus a substantial front cross-member. Although the two models shared the same wheelbase, the 365 GT 2+2 has a 90mm (3.54in) wider front track at 1438mm (56.61in)

and a 69mm (2.72in) wider rear track at 1468mm (57.80in). The floor pan, footwell boxes and firewall are glass-fibre units bonded to the chassis frame, which is painted satin black.

The 365 GT 2+2's body bears no resemblance to its predecessor, being more akin to the 500 Superfast and the concurrent 365 GTC, although the tail treatment is unique and the glass area profile is not dissimilar to the 250 GT 2+2 of the early 1960s. The body is constructed of welded steel panels, with an aluminium bonnet and boot lid on steel frames. Whereas the 365 GTC has the engine bay air vents in the rear corners of the bonnet, the 365 GT 2+2 has them alongside the rear end of the bonnet, mounted in the top face of each front wing. The radiator grille opening is a similar shape to that of the 365 GTC and quarter

DIMENSIONS & WEIGHT

	mm	in
Overall length	4974	188.74
Overall width	1786	70.31
Overall height	1345	52.95
Wheelbase	2650	104.33
Front track	1438	56.61
Rear track	1468	57.80
Weight (dry)	1580kg	3483lb

Details show one of the two engine bay exhaust air louvres next to the bonnet and the internally released fuel filler flap in the left rear wing.

no longer permitted on cars sold in the USA, the feature was dropped for all markets.

Apart from the chrome-plated bumpers, the body is very clean and virtually devoid of brightwork. This is confined to the chrome-plated screen and glass surrounds, slim headlamp rims, windscreen wiper arms and blade frames, rectangular rear light panel, plus arrowhead-shaped door handles with a front pull section and lock barrel in the trailing end. Access to the boot is via a lockable chrome-plated lever on the trim panel alongside the left rear seat, with adjacent matching fuel filler flap release.

Plain glass is fitted and the windscreen is laminated. The two-speed self-parking wipers normally park on the right on left-hand-drive cars and on the left on right-hand-drive examples. The door windows are provided with electrically-operated swivelling quarterlights, which are controlled by switches on the centre console, forward of the main door window switches. The rear screen contains heater elements for demisting, actuated via a switch on the centre console, with a warning light in the rev counter.

Paintwork

As mentioned in the chapters on the 275 GTB and 365 GTB/4 models, a vast range of colours was available for Ferraris at this time and the same comments made there apply to the 365 GT 2+2. This Pininfarina-built model should have a paint colour manufactured by either PPG or Duco. The tables in the *275 GT Berlinetta* and the *365 GTB/4* chapters list the full range of colours offered for the respective model years.

Interior Trim & Fittings

The standard seat upholstery material is full leather and the range of colours available is shown in the tables in the *275 GT Berlinetta* and the *365 GTB/4* chapters, relative to the respective model years. The front seats are mounted on runners with adjustment via a lever under the inner front edge of the cushion; a second lever on the outer lower edge of the squab alters its rake. The backrest can be tilted forward for access to the rear seats. Rear seating features a deep central upholstered armrest, effectively providing individual bucket seats, with stowage compartments in the outer panel trim. Each seat, front and rear, is provided with a static lap-and-diagonal seat belt.

The door armrests incorporate pulls angled upwards at the front end, with a chrome-plated door opening lever in the door panel, above the forward end of the armrest section. The armrest section is normally trimmed either in black vinyl to match the upper door trim panel or to match

bumpers are also fitted to the front, although they have large side/turn indicator lamps incorporated in the forward face. A full-width chrome-plated rear bumper has rubber-faced vertical overriders. An entirely new rear lamp assembly consists of three circular lenses in a horizontal rectangular chrome-plated surround.

Body Trim & Fittings

The front of the 365 GT 2+2 features a wide, shallow, projecting, elliptical radiator opening with an aluminium trim surround to its inner lip. The inset aluminium egg-crate grille carries a chrome-plated *Cavallino Rampante* at its centre. The bulbous divided front bumpers, of chrome-plated steel, wrap around the wings and run into the grille extremities and have large rectangular side/turn indicator lights on the front face, with small elliptical turn indicator lights near the trailing edge. At the rear a full-width chrome-plated steel wrap-around bumper is provided, fitted with vertical black rubber-faced overriders. A rectangular enamel Ferrari badge is fitted on the upper nose panel between the grille and leading edge of the bonnet and a chromed Ferrari script badge is mounted centrally close to the trailing edge of the boot lid. Slim horizontal rectangular Pininfarina badges, with Pininfarina enamel shield badges above them, are fitted centrally on the lower sides of the front wings. The front-hinged bonnet is plain and is supported by a manually-positioned sprung stay on the left front side. The fuel filler flap is on the left rear wing, irrespective of whether the car is left- or right-hand drive. Early cars have screw-retained plain Perspex headlamp covers, without a trim ring. When headlamp covers were

PAINT & TRIM COLOURS

For Paint Colours, Leather Upholstery Colours and Carpet Colours see the *275 GT Berlinetta* chapter for cars up to mid-1969 and the *365 GTB/4* chapter for cars from mid-1969 onwards.

the upholstery colour. A circular removable plug in the door panel, forward of the armrest, is provided to allow emergency winding of the electric windows and quarterlights in the event of motor failure. Control switches for the electric windows and quarterlights are in the centre console between the gear lever and the ashtray. Polished aluminium kick strips are fitted to the base of the door trims and the shut face of the sill panels.

The floor and rear seat support panel are carpeted, with black rubber heelmats incorporated for both driver and passenger. The range of carpet colours is provided in the tables in the *275 GT Berlinetta* and the *365 GTB/4* chapters (see pages 32 and 89), relative to the year of manufacture. Normally the centre section of the firewall has a grey vinyl covering, with the transmission tunnel console, front and rear inner wheelarches, facia top and bottom roll trimmed in a mixture of vinyl and leather. The facia top is black, with the other panels either black or the upholstery colour. The headlining is plain ivory vinyl retained by cant rails upholstered in the same material, as are the rear screen pillars. The rear parcels shelf is trimmed in black vinyl or matches the upholstery.

Vinyl-covered sun visors are provided, the passenger's side one incorporating a vanity mirror. Also mounted on the upper screen rail is the dipping interior mirror.

The chrome gear lever, topped by a black plastic knob, has a leather gaiter with a chrome-plated retaining ring at its base and is mounted centrally at the front of the centre console. The knob on US and late-series European models has the gearchange pattern engraved in white on its top face. To the rear of the gear lever is a bank of four switches for the electric windows and quarterlights, two per side, with a chrome lidded ashtray to their rear. The central glove tray behind the ashtray has a cigar lighter at each end. The chrome-plated handbrake, with leather gaiter, is vertically mounted alongside the transmission tunnel on the driver's side. The bonnet release lever is below the facia at the outer end, with an emergency ring-pull release alongside, and the choke lever is also suspended below the facia inboard of the steering column. Two interior

Dashboard design has a wide centre console sweeping upwards to join it, and a glove locker on the passenger side. Switches between the gear lever and ashtray are for electrically operated quarterlights and door windows. Detail view shows central arrangement of auxiliary instruments, ventilation control levers and switchgear.

lights, mounted on the cant rail above the rear side windows, are operated automatically by the doors or manually by a rocker switch in each lens. Cabin air is extracted via an outlet in the base of each rear screen pillar and exits through the black external louvre behind each rear side window. If additional air throughput is required then the rear quarter windows, hinged at their forward edges, can be opened by means of over-centre catches.

Facia & Instruments

The facia and centre console of the 365 GT 2+2 are integrated, with the console's side rolls running up to the top of the facia. A separate oval instrument nacelle in front of the driver contains the speedometer and rev counter. Between them are the oil temperature and pressure gauges (at the top) and the water temperature gauge centrally below them. This triangular arrangement is very similar to that of the 365 GTC but more compact. Below and to either side of the water temperature gauge are the trip meter reset button and instrument lighting rheostat switch. The speedometer dial contains an odometer and trip recorder, plus red turn-indicator and green sidelamp warning lights. The rev counter dial has warning lights for choke, heated rear window, main beam, electric fuel pump and braking system. The latter can be illuminated for one of three reasons: handbrake on, brake light bulb failure, or loss of pressure in either front or rear brake hydraulic circuits. The vertical section of the centre console forms the centre portion of the facia and houses auxiliary instruments: fuel gauge with warning light for low level, clock and ammeter. All gauges have white digits on a black background.

Either side of this bank of dials is a sliding vertical lever. One controls air distribution on the passenger's side, to provide air to the circular facia top demister outlet or the low-level outlet on the side of the centre console. The other regulates the heat output to that side of the car. A similar pair of levers at the extremity of the facia on the driver's side performs the same functions for that side. Between the demister outlets on the facia top panel is a matching fresh air inlet, with its control switch in front of it.

Below the dials on the centre console is a row of seven switches, with circular black plastic levers, controlling ignition, electric fuel pump, left-side ventilation fan, rear window demister element, right-side ventilation fan, interior lights and either hazard warning lights or remaining spare, dependent upon market. Below the switches is a radio, under which are three circular ventilation outlets for the optional air conditioning system, with integral central control switches. A lockable glovebox with interior light is pro-vided on the passenger's side of the facia, the key-operated lock plate being sited in the top corner of the centre console.

The instrument nacelle surround, facia top, glovebox lid and bottom padded roll section are all black-vinyl covered. Teak veneer covers the faces of the instrument nacelle and combined driver's side lower facia and centre console panels.

The wood-rim steering wheel has an aluminium boss with plain aluminium spokes featuring an engraved pattern. The central yellow horn push, with black plastic rim, contains a *Cavallino Rampante* emblem. This was the last new Ferrari model to be fitted with a wood-rim steering wheel as standard. A pair of slender chrome-plated stalks, with black plastic finger pads, project from the left of the steering column; one controls the direction indicators and the other the sidelamp plus headlamp main/dipped beam and flasher functions. A stalk on the right operates the two-speed windscreen wipers and the washers by pulling it towards the driver. The key-operated ignition/starter switch, incorporating a steering lock, is mounted on the lower facia to the right of the steering column shroud, irrespective of whether the car is right- or left-hand drive.

Luggage Compartment

Beneath the boot floor are the twin aluminium fuel tanks, spray coated with glass-fibre, which form the sides of the spare wheel well, with a removable cover panel. Fuel capacity is 112 litres (24.6 Imperial/29.5 US gallons). The fuel filler cap is on the left rear wing beneath a cover flap, opened by a lockable lever on the trim panel alongside the left rear seat. An emergency release pull for the fuel filler flap is provided in the forward left part of the boot. On late-model US-market cars a 'Fuel Evaporative Emission Control System', basically as described in the *365 GTB/4* chapter (see page 90), is fitted to comply with American legislation.

The boot floor and sides are lined with black carpet and all plain metal surfaces are painted satin black. A light, mounted on the ceiling of the boot, is actuated by a switch plate on the self-supporting lid, when the boot is opened. Access to the boot is via a lockable lever, on the left of the one for the fuel filler flap, on the trim panel alongside the left rear seat.

Engine

The 365 GT 2+2 has a 4390cc (267.9cu in) wet-sump 60° V12 engine, type 245, with a single overhead camshaft per cylinder bank. Power output is 320bhp (DIN) at 6600rpm, with maximum torque of 37kgm (267lb ft) at 5000rpm.

TOOL KIT

- Scissor-type jack with ratchet handle
- Sparking plug spanner
- Phillips screwdriver for screws up to 4mm (0.16in)
- Phillips screwdriver for screws 7-9mm (0.27-0.35in)
- Flat-bladed screwdriver
- 190mm (7.5in) long pliers
- 10x11mm open-ended spanner
- 13x14mm open-ended spanner
- Oil filter cartridge wrench
- Front hub extractor
- Rear hub extractor
- Lead mallet
- Wheel chock
- Generator belt
- Air conditioning drive belt
- Water pump belt
- Spare bulb and fuse container with six bulbs and four fuses
- Grease gun extension tube
- Warning triangle

This engine was always fitted with Weber 40DFI/5 carburettors and a Fispa Sup 150 mechanical fuel pump with a Bendix 476087 auxiliary electric pump. Apart from minor differences, due to model specification variations, the construction materials, operation and component layout are identical to the 365 GTC/S engine (see page 67). Although the 365 GTC/S models were the last new Ferrari production cars to receive a single-camshaft-per-bank engine, the 365 GT 2+2 was the last production model to use this form of engine, as it outlived the 365 GTC by a year.

The engine used in the 365 GT 2+2 was fitted with an air pollution control system for the US market, with a fast-idle device on the throttle control rod linkage to alter the idling speed relative to engine temperature. This was arranged via an oil temperature-operated thermostatic valve with a cam bearing on an arm on the throttle rod. Concurrently a microswitch, actuated by a separate cam on the throttle linkage, retarded the ignition timing below 3000rpm by using slow-running contact breakers in the distributors up to this speed. An air injection system is also provided for US-market models, to minimise release of unburned exhaust gases. An air pump, driven by a vee-belt from the alternator pulley, supplies air under pressure to a manifold for each cylinder bank. From there the air is injected into the individual exhaust manifold outlet from each cylin-

ENGINE

Type	60° V12
Type number	245
Cubic capacity	4390.358cc (267.9cu in)
Bore and stroke	81x71mm (3.19x2.80in)
Compression ratio	8.8:1
Maximum power	320bhp (DIN) at 6600rpm
Maximum torque	37kgm (267lb ft) at 5000rpm
Carburettors	3 Weber 40DFI/5

TIMING DATA

Inlet valves open	13°15' BTDC
Inlet valves close	59° ABDC
Exhaust valves open	59° BBDC
Exhaust valves close	13°15' ATDC
Firing order	1-7-5-11-3-9-6-12-2-8-4-10

Valve clearances with a cold engine should be 0.2mm (0.0079in) for inlets and 0.25mm (0.0098in) for exhausts, measured between the valve pads and rocker arm.

SYSTEM CAPACITIES

Fuel tank	112 litres (24.6 Imperial/29.5 US gallons)		
	Litres	Imp Pints	US Pints
Cooling system	13.0	22.9	27.5
Washer bottle	1.0	1.8	2.1
Engine oil	10.75	18.9	22.7
Gearbox oil	5.0	8.8	10.6
Differential oil	2.5	4.4	5.3

The 4.4-litre engine is dominated by the large pressed steel air filter box and inlet nozzles. Cylinder firing order plate can be seen on the front of the camshaft cover, and the screen washer bag tank on the far inner wing panel. Crackle-black paint finish should cover the Ferrari motif on the camshaft cover.

der, with test points in the individual manifold branches. An electro-magnetic clutch disengages the pump when the engine speed reaches 3100rpm. This arrangement necessitates the use of different camshaft covers, which have additional support lugs for the equipment and its brackets. US-market cars have a Marelli S138B distributor for each cylinder bank, each operating in conjunction with a Marelli Dinoplex AEC101EA high-tension transistor unit. Emergency override switches, in case of unit failure, allow the engine to be fed by the normal coil, bypassing the transistor unit.

If the optional air conditioning is fitted, the pump is mounted on the lower right front of the timing chain casing, with its own twin-belt drive direct off the crankshaft pulley and a condenser coil mounted on a bracket forward of the radiator. The evaporator coil is positioned behind the vents in the centre console, which have the operating switches in their centres.

The normal oil pressure with an oil temperature of 120°C should be 4.5kg/cm^2 (64psi) at 6600rpm, with a minimum of 4kg/cm^2 (57psi) under the same conditions. The minimum slow running pressure (at 700-800rpm) should be 1.0-1.5kg/cm^2 (14-21psi). The oil cooler is integral with the water radiator, as on the 365 GTC/S.

Transmission

Although all the other concurrent front-engined Ferrari models were fitted with transaxle units, the 365 GT 2+2 stayed with a conventional aluminium-cased gearbox mounted to the engine bellhousing – but part of the transaxle development from the other models in the family did rub off on the 365 GT 2+2. The tailshaft of the gearbox has a flange to which the rigid propeller shaft's torque tube is bolted and there is a similar flange on the differential casing, thus making the engine, gearbox, propeller shaft and differential one solid unit – as on the late 275 GTB and 275 GTB/4 models. The 365 GT 2+2 also features independent rear suspension – employed for the first time on a Ferrari 2+2 model.

The gearbox is an all-synchromesh five-speed unit, with a cable-operated clutch. This single-plate Borg & Beck unit is mounted on the flywheel in the bellhousing, with a spring diaphragm plate. There is an assister spring at the pedal box to reduce pressure.

The gearbox casing is in two halves bolted together, the forward part containing the main and secondary gear shafts running in roller bearings, plus the reverse gear transfer shaft. The gearbox filler/level plug is on the front left side and the drain plug in the lower left rear corner. There is a removable top cover to the front section with a second rearward removable cover, incorporating the gearbox turret, spanning the front and rear sections of the gearbox. The rear part contains the lever linkage selector rod connec-

FACTORY LITERATURE

1967
• Sales brochure for 365 GT 2+2; factory reference 19/67.

1968
• Sales brochure for 365 GT 2+2; factory reference 19/68.
• Mechanical spare parts catalogue for the 365 GT 2+2, with factory print reference 23/68 and black/white/orange cover. Later issued with extra information to cover the air pollution control system.
• Owner's handbook for the 365 GT 2+2; with factory reference 24/68 with black/white/orange cover. Reprinted with black & white cover.

1969
• The 1969 model-range brochure includes two pages on the 365 GT 2+2, with photograph and specifications in Italian/French/English; factory reference 27/68.
• Mechanical spare parts catalogue for the 365 GT 2+2, from chassis number 12811, with factory print reference 35/69 and grey/white/red cover. Reprinted with black/white/red cover.

GEAR RATIOS

	Gearbox	Overall
First	2.536:1	10.778:1
Second	1.701:1	7.229:1
Third	1.256:1	5.338:1
Fourth	1.000:1	4.250:1
Fifth	0.79:1	3.357:1
Reverse	3.218:1	13.676:1
Final drive	4.25:1 (8:34)	

tions, from where the rods run to the selector forks in the forward section of the casing. The gearbox oil pump, with mesh filter screen, is in the lower part of the casing and is driven off an extension from the secondary shaft in the front of the casing. An oil pressure relief valve is provided in the front face of the gearchange turret casing. There is a tapping on the upper left side of the front of the gearbox for the reversing light switch, which is operated by the selector rod. The speedometer drive cable is taken from a tapping on the rear section of the gearbox. On the lower rear portion of the casing, below the output shaft connection flange, is a boss for the tie-rod connection to the chassis frame to prevent fore and aft movement.

The gearchange provides first to fourth gears in an 'H' pattern; first at top left, second at bottom left, third at top right and fourth at the bottom right. Fifth is outside the 'H', to the right and forward alongside third gear, while reverse is opposite fifth and alongside fourth. From chassis number 11799 the gearchange pattern is engraved in white digits on the top of the gear knob.

Drive is carried from the gearbox output shaft via a splined solid propshaft, running in a flanged torque tube containing a central lubricant-free roller bearing, to the differential. The differential casing houses a ZF-type limited slip differential and has a rubber block support on each side at the forward end. These two supports, plus a similar pair on the engine block, carry the entire engine, gearbox and differential as a rigid unit. The casing has an oil filler plug and a drain plug on the rear face. The flanged one-piece half-shafts, which take the drive to each rear wheel, are of the maintenance-free Lobro type and incorporate constant-velocity sliding joints.

Electrical Equipment & Lights

The electrical system is 12-volt, negative earth, served from a 74amp/hour battery sited in the rear corner of the engine bay on the opposite side to the driver. The Lucas alternator, mounted on the front of the engine, is driven by a vee-belt from the crankshaft pulley. The starter motor is mounted on the lower right section of the flywheel bellhousing, integral with its solenoid suspended below it. Twin air horns are mounted on

Battery	12-volt SAFA 65SNS, 74amp/hour
Alternator	Marelli 50.35.014.1
Starter motor	Marelli MT21T-1.8/12D9
Ignition	Twin Marelli S85A-12v-15° distributors (S138A in US), each with a Marelli BZR201/A-12v-15° coil
Sparking plugs	Champion N6Y

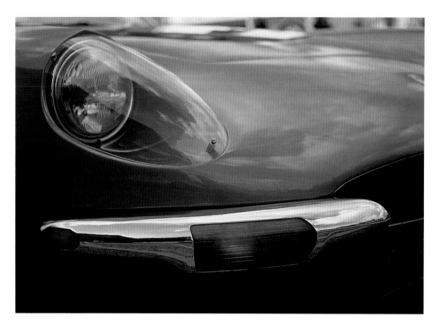

Front side/turn indicator light units are unique to the 365 GT 2+2; Perspex headlamp cover was omitted on later cars. Rear lights are influenced by 330 GTC 'Speciale', with three individual units on a chromed backplate.

the inner wing panel in the engine bay, actuated by the horn push in the centre of the steering wheel. Specifications for the major electrical components are provided in the table. The fuse and relay board is mounted on the firewall.

Lighting is all by Carello and remained constant throughout the production run. The only variations were left-hand dipping headlamps for right-hand-drive cars, yellow headlamp bulbs for French-market cars, the colour of the front side/turn indicator lenses (white or orange dependent upon market) and the addition of small orange side marker lights on the rear wings of late-model US-market cars as required by law. The front side/turn indicator lights are mounted in the forward face of the divided bumpers; the small orange turn repeater lights in their trailing edges

became side-marker lights on late-model US-market cars. 'Door open' warning lights are provided in the trailing edge of the door frames.

At the rear, a pair of horizontal, rectangular, chrome-plated housings each contain a row of three separate circular units. The outer one is the orange turn indicator (red on US-market cars), in the centre is the combined stop/tail lamp, and the inner is a matching reflector. The number-plate light is a twin-bulb unit housed in a slim chrome-plated rectangular casing on top of the bumper. A reversing lamp, mounted centrally on the underside of the bumper, is actuated by a switch on the gearbox upon engagement of reverse gear. An electric radio aerial is provided on the rear wing, automatically extended or retracted when the radio is switched on or off.

Suspension & Steering

The independent front suspension is virtually identical in layout to that of the 330 GT 2+2 and uses unequal-length forged steel upper and lower wishbones, joined by the hub carrier at the outer end and mounted to the chassis via rubber bushes at the inner end. There is a coil spring between the wishbones and a telescopic damper between the top wishbone and a chassis bracket; an anti-roll bar links the two front suspension units, via brackets on the lower spring-retaining buckets. Each suspension unit has a pair of chassis-mounted rubber bump stops.

The independent rear suspension of the 365 GT 2+2 is the first on any Ferrari model to feature self-levelling. Unequal-length combined forged and pressed steel upper and lower wishbone assemblies are joined by the hub carrier at the outer end and mounted to the chassis via rubber bushes at the inner end. Rearward of the hub there is a coil spring with the damper mounted co-axially within it, fixed between the lower wishbone and an upper chassis mounting bracket, incorporating the bump stop. Forward of the hub is a sealed Koni-type 4454-04 hydraulic self-levelling unit, mounted in the same manner as the spring/damper assembly. These units are designed to maintain a constant ride height regardless of speed, load or road conditions. An anti-roll bar

SUSPENSION SETTINGS

Front toe-in	0 to −3mm (0 to −0.118in)
Front camber	+1°
Rear toe-in	None
Rear camber	0°50′ to −1°15′
Castor angle	2°30′
Dampers: front	Koni OFF1299
rear	Koni 82N1573 initially with a Koni 4454-04 automatic levelling device, succeeded by a type 7100-1004 unit in 1969

mounted on rubber bushes couples the two lower wishbones and is fixed to rubber-bushed brackets on the main chassis tubes.

Each front hub carrier is machined from forged steel and carries a stub axle on which the brake disc and a splined hub assembly run on roller bearings. The rear hub carriers are machined cast steel, with a central hole through which the splined hub shaft passes to the driveshaft connection, running in roller bearings and retained by a bolted flange to the brake disc.

The 365 GT 2+2 was the first production Ferrari road car to feature power-assisted steering as standard. The hydraulic pump, incorporating a reservoir with a dipstick in the cap, is mounted on a bracket on the upper part of the camshaft cover and is driven by a vee-belt from the alternator pulley. The hydraulic circuit is provided with its own cooling radiator at the front of the engine bay. The steering box is mounted on the front chassis cross-member at the lower end of the universally-jointed steering column.

Track control adjustment is provided on the track rod arms. The steering ball joints are non-adjustable and require no lubrication. The steering has a turning circle of 13.6 metres (44ft 7in). Left- or right-hand drive was available throughout the production period.

Brakes

The braking system is much improved over that of the preceding 330 GT 2+2, with the use of ventilated cast iron discs front and rear. There is vacuum-operated servo assistance, with a tandem master cylinder feeding separate front and rear circuits, with their own reservoirs; a pressure-regulating valve balances braking effort between front and rear wheels. A pressure switch illuminates a facia warning light if a loss of pressure is detected in either circuit. From chassis number 118013 a Bonaldi Z4 servo, with revised reservoir assembly, was fitted but the system's method of operation remained unaltered. Recommended brake pads for normal touring conditions are Ferodo 2426 F, front and rear.

A floor mounted handbrake, sited alongside the transmission tunnel on the driver's side, operates its own set of pads on each rear wheel disc via rods and cables. From chassis 118013, the handbrake operation was also changed to all-cable, with a main cable from the handbrake actuating a central mechanism that controlled the cables to each rear wheel.

The pedal box provides a suspended pedal arrangement, with a facility on the pedal pad pins for height adjustment as on the 275 series models. The switch for the brake lights is actuated by the movement of the pedal arm.

Wheels & Tyres

Borrani 7.5x15in light alloy wheels of the ten-hole design are the standard equipment on the majority of cars built. Finished in silver with a clear lacquer coat and with a single centre-nut fixing on a splined hub, they are very similar, apart from size, to those fitted to the 365 GTC/S models. Late in the production run five-spoke light

The spare wheel, housed in a covered well in the boot floor, shows the design of the inner face of the standard alloy wheel, the ribs providing strength and aiding heat dissipation.

alloy wheels, similar in design to those fitted to the 365 GTB/4, were provided. Borrani wire wheels with polished aluminium rims in the same size were optional equipment. The hub spinners for the Borrani wire wheels normally have triple angled ears with a Borrani crest in the centre, as opposed to the straight-eared variety with a *Cavallino Rampante* emblem used on the alloy wheels.

The spare wheel is mounted horizontally in a well between the twin fuel tanks, under a removable panel in the boot floor.

Identification plate fixed to the inner wing panel gives model type, engine type and chassis number. Lubrication plate is alongside and engine bay light above.

Chapter 8
365 GTB/4 & 365 GTS/4

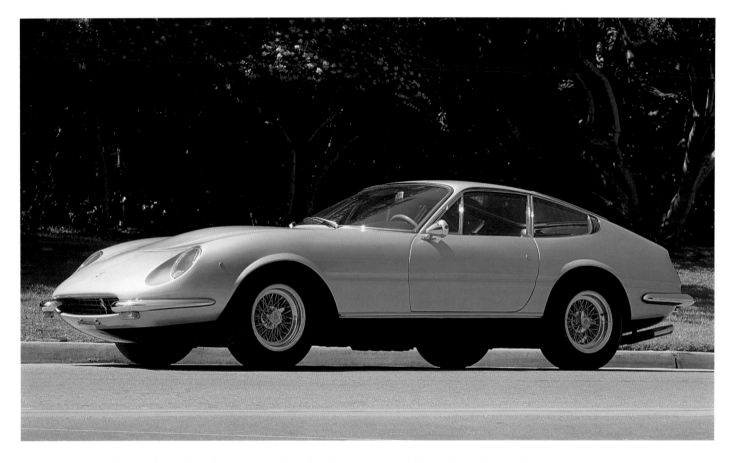

The Pininfarina-designed 365 GTB/4, announced at the 1968 Paris Salon, was powered by the first Ferrari 4.4-litre four-camshaft production engine and superseded the 3.3-litre 275 GTB/4 as the top performance model in the range. Like its predecessor, the 365GTB/4 featured a five-speed transaxle, independent rear suspension and was constructed at the Scaglietti works in Modena.

Two of the prototypes, chassis numbers 10287 and 11001, featured frontal treatment like the 275 GTB/4. The former had a prototype three-valve-per-cylinder engine with combustion chambers in the piston crowns and flat cylinder heads, while the latter was fitted with the 3.3-litre engine of the 275 GTB/4. The definitive production model had a much more angular, long, wedge nose with fixed twin headlamps under a full-width Plexiglas cover that ran into the sidelamp/indicator assemblies, which extended around the leading edges of

the front wings. Although it shares the same wheelbase as the 275 GTB/4, the 365 GTB/4's wider front and rear tracks and its dominant long flat bonnet expanse give it a bulkier appearance.

The 365 GTB/4 was dubbed the Daytona by Ferrari enthusiasts and journalists in recognition of Ferrari's 1-2-3 victory in the 1967 24 Hours of Daytona race. This unofficial nickname has stuck, probably because it is less of a mouthful and easier to remember than 365 GTB/4. There is an unconfirmed rumour that Ferrari was originally going to call the model the Daytona but that the name was leaked prior to its release and so was dropped. The choice of 365 GTB/4 as the designation continued the long-standing theme of its predecessors, with the model name signifying a single cylinder's displacement in cubic centimetres.

Initially the 365 GTB/4 had been intended as a stop-gap model between the 275 GTB/4 and the

Nose styling of the 365 GTB/4 prototype (chassis number 11001) shows clear influence from the preceding 275 GTB/4, although the tail treatment is almost definitive 365 GTB/4.

An early left-hand-drive 365 GTB/4, with the full-width Plexiglas nose panel with pinstripe effect. Radical changes were made to the nose styling between the prototype stage and production.

British-registered right-hand-drive car (with Plexiglas nose) illustrates the styling theme of long bonnet and set-back cabin, with the front wing line running into the side glass to form an elegant 'S' as the glass sweeps into the rear screen pillar.

mid-engined replacement that was under development and would be announced as the 365 GT/4BB in 1971, eventually going into production in 1973. However, finances were tight at Ferrari at this time and it was less costly to upgrade an existing design than to embark upon a radically different proposal, which might not find favour with the established clientele. It should be remembered that customer uptake on the 250/275 LM had been very slow, with only 32 examples produced in two years – partly because of the homologation problems but also because it was

mid-engined and thus radically different from previous models. The 365 GTB/4 had also been intended as a tyre test bed for the forthcoming 365 GT/4BB as Ferrari was concerned about road tyre technology for a powerful mid-engined car, bearing in mind the reported problems that the Lamborghini Miura encountered with its Pirelli rubber. Michelin was developing a new high-speed radial tyre, the XWX, which Ferrari tried on the 365 GTB/4 and found to be ideal. The XWX provided good grip, longevity and was able to cope with the stresses imposed by transmitting 352bhp

The prototype 365 GTS/4 (chassis number 12851), which was first exhibited at the 1969 Frankfurt Salon.

Retractable headlamps were introduced in 1971 to comply with US lighting legislation and standardised on cars for all markets. Early versions had an aluminium paint finish on the nose panel to give the impression of the old Plexiglas arrangement, but the idea was soon dropped.

On the prototype 365 GTS/4 the semi-circular indent line along the body sides and across the tail panel has always been painted black, whereas on all production cars it is left in the body colour.

to the road. However, this 'interim' test-bed model proved so popular with customers that production continued for five years and eventually more examples were built than of any other V12 Ferrari up to that time; only the concurrent V6 Dino series exceeded it in sales volumes.

During the late 1960s the US Government was introducing a string of legislation relating to automobile construction, known as the USA Federal Safety Standards. Among other things, this resulted in the covered headlamp arrangement having to be replaced by paired retractable units in mid-1971, an alteration made for all markets for the sake of uniformity. To meet the new legislation, US-market cars also had rectangular side marker lamps cut into their rear wings, and there were mechanical and electrical additions to meet pollution requirements.

The 365 GTS/4 spider version, with a neat folding soft-top and flat boot lid replacing the berlinetta's fastback, was announced at the 1969 Frankfurt Motor Show. The majority of these were sold on the North American market and today command a price premium over the berlinetta. A number of berlinettas have been converted to spider configuration over the years, particularly in the USA and UK. This was a relatively simple operation for a competent panel shop due to the separate tubular chassis, which ensured rigidity of the body even without a fixed roof. Competition versions of the berlinetta were built for private

customers at the factory's *Assistenza Clienti* in Modena; details are given in the *Competition Derivatives* chapter (pages 118-126).

When the 365 GTB/4 was tested by the British magazine *Autocar* in its issue of 30 September 1971 the sub-title was 'Fastest Road Car In The World?' and the magazine achieved a mean top speed of 174mph. The test concluded: 'It is a hard task to capture in mere words all the excitement, sensation and sheer exhilaration of this all-time great among cars… We know it will be many years before the figures we record here are beaten…' In *Autosport* Patrick McNally called it 'the most desirable car in the world'.

Body & Chassis

There was no radical departure from Ferrari's tried and tested principle of a substantial tubular steel chassis, which employs two large oval-section main tubes running front to rear, a built-up front cross-member and cross-bracing under the cabin section. Circular- and square-section sub-units welded to the main frame are used to support the mechanical and body components. The chassis retains the 2400mm (94.49in) wheelbase of the preceding 275 GTB/4, but the front and rear track are greater at 1440mm (56.70in) and 1453mm (57.20in) respectively. The Ferrari type number for the chassis is 605.

The use of glass-fibre for hidden panels, which

DIMENSIONS & WEIGHTS

	mm	in
Overall length	4425	174.2
Overall width	1760	69.3
Overall height	1245	49.0
Wheelbase	2400	94.5
Front track	1440	56.7
Rear track	1453	57.2

Weight (dry)	kg	lb
Berlinetta		
(Europe)	1280[1]	2822
(US)	1543	3402
Spider		
(Europe, US)	n/a	n/a

[1] Later berlinettas with steel doors had a kerb weight (with fuel, oil and water) of 1600kg (3527lb)

Evening sunlight reflects off a right-hand-drive 365 GTB/4 with the definitive style of retractable headlamp front. Reversing lights are suspended below the quarter bumpers, whereas US-market cars had a single light fitted to the body between the bumpers.

had started on the 275 GTB, continued in the 365 GTB/4. This material was used for the floor sections on either side of the transmission tunnel, incorporating the inner sills, front firewall and rear cabin bulkhead.

The body construction is in pressed steel – the larger panels being made up of a number of smaller panels welded together – with aluminium doors, bonnet and boot lid on steel frames. Later in the production run, from chassis 15701 according to the factory homologation papers, the door panels were changed from aluminium to steel. At around the same time US-market cars received horizontal side-impact bars in the door frames, again to meet legislative requirements, so it is likely that the change to steel doors was part of this process.

This 365 GTB/4, fitted with optional Borrani wire wheels, shows the special features for the US market – hexagonal wheel nuts, full orange front side/turn lights and side marker lights recessed in the rear wings.

This gorgeous view of a US-market 365 GTS/4 confirms that the model is equally attractive as a berlinetta or spider. Despite being outlawed by US legislation, triple-ear hub nuts are fitted to the optional Borrani wire wheels.

For economy and uniformity the changes were made for all markets. The body panels were delivered from Pininfarina in Turin to the Scaglietti works in Modena, where the body/chassis units were constructed, prior to shipment to the Ferrari factory in Maranello for fitment of the mechanical components. One example, on chassis 12547, was manufactured with an all-aluminium body for Luigi Chinetti, Ferrari's American importer, and the first series of five competition versions also had aluminium bodies.

The most striking feature of the body is the massive bonnet area, with twin rectangular air outlets, running from the wedge-shaped nose for almost half the car's length to the very rear-set cabin. Other distinctive styling features include a truncated tail and the semi-circular indent that runs from the trailing edge of the front wings on the body sides and right around the tail panel.

The only body changes during the five-year production run were the introduction of a spider model with a folding canvas soft-top at the 1969 Frankfurt Show and the replacement of the fixed Plexiglas-covered headlamps by paired retractable units in 1971 to satisfy US safety legislation.

The bonnet is forward hinged with twin hydraulic support struts and the trailing edge curves upwards to hide the windscreen wipers in their parked position. After the external boot lid hinges of the 275 GTB/4, the 365 GTB/4 saw a return to more conventional concealed hinges, with a single self-locking telescopic support on the left side. Access to both compartments is via control levers in the cabin. The spider version has a boot lid with a horizontal top face, with the fuel filler on the top of the rear wing near the left corner of the lid, whereas the berlinetta's fuel filler is on the left rear quarter panel. Control of the fuel filler flap is also from a lever within the cabin. On the spider, the soft-top is fastened by over-centre catches at the extremities of the screen rail; a shaped vinyl cover retains and covers the soft-top when in the folded position.

Body Trim & Fittings

The body of the 365 GTB/4 carries virtually no adornment to detract from its smooth lines. The front of the early cars is dominated by the full-width Plexiglas headlamp cover that runs into the side/turn lights. The centre portion between the headlamps is etched with vertical white pin-stripes, surrounding a small central rectangular clear section over the enamel Ferrari badge. On later cars retractable twin-headlamp pods are fitted. They and the upper-nose section between them are body colour, with a centrally mounted enamel Ferrari badge in a shallow recess.

Below the leading edge of the wedge nose is a full-width shallow rectangular radiator opening, with a plain aluminium egg-crate grille in the centre. On either side of the grille are chrome-plated steel quarter bumpers with black rubber strips, a treatment repeated at the rear of the car. Further badging comprises a rectangular aluminium 'Disegno di Pininfarina' badge low on each front wing side and a Ferrari script badge close to the trailing edge of the upper face of the boot lid. Further brightwork, initially chrome but later stainless steel, is confined to front and rear screen surrounds, rain channel trim and window frames, chrome-plated rectangular rear number plate shroud, tiny unobtrusive door handles that blend into the window frames, and circular keylocks in the door panels. A chrome-plated circular driver's

door mirror is standard on US-market cars to comply with legislation.

The cabin air extraction vents are subtle matt black curved units integrated just behind the rear quarter windows. The 365 GTS/4 spider does not have these louvres or the quarter windows as its canvas soft-top replaces the rear quarter panels. The folding soft-top features a large rectangular clear PVC panel in the rear face and is retained by two over-centre catches on the screen rail. Usually the soft-top was finished in black, although other colours could be specified; the two most popular alternatives were beige or blue. The standard fuel filler location is beneath a body-coloured flap on the left rear quarter panel on the berlinetta and on the upper face of the left rear wing on the spider.

Plain glass is fitted all round, the windscreen is laminated and the heated rear screen on the berlinetta is controlled by a facia switch. The two-speed self-parking wipers, with non-glare silver-finish arms, park centrally, left above right, on all models. The door windows are provided with swivelling quarterlights with a chrome-plated retaining catch at the rear lower corner.

Paintwork

As noted in the *275 GT Berlinetta* chapter, a vast range of colours was available for Ferraris at this time. Indeed, when specific customer requests are taken into consideration it could be said that a standard range did not exist in the true sense of the words. The Scaglietti-built cars, such as the 365 GTB/4 in this chapter, were normally delivered with paint manufactured by Glidden & Salchi but the comments made in the *275 GT Berlinetta* chapter also apply here.

The tabulated chart lists all known colours available during the period; where a code number is not provided, this is because the manufacturer did not issue one.

The chassis, engine bay, boot compartment, unseen inner surfaces, under-wing areas and underside were always painted in a satin black finish, as was the section of bodywork underneath the Plexiglas front panel. Early post-Plexiglas cars had the panel between the headlamps, plus the headlamp shrouds, painted in satin silver to imitate the appearance of the original concept but this idea was soon dropped.

Interior Trim & Fittings

The standard seat upholstery is full Connolly leather, although a customer could have cloth centre inserts to special order. The hammock-style seats feature bolstered sides and the centre sections are separate removable panels. These

PAINT COLOURS

Argento Auteuil 106-E-1
Amaranto Bull Lea 2.443.413
Amaranto Ferrari 20-R-188
Arancio Vaguely 95.3.2943
Avorio Le Tetrarch 2.662.016
Azzurro Hyperion 2.443.648/106-A-32
Bianco Polo Park 9.265.470/20-W-152
Blu Caracalla 2.666.901
Blu Chiaro Met 106-A-38
Blu Dino Met 106-A-72
Blu Ferrari 20-A-185
Blu Ortis 95.3.6159
Blu Ribot 2.443.631
Blu Sera Met 106-A-18
Blu Scuro 95C.6159
Blu Tourbillon 2.443.607
Celeste Gainsborough 2.443.625
Celeste Met 106-A-16
Giallo Fly 20-Y-191
Giallo My Swallow 95.3.2643
Grigio Argento 2.443.048
Grigio Le Sancy 2.443.009
Grigio Orthello 2.448.813
Grigio Mahmoud 2.443.931
Marrone Colorado 2.443.221
Marrone Dino Met 106-M-73
Nero 20-B-50
Nero Dark Ronald
Nocciola Met 106-M-27
Oro Chiaro Met 106-T-19
Oro Kelso 2.443.214
Oro Nashrullah 2.443.248
Rosso Chiaro 20-R-190
Rosso Cina 'Duce' 812.69484
Rosso Cordoba Met 106-R-7
Rosso Dino 20-R-351
Rosso Ferrari 20-R-187
Rosso Nearco 2.664.032
Rosso Sir Ivor 95.3.9301
Rosso Rubino 106-R-83
Turchese Molvedo
Verde Medio Met 106-G-29
Verde Medio Nijinsky
Verde Pino Met 106-G-30
Verde Pino Blenheim
Verde Seabird
Viola Dino Met 106-A-71

In addition to this wide range of body colours, many of which are named after famous racehorses, customers could order any colour to suit their specific requirements.

As well as applying to the 365 GTB/4 and GTS/4, these colours were also used for 365 GTC/S cars built after mid-1969 and for 365 GT 2+2, 365 GTC/4 and 365 GT4 2+2 models.

A one-off special hard-top with brushed stainless steel rear screen surround, fitted to 365 GTS/4 chassis number 14547.

The simple door release catch fitted to all cars in the series, seen on a 365 GTS/4.

An early series car, as revealed by the wood-rim steering wheel. Optional duo-tone leather treatment highlights the attractive seat design pattern.

feature a thin central strip from top to bottom, with lateral strips on either side alternating between a solid wide strip and a thin strip punched with three ventilation holes. The punched strips of leather are often of a different colour to the main body of the seat. Each seat has a height-adjustable head restraint, with a curved profile,

trimmed in matching leather. The colours available are shown on page 89. The seats are mounted on runners with adjustment via a lever under the inner front edge of the cushion. There is a small lever on the outer lower side of the seat to facilitate angle adjustment of the complete unit. Three-point lap-and-diagonal static seat belts are

provided. For US-market models inertia-reel seat belts were mandatory from 1 January 1972, incorporating a seat belt warning light and buzzer.

The door pulls incorporate armrests, with an elliptical chrome-plated opening lever to the rear of the pull section in a fluted trim panel. A trapezoidal ribbed aluminium kick plate is fitted to the lower front corner of the door trim panel, with a speaker mounted in the forward lower corner. Electrically-operated windows are standard, with the control switches on the centre console beside the gearchange. An emergency window winding handle is provided and fits into a circular hole in the door trim after removing a cover plug.

The floor, inner sills, lower rear parcels shelf and bulkhead are carpeted, with ribbed black rubber heelmats incorporated for both driver and passenger. Carpet colours are given on page 89. Circular air outlets are provided on the outer face of each footwell. The centre console and door panels are trimmed in leather to match the seats, with black vinyl strips on the fluted section of the door panel, which has a chrome-plated strip along the top edge of the fluting. The rear upper parcels shelf (berlinetta only), the front and rear wheel-arches and upper sill faces are trimmed in vinyl, although the latter were normally leather if the seat colour was other than black. Fixed to the

lower rear shelf is a pair of leather luggage retaining straps with chrome-plated support brackets. In the side trim pad, to the rear of the left door, are two vertical chrome-plated levers; the forward one opens the boot lid and the rear one the fuel filler flap. The latter has an emergency release

Instrument layout in the deeply hooded nacelle remained constant throughout the production run. This is a later series car, with leather-rim steering wheel.

Ventilation control levers and switch bank in the centre of the dashboard.

LEATHER COLOURS

Beige VM846
Beige VM3218
Beige VM3234
Black VM8500
Blue VM3015
Blue VM3282
Grey VM3230
Marrone VM487
Red VM3171
White VM3323

The above code numbers all refer to Connolly's Vaumol leather which was fitted as standard. This is now available again under the name Connolly Classic. As with the external colours, customers could order a specific colour to their requirements.

As well as applying to the 365 GTB/4 and GTS/4, these colours were also used for 365 GTC/S cars built after mid-1969 and for 365 GT 2+2, 365 GTC/4 and 365 GT4 2+2 models.

CARPET COLOURS

Beige
Black
Blue (Light or Dark)
Grey (Light or Dark)
Red (Light or Dark)
Tan

Specific colours to a customer's requirements were also available. As well as applying to the 365 GTB/4 and GTS/4, these colours were also used for 365 GTC/S cars built after mid-1969 and for 365 GT 2+2, 365 GTC/4 and 365 GT4 2+2 models.

lever in the boot, and an emergency ring-pull for the boot lid is provided under the fuel filler flap.

The roof lining is fluted ivory-coloured vinyl, glued to the underside of the roof panel and bordered by upholstery-coloured cant rails. Matching upholstered sun visors, with a vanity mirror for the passenger, flank the dipping rear-view mirror on the berlinetta. On the spider version, the sun visors are retractable fine-weave semi-opaque roller blinds, housed in the upper screen rail and held on the screen by suction cups when in use.

The gear lever moves in an open chrome-plated gate sunk in a recess in the top left face of the transmission tunnel on all models, whether right- or left-hand drive. First gear is a dog-leg in the left rear corner with reverse immediately opposite; second to fifth gears form an 'H' pattern to their right. The chrome-plated lever is surmounted by a circular black plastic ball, which was plain initially. However, when US legislation decreed that the gear shift pattern should be engraved in white lettering on the upper surface, this feature was applied to all cars. Immediately behind the gear lever is a cigar lighter, with a chromed lidded ashtray to its right. Forward of the ashtray, alongside the gear lever, are the electric window switches, with a longitudinal radio panel to their right. The section of console between the seats is a shallow oddments tray, from which the chrome-plated handbrake, fitted with a ribbed black plastic grip, protrudes in an upholstery-coloured gaiter. Two under-dash courtesy lamps are actuated by door switches, while coupé models also have a rectangular interior light, with rocker switch integral with the lens, positioned centrally on the rear screen rail.

Facia & Instruments

The facia top, instrument nacelle surround and glovebox lid are trimmed in black Alcantara suede, although some very early production examples had black vinyl. Central on the facia top are four circular black plastic adjustable air outlets. The outer pair provide fresh or warmed air, while the central pair supply cooled air from the air conditioning unit, the control console for which is in the centre section of the facia. A bank of four vertical sliders controls heating and ventilation for the left and right of the car, with the outer pair of three toggle switches below operating the ventilation fans on the left and right side. The central switch controls the heated rear window. On the lower facia to the right of the steering column is the ignition/starter switch, with the choke lever below the facia adjacent to the steering column. The only other controls outside the instrument nacelle are the bonnet release lever (with emergency ring-pull alongside) below the outer edge of

the facia, and the instrument lighting rheostat between the instrument nacelle and door pillar. On the passenger's side, the glove compartment has a triangular-profile lid which projects from the facia and incorporates a circular finger-pull hole on the inner edge. An internal light is switched on when the lid is opened. Two courtesy lights are fitted below the facia, one at each extremity, and an emergency power socket is provided below the facia close to the bonnet release catch.

The steering wheel, which always has its three spokes and boss in aluminium, has plain spokes and a wood rim on early cars but pierced spokes (with two circular holes in each) and a leather rim on later cars. A central yellow horn button, with black surround, contains a *Cavallino Rampante*. Two stalks project from the left of the steering column; the shorter one controls the direction indicators and the longer one the sidelamp and headlamp main/dip beam functions. A stalk on the right of the column actuates the two-speed windscreen wipers, and the washers by pulling it towards the driver.

The instruments are laid out symmetrically in a matt-finished aluminium nacelle immediately in front of the driver. The speedometer and rev counter are positioned on either side of the steering column, with a bank of four smaller supplementary gauges between them. The upper pair is for water and oil temperature, with the oil pressure gauge and ammeter below them. In the centre of this bank is the trip meter zero button. To the left of the speedometer is the fuel gauge, incorporating a red reserve warning light, and there is a matching clock to the right of the rev counter. The speedometer incorporates a trip meter and an odometer, together with a green 'lights on' warning lamp, which has a pair of small triangular green direction indicator warning lights on either side of it. The rev counter incorporates four further warning lights: yellow for the choke, orange for the heated rear window, blue for headlamp main beam, and red indicating that the handbrake is on, that brake fluid level is low or that the brake lights have failed. All instruments have white characters on black faces and are mounted in the same locations in the nacelle for right- or left-hand drive.

Cars for the US market received additional warning lights and labels in line with changes to legislation. Introduced for 1971 were a letter 'C' engraved on the choke knob, a hazard warning light switch below the heating/ventilation slider controls (also added to late-model European cars), particular windscreen wiper sweep speeds, and an audible signal if the driver's door was opened with the key still in the ignition. From January 1972, a 'fasten seat belt' warning light was added to the facia on the right of the steering column, operating in conjunction with a buzzer if the ignition was switched on with the seat belt buckles unfastened. Also the choke control lever was repositioned in a more visible location, on the top of the centre console in front of the electric window switches.

The fuse and relay board is mounted in the engine bay on the inner wing panel in front of the battery, which is on the left on right-hand-drive cars and on the right on left-hand-drive models.

Luggage Compartment

Twin aluminium fuel tanks, spray coated with glass-fibre, are sited in each rear wing and incorporate a balance pipe. Total fuel capacity is 128 litres (28.1 Imperial/33.8 US gallons), with the fuel filler in the left rear quarter panel on the berlinetta and in the top of the left rear wing on the spider. On US-market cars a 'Fuel Evaporative Emission Control System' is fitted to comply with legislation to prevent vapours from the fuel tank escaping to atmosphere. To effect this the filler neck has a sealed cap, a liquid vapour separator is mounted above the left-hand fuel tank and the vapour is piped to an adjacent Borg-Warner CVX2219 three-way valve, from which a pipe runs to an activated charcoal filter canister at the front of the engine bay. This canister is purged by hot air from the left exhaust manifold and the vapour is fed into the front carburettor on the right-hand manifold.

The spare wheel is housed in a covered recess in the boot floor and the tool kit is contained in a soft roll between the rear suspension enclosures. The boot has black carpet as standard, but this could be matched to the interior carpet. All other internal boot surfaces are painted satin black.

The boot lid is opened by a lever within the cabin and is supported by a self-locking telescopic strut on the left-hand side. A light is provided, actuated by a switch on the lid.

Engine

The basic structure and materials of the 365 GTB/4 engine, type 251, are virtually identical to those of the 275 GTB/4, although one third bigger at 4390cc (267.9cu in) and producing another 52bhp. The maximum power of 352bhp (DIN) was developed at 7500rpm with 44kgm (318lb ft) of torque at 5500rpm. The cylinder block also has two mountings, located on the sides of the block in line with the third cylinder from the front. A rigid torque tube connects the engine to the rear transaxle, which again has two mounting points.

The twin camshafts on each head run above their respective inlet or exhaust valves and each has its own slim crackle-black finished cover bearing the Ferrari script logo. The cam covers are joined by the top timing chain cover at the forward end. The camshafts are supported and driven in exactly the same way as on the 275 GTB/4 and the timing chain has a tensioner fitted on the lower right of its casing.

The valves are actuated via steel bucket followers, fitted with shims upon which the camshaft lobes operate. The inlet valves, on the inner side of each head, are fed by a cast alloy manifold from the carburettors positioned in the vee. All models were fitted with six Weber carburettors, of type 40DCN20 or 21 for Europe and type 40DCN21/A for US-market cars. The petrol feed pipe runs on the right of the carburettor assembly, above the throttle linkage rod, irrespective of whether the car is right- or left-hand drive. Fuel feed is via twin Bendix electric pumps, type 476087, mounted on the chassis frame close to the fuel tanks at the rear of the car. These pumps are set to provide fuel at a pressure of about 0.3 kg/cm^2 (4psi) and operate as soon as the ignition is switched on.

The exhaust valves are on the outside of the vee and exhaust gases from each cylinder bank pass into a pair of triple-branch free-flow steel manifolds, with heat shields above. Heat shields are also fitted above the main manifold/exhaust connections and the two main silencer boxes for each bank of cylinders beneath the cabin. US-market cars have manifolds with pressed steel shrouds containing insulation and tappings for exhaust gas analysis, plus insulated steel shrouds

TOOL KIT

Scissor-type jack with ratchet handle
500g (1.1lb) hammer
2.3kg (5lb) lead mallet (European models)
Special hub-nut spanner (US models), plus late NL, D and S models
Pliers
Set of seven open-ended spanners 8-22mm
120mm (4.7in) long flat-bladed screwdriver
150mm (5.9in) long flat-bladed screwdriver
Phillips screwdriver for screws up to 4mm (0.16in)
Phillips screwdriver for screws 5-9mm (0.20-0.35in)
Emergency warning triangle
Oil filter cartridge wrench
Sparking plug spanner
Weber carburettor spanner
Generator belt
Bulb and fuse holder containing 12-volt bulbs, one each of: 3W, 4W, 5W, 21W and 5/21W

ENGINE

Type	60° V12
Type number	251
Cubic capacity	4390cc (267.9cu in)
Bore and stroke	81x71mm (3.19x2.80in)
Compression ratio	8.8:1
Maximum power[1]	352bhp (DIN) at 7500rpm
Maximum torque[1]	44kgm (318lb ft) at 5500rpm
Carburettors: Europe	6 Weber 40DCN20 or 21
US	6 Weber 40DCN21/A

[1] European specification cars

TIMING DATA

Inlet valves open	45° BTDC
Inlet valves close	46° ABDC
Exhaust valves open	46° BBDC
Exhaust valves close	38° ATDC
Firing order	1-7-5-11-3-9-6-12-2-8-4-10

Valve timing should be measured with a clearance of 0.5mm (0.0197in) between the tappet thimbles and camshaft. Valve clearances with a cold engine should be 0.25mm (0.0098in) for inlets and 0.45-0.5mm (0.0177-0.0197in) for exhausts, measured between the valve pads and camshaft.

SYSTEM CAPACITIES

Fuel tank		128 litres (28.2 Imperial/33.8 US gallons)	
	Litres	Imp Pints	US Pints
Cooling system	17.5	30.8	37.0
Washer bottle: Europe	1.0	1.8	2.1
US	2.0	3.5	4.2
Engine oil	14.62	25.7	30.9
Gearbox/differential oil	4.5	7.9	9.5

Engine bay of a right-hand-drive example, with paired camshaft covers clearly visible and plug leads running between. On the far side are flexible tube and intake port to the air filter casing, and the brake booster.

over the complete under-cabin silencer assemblies. Initially European cars had manifolds with push-fit connections to the silencer boxes, but these were replaced by flanged connections from chassis number 15065; tailpipe connections to the silencer remained a push-fit. The US-market silencer boxes are all flanged front and rear, and the exhaust system is supported by rubber rings on hooks bolted to the chassis. On European cars the fixing is more elaborate with rubber-bushed bolts. All cars have paired chrome-plated twin tailpipes, cut at an angle, so that the top edge protrudes further than the bottom.

The standard carburettor air filter box is black-painted pressed steel, with the top panel retained by three knurled nuts on early cars and eight on later ones. A single inlet pipe, with a manually-operated summer/winter flap, is fed by a flexible hose on the right-hand side of the engine. A single filter element extends around the inner perimeter of the casing. A plate giving the cylinder firing order and a direction label for the summer/winter flap are attached to the top face of the inlet tract.

US-market cars have a fast-idle device on the throttle control rod linkage; a bi-metallic spring acts on a cam with an arm to the throttle-control rod, which alters the engine idle speed relative to engine temperature. An air injection system is also provided for US models, to minimise release of unburned exhaust gases. An air pump, driven by a vee-belt from the alternator pulley, supplies air under pressure to a manifold for each cylinder bank. From there the air is injected into the individual exhaust manifold outlet from each cylinder. An electro-magnetic clutch disengages the pump when the engine speed reaches 3100rpm.

On European models a Marelli S85F distributor, mounted at an angle towards the centre of the car, is provided for each bank of cylinders and driven off the rear end of each exhaust camshaft. Each distributor is fed by its own Marelli 12v BZR201A coil. US-market cars have a Marelli S138B distributor for each bank of cylinders with three changes of coil type, depending upon the year of manufacture; details are given in the *Major Electrical Equipment* table on page 93. The US-market cars' ignition systems incorporate twin Marelli Dinoplex high-tension transistor units, one for each cylinder bank; they are type CAEC101DAX on 1971 models and AEC103A units on 1972 models onwards. In case of unit failure, there are emergency override switches that allow the engine to be fed by the normal coil, bypassing the unit. From the twin distributors, the high-tension leads run in insulated brackets bolted to the inlet cam covers, serving each plug via an insulated snap-on cap. The sparking plugs, one per cylinder, are located centrally in the heads between the cam covers.

The reciprocating parts of the engine (crankshaft, pistons, connecting rods and flywheel) and the dry-sump lubrication system are all very similar in design, materials and layout to the 275 GTB/4 model, apart from differing dimensions due to the larger engine capacity. On the 365 GTB/4 an oil cooler, mounted in the water radiator frame, is incorporated. A crankcase-breather emission control system is fitted, whereby any fumes are carried through a flexible tube to the neck of the dry-sump tank, from where another flexible tube runs to 12 jets on the induction manifolds, with a branch tube into the carburettor air filter housing. The system fitted to US-market cars differs in that the scavenge pump conveys the gases back to the dry-sump tank, maintaining a negative pressure in the sump. A flexible breather tube runs from the sump to the neck of the dry-sump tank and another from there to the carburettor air filter. Oil pressure at an oil temperature of 110-120°C should be 5.5-7.0kg/cm^2 (78-100psi) at 6800rpm and a minimum of 4.5kg/cm^2 (64psi). If the engine is running at the minimum pressure, it is recommended that engine speed should be reduced by at least 1000rpm and the cause established as soon as possible.

The water pump is driven directly off the timing chain, as on the 275 GTB/4, and draws coolant through a flexible hose from the base of the radiator into the engine waterways. Coolant leaves the engine on the top front centre of the block and passes via a flexible hose to a thermostat housing. From there a by-pass hose runs to a 'T' in the pump suction hose, allowing coolant to go straight back into the engine until temperature reaches 83°C, above which it passes through the radiator matrix. This has twin electric fans, controlled by a thermostatic switch in the lower part of the radiator and the air conditioning control switch. An expansion tank with pressure relief cap is fitted to the right of the radiator.

An air conditioning pump is fitted on a bracket on the right front face of the block, driven by vee-belt off the crankshaft via a double pulley; the second forward part of the pulley drives the alternator mounted on the upper front left of the engine. The air conditioning evaporator coil is mounted on the front face of the radiator, which is why the cooling fans are interlocked with the air conditioning controls.

Transmission

The transmission layout uses a flywheel-mounted clutch, a rigid torque tube carrying the propshaft and a five-speed transaxle, and is virtually identical to that used on the 275 GTB/4 model that preceded the 365 GTB/4. The only major differences are that the clutch is operated mechanically rather than hydraulically and the individual gear and final drive ratios are different (see the *Gear Ratios* table) to suit the characteristics of the larger and more powerful engine. Alternative gear and final drive ratios were homologated for competition use. The internal layout of the gears, shafts running in needle-roller bearings, synchronisers and the gear-driven oil pump mirror the 275 GTB/4. The method of support is also identical with a pair of rubber mountings on the engine and another pair on the transaxle casing, the two being rigidly connected by the torque tube. The bellhousing also has a tie rod attached to the chassis via a rubber bush. A connection for the gear-driven speedometer cable is sited on the top right of the transaxle's front cover plate.

The flywheel-mounted single dry-plate clutch features a multi-spring pressure plate and is cable-operated via an adjustable rod linkage to the sealed ball thrust race. An assister spring is fitted to the pedal pivot assembly to reduce effort. As on the 275 GTB/4, the pedal has a height adjustment facility via a bolt at the base of the lever arm. This bolt can be removed to adjust the pedal shaft location to one of three height settings using semi-circular cut-outs along its length.

Electrical Equipment & Lights

The electrical system is 12-volt. A 74amp/hour battery (originally a Fiamm 6B5), sited in the rear of the front wing on the opposite side to the driver, is charged by a Marelli alternator. This is mounted on the front of the engine and driven by a vee-belt off a crankshaft pulley. The Marelli starter motor, integral with its solenoid suspended below it, is bolted to the flywheel bellhousing at the lower right. Twin air horns are provided, mounted in the front of the engine bay and activated by the central push-button in the steering wheel.

The lighting equipment is all of Carello manufacture and underwent one major change in 1971, with the introduction of the US-market

Traditional open-gate gear lever controls five-speed transaxle carried over from the 275 GTB/4; engraved markings giving the pattern were adopted during production as a result of US legislation.

PRODUCTION

365 GTB/4 between 1968 and 1973, chassis numbers 12301-17615. Total production 1284.

365 GTS/4 between 1969 and 1973, chassis numbers 14365-17073. Total production 122.

GEAR RATIOS

| | Gearbox | | Overall | |
	Standard	Optional[1]	Standard	Optional[1]
First	3.075:1	2.467:1	10.147:1	8.141:1
Second	2.120:1	1.842:1	6.996:1	6.079:1
Third	1.572:1	1.455:1	5.188:1	4.801:1
Fourth	1.250:1	1.200:1	4.125:1	3.960:1
Fifth	0.963:1	0.963:1	3.178:1	3.178:1
Reverse	2.667:1	2.667:1	8.801:1	8.801:1
Final drive	3.300:1 (10:33)			
Optional final drive	4.714:1 (7:33), 4.375:1 (8:35), 4.250:1 (8:34), 4.125:1 (8:33), 4.000:1 (8:32),			
	3.889:1 (9:35), 3.667:1 (9:33), 3.444:1 (9:31) and 3.500:1 (10:35)			

[1] Optional gear ratios were intended for competition use

The pattern of the side/turn indicator light units differed according to market. Cars for most markets had a white sidelight lens and a *Cavallino Rampante* in the circular side reflector, but for the US there was an all-orange lens and a plain reflector. British cars were an anomaly, generally having all-orange lenses.

Rear light layout, seen on 365 GTS/4 models, for European cars (right) and US cars (below), the latter having red indicator lenses, rectangular reflectors in the indent line below the lights, and a single central reversing light.

MAJOR ELECTRICAL EQUIPMENT

Battery		12-volt Fiamm 6B5, 74amp/hour
Alternator		Marelli GCA113A
Starter motor		Marelli MT21T-1.8/12D9
Ignition:	Europe	Marelli 50.10.141.1 (S85F) distributor
		Twin Marelli BZR201A coils
	US	Twin Marelli S138B distributors
		Twin Marelli BZR205A coils (1971),
		BAE200A coils (1972-73),
		BAE203A coils (from chassis 16569)
Sparking plugs		Marelli CW89LP or Champion N6Y

lighting layouts on European-market models, mainly in respect of the front sidelamp/turn indicator lens colours. All cars have two automatic lights under the bonnet and one in the boot.

As the European arrangements are the most confusing, it is probably best to clarify them first. Standard European-market cars with fixed paired headlamps under Plexiglas covers are provided with a white forward section to the sidelamp/turn indicator lens, with a vertical pin-stripe effect, and an orange side/rear section incorporating a circular reflector with an embossed *Cavallino Rampante*. Those cars destined for France have yellow headlamp glass. However, British-market examples of the period have all-orange turn indicator lenses, with sidelamps incorporated in the headlamps. When retractable headlamps were introduced, main European-market cars continued with white sidelamp lenses, but cars for Britain retained full orange lenses and received small rectangular sidelamps in chrome-plated cases mounted on top of the quarter bumpers. This might sound reasonably straightforward, but there are numerous exceptions to this arrangement, without any apparent rhyme or reason – British cars with white sidelamp lenses or with retractable headlamps but no rectangular sidelamps on the bumpers. It seems that it may have been a case of fitting whatever was available at a given time! The headlamps are fitted with 55-watt quartz iodine bulbs, the outer one of each pair being for main beam and the inner for dipped beam. A flashing facility is provided on cars for the British, German and Swiss markets. The retractable headlamp pods are raised by an electric motor when the headlamps are switched on and have a manual raising facility via a knurled knob on the motor casing, in the event of a motor failure. Red 'door-open' warning lights are provided in the trailing edge of each door.

At the rear there is fortunately more harmony in the lighting equipment. There is a pair of circular lamps on each side of the tail panel, the outer being an orange turn indicator and the inner a red combined stop/tail lamp with central circular reflector. A twin-element number plate light is provided on the boot lid in a rectangular chrome-

model, when fixed twin headlamps under clear Plexiglas covers were replaced with retractable units. The US-market lighting arrangement is the most clear-cut and remained constant through the production run, whereas there are vagaries in the

plated shroud and a small rectangular reversing light is suspended below each quarter bumper. Reversing lights are actuated by a switch on the lever mechanism when reverse gear is engaged.

The lighting on US models is specific to that market and all cars have retractable headlamps. The sidelamp/turn indicator/side marker lens is full orange, but the integral circular reflector is plain, without the *Cavallino Rampante*. Headlamp arrangement, bulb power and door open warning lights are as for other markets. In the sides of each rear wing are cut-outs housing chrome-framed rectangular red side marker lamps/reflectors. The rear side/turn indicator lamp layout is similar to European-market cars, but all lenses are red and a small rectangular reflector is fitted in the body indent line below each pair of lights. A single rectangular reversing light is mounted centrally on the body, between the quarter bumpers.

Suspension & Steering

Suspension and steering follow the same principles as on the 275 GTB/4. The suspension is all-independent with unequal-length wishbones, coil springs around double-acting telescopic dampers and anti-roll bars front and rear, while the worm and roller steering is unassisted. Although the suspension layout is similar on both models, the components are not interchangeable due to both dimensional and constructional differences.

Unequal-length forged steel upper and lower wishbones are used all round. They are joined by the hub carriers at the outer end, with ball joints at the front and bronze bushes at the rear, and mounted to the chassis via rubber bushes. Front hub carriers are manufactured from machined forged steel, while those at the rear are machined cast steel units. At the front, the dampers are mounted co-axially within the coil springs, which are between the wishbones. At the rear the half-shafts preclude this arrangement, so the dampers, again mounted co-axially within the coil springs, are fitted above the top wishbones, between them and a substantial support frame from the main chassis tubes. Rubber bump stops for maximum suspension travel are within the damper assemblies, which are Koni type 82T1633 at the front and Koni type 82P1634 at the rear.

SUSPENSION SETTINGS

Front toe-in	−2 to −3mm (−0.079 to −0.118in)
Front camber	+ 0°50′ to 1°10′
Rear toe-in	−2 to −3mm (−0.079 to −0.118in)
Rear camber	−2°15′ to −2°30′
Castor angle	Fixed 1°30′
Dampers: front	Koni 82T1633
rear	Koni 82P1634

The splined front and rear hubs are attached to the brake discs by eight-bolt flanges, with tappings in the bell of each disc for the retaining bolts. Anti-roll bars, supported in rubber-bushed brackets, are of 22mm (0.87in) diameter at the front and 20mm (0.79in) at the rear.

Steering is unassisted with a worm and roller steering box, mounted on the front chassis cross-member at the lower end of the universally-jointed steering column. The box has a screw and lock-nut facility for adjustment of any play on the upper face, and track control adjustment is provided on the track rods. The steering ball joints are non-adjustable and require no lubrication. The steering has 2.8 turns from lock to lock, with a turning circle of 13 metres (42ft 8in). The high-geared steering without power assistance makes the 365 GTB/4 hard work at parking speeds and around town, but comes into its own at high speed, when it lightens considerably, proving perfectly weighted to enjoy the handling to the full. Left- or right-hand drive was available for both berlinetta and spider variants.

Brakes

The braking system employed on the 365 GTB/4 is a vast improvement on that used on the preceding 275 GTB/4 model. Ventilated cast iron discs, of 287mm (11.30in) diameter at the front and 295mm (11.61in) at the rear, are each fitted with a single four-pot caliper. Twin master cylinders, with vacuum servo assistance, each supply a separate circuit to the opposing pair of cylinders on each wheel, so there is in effect a duplicated braking system. A pressure-limiting valve is fitted to regulate rear-wheel braking. Both hydraulic circuits have a pressure-sensing switch; a loss of pressure causes a facia warning light to illuminate.

A cable-operated handbrake, situated between the seats, operates on its own set of shoes inside the hub on each rear wheel disc. Shoe adjustment in each disc is via a pair of holes (at one o'clock and seven o'clock on the left, 11 o'clock and five o'clock on the right) through which a screwdriver can be inserted to turn a toothed adjuster. Handbrake cable adjustment can be effected by screws where the twin cables join the lever arm below the cabin. The brake pedal has the same height adjustment facility as the clutch pedal, as described in the *Transmission* section.

The recommended brake pads for normal touring conditions were Ferodo I/D330 (with three radial slots) at the front and Ferodo I/D330 (with a single radial slot) at the rear.

The improvement that the system provided over that employed on the 275 series can be gauged from the comment in *Autocar*'s road test of 30 September 1971 where it stated: 'There was

FACTORY LITERATURE

1968
- Sales brochure for 365 GTB/4, with factory reference 25/68, compression ratio 8.8:1 and 128-litre fuel tank.
- Sales brochure for 365 GTB/4, with factory reference 25/68, compression ratio 9.3:1 and 100-litre fuel tank.

1969
- Mechanical spare parts catalogue for the 365 GTB/4, with factory print reference 33/69 and orange/white/black cover. Reprinted a number of times with various updates, modifications and supplements, up to September 1972.
- Owner's handbook for the 365 GTB/4, factory reference 34/69, with red and white cover.
- The 1969 model-range brochure includes two pages on the 365 GTB/4, with photograph and specifications in Italian/French/English; factory reference 27/68.

1971
- Sales brochure for 365 GTB/4; factory reference 49/71.
- Chassis service manual abstract, with factory reference 46/71, dark red cover. Reprinted a further three times.
- Additional instructions for the US-version 365 GTB/4, supplement to the owner's handbook; factory reference 47/71.

1972
- Additional instructions for the 1972 US-version 365 GTB/4, supplement to the owner's handbook; factory reference 47/71.
- US consumer information booklet for 365 GTB/4; factory reference 62/72. Three different printings.
- Sales brochure for 365 GTB/4; factory reference 64/72.
- Mechanical spare parts catalogue for the 365 GTB/4, with factory print reference 70/72 and red/white/black cover. Reprinted twice with 1974 sticker on cover.
- Sales brochure for 365 GTB/4; factory reference 73/72.

1973
- Owner's handbook for the 365 GTB/4; factory reference 74/73, with red/white/black cover.
- Additional instructions for the 1973 US-version 365 GTB/4, supplement to the owner's handbook; factory reference 47/71.

The standard 7.5x15in five-spoke alloy wheel (far left), with the triple-ear hub nut used on European versions. The optional 9x15in rim (left) has a more pronounced curve to the spokes.

no fade at all during 10 stops in succession from 70mph nor after four runs to 150mph and down to 50mph during acceleration tests. At all times the brakes gave supreme confidence and qualify as a perfect match for the performance.'

Wheels & Tyres

The standard wheels are five-spoke 7.5x15in alloys with a satin-silver paint finish under clear lacquer. The splined hubs are retained by a single chrome-plated nut with triple angled ears. Wider wheels were homologated for competition purposes, as detailed in the table, and a number of road cars feature these, particularly at the rear. The standard tyres are also listed in the table. All cars for the USA, plus later models for the Dutch, German and Swedish markets, have special octagonal chrome-plated hub nuts, as the triple-eared spinners did not comply with Federal Safety Standard 110, and the tool kit contains a spanner for these in place of the lead mallet for other markets.

As an option Borrani wire wheels with chrome-plated spokes and polished aluminium rims were offered, size 7.5x15in. As on the 275 series, these more open wheels undoubtedly provide better brake cooling and heat dissipation but need regular checks for spoke tightness and rim alignment – especially important with the 365 GTB/4 because of the power available and cornering forces possible.

Identification plate fixed to the inner wing panel gives model type, engine type and chassis number, with lubrication plate below.

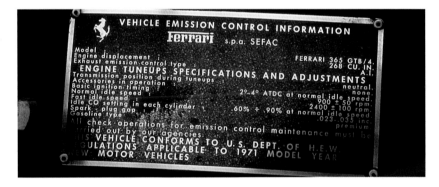

US-market vehicle emission control plate fitted in the engine bay.

WHEELS & TYRES

Wheels, front & rear 7½x15in five-spoke cast alloy
Optional Borrani wire wheels in the same size type RW4075
Tyres, front & rear Michelin X or XVX 215/70VR-15
Note: 8in, 8½in and 9in wide front and rear wheels were homologated for this model, plus 11in wide rear wheels, mainly for competition use, but some road cars have also been fitted with wider rims, particularly at the rear.

IDENTIFICATION PLATES

1. Chassis number stamped in frame above front spring mounting.
2. Engine number stamped on right side of block adjacent to flywheel housing.
3. Vehicle data plate mounted on engine bay valance panel.
4. On later models there is also a vehicle type and chassis number plate on the upper face of the steering column shroud in the cabin. This plate is common to all US-market cars. US-market cars have the following additional identification plates:
5. US Safety Standard conformity plate on the driver's door shut post below lock striker plate, giving year and month of manufacture, chassis number and car type.
6. US Safety Standard 110 tag, giving tyre data and vehicle capacities; on driver's sun visor for 1971 models and on inner face of glovebox lid for 1972-73 models.
7. Air pollution plate showing the main details for correct engine tuning to meet regulations, mounted on left side engine bay valance panel.
8. Cars registered in California also had to have a 'State emissions standard' label located in the rear screen.

Vehicle safety compliance plate on cars for the USA was fitted to the driver's door shut post.

Chapter 9

365 GTC/4

The 365 GTC/4 joined the Ferrari range at the 1971 Geneva Salon, ostensibly as a replacement for the 365 GTC but with nominal 2+2 seating on a 2500mm (98.42in) wheelbase. The model attempted to some degree to fill the gap left by the cessation of 365 GT 2+2 production. The 365 GTC/4 has a four-camshaft 4.4-litre engine, similar to that of the 365 GTB/4, albeit with side-draught rather than downdraught carburettors. However, transmission is a conventional five-speed gearbox mounted on the engine, with a rigid driveline to a limited slip differential, as on the 365 GT 2+2, with which it also shares the power-assisted steering and the hydraulic self-levelling device on the rear suspension. Like the 365 GT

2+2 it was constructed at the Pininfarina plant in Turin and then shipped to Ferrari in Maranello for the mechanical components to be added.

Visually the GTC/4 has no connection with the 365 GT 2+2, but has a slight resemblance to the 365 GTB/4, although that is mainly relative to the wedge styling, retractable headlamps and the five-spoke 'star' wheels. There are no common body panels between the two models. The 365 GTC/4 has a distinctive black rubber bumper surrounding the grille that forms the leading edge of the nose, from which the bonnet and front wings run smoothly rearward to the cabin section. From there the roofline runs gently to a shallow Kamm tail, featuring a pair of triple-lens lamps.

The 365 GTC/4 in profile: this is a US-registered European model, with the all-red rear lights required for that market but not the side marker lights. Wheels are optional Borrani wires.

The 365 GTC/4 has a distinctive wedge shape that is unique to this model. The only body detail elements carried through from the preceding 365 GT 2+2 are the arrowhead-shaped door handles and a triple rear light layout.

The production period only lasted for around 18 months, in which time 500 examples were manufactured. It was succeeded by the true 2+2 replacement, the 365 GT4 2+2 in 1972.

Body & Chassis

The 365 GTC/4 chassis, type F101 AC 100, is the first in a new Ferrari type-numbering system and was developed from that of the 365 GT 2+2. The model has a 2500mm (98.24in) wheelbase and is constructed following the usual Ferrari practice for the period with two main longitudinal oval steel tubes. These have sub-structures welded to them, plus a substantial front cross-member. The floor pan, footwell boxes and firewall are glass-fibre units bonded to the chassis frame, the standard finish of which is satin black paint.

The body, designed and built by Pininfarina, is unique to the model, carrying no styling cues from its predecessor and with nothing from its shape carried over to any succeeding models. The only features that came from the 365 GT 2+2 are the door handles and a similar rear light arrangement, and these also carried over into the 365 GT4 2+2. The full-width radiator grille opening incorporating the front bumper is the dominant feature of the design, from which the remainder of the body flows. The shape is distinctively wedge in profile. Starting at the projecting radiator opening with its peripheral rubber bumper, the theme continues through the nose panel with retractable headlamps to a flat bonnet with a pair of radiator exhaust air outlets. The steeply raked screen forms an ellipse with the cabin roof and the styling then follows a virtually straight line over the rear screen and boot lid to the shallow Kamm tail. The body is constructed of welded steel panels, with an aluminium bonnet and boot lid on steel frames.

Body Trim & Fittings

The front of the 365 GTC/4 features a projecting, almost rectangular, radiator opening, which is wide and shallow with slightly rounded ends. The opening is surrounded by a black rubber lip, which serves as a bumper. An inset aluminium egg-crate grille carries a chrome-plated *Cavallino Rampante* at its centre and has an aluminium trim surround. Within the opening, at the extremities, are the side/turn indicator lights, which have rectangular driving lights inboard of them. The full-width steel rear bumper is finished in satin black.

A rectangular enamel Ferrari badge is fitted on the upper nose panel between the grille and leading edge of the bonnet, and a chromed Ferrari script badge is mounted centrally close to the trailing edge of the boot lid, with a chrome-plated *Cavallino Rampante* on the right side of the tail

panel inboard of the lights. Slim horizontal rectangular Pininfarina badges, with Pininfarina enamel shields above them, are fitted to the lower sides of the front wings. The front-hinged bonnet has a pair of rectangular depressions in the top face for the radiator hot air extraction slots and is supported automatically by a pair of hydraulic struts when opened. The fuel filler flap is on the left rear wing, irrespective of whether the car is left- or right-hand drive.

The body is very clean and virtually devoid of brightwork, which is confined to the stainless steel screen and glass surrounds, plus chrome-plated arrowhead-shaped door handles with a front pull and a lock barrel in the trailing end. The windscreen wiper arms and blade frames are finished in satin black paint. Access to the boot is via a chrome-plated lever, with keylock, on the left side inner sill panel alongside the seat; the matching fuel filler release is located forward of it.

Plain glass is fitted and the windscreen is laminated. The two-speed self-parking wipers normally park on the right on left-hand-drive cars and on the left on right-hand-drive examples. The door windows are provided with swivelling quarterlights, operated by knurled knobs on the inner door panel. The rear screen is heated and has a switch on the centre console, with a warning light in the rev counter.

Paintwork

As mentioned in the chapter on the 365 GTB/4 models, a vast range of colours was available for Ferraris at this time and the same comments made there apply to the 365 GTC/4. As the bodies were built by Pininfarina they should have a paint colour manufactured by either PPG or Duco. The table on page 86 in the *365 GTB/4* chapter lists the full range of colours offered. The standard finish of the inset tail panel is satin black.

Interior Trim & Fittings

The 365 GTC/4 is the only Ferrari of the period to have been offered with anything other than leather as the standard seat upholstery material. Customers had the option of Connolly full-leather upholstery, or plaid cloth for the seat centres, with leather surrounds, and part of the door panel. The range of plaid trim material is unique to this model. The range of upholstery colours available is shown in the table provided in the *365 GTB/4* chapter (see page 89). The front seats are mounted on runners with adjustment via a lever under the outer front edge of the cushion. A lever on the outer lower edge of the backrest allows the rake to be altered rapidly through large arcs, with an adjacent knurled black plastic knob

DIMENSIONS & WEIGHTS

	mm	in
Overall length	4550	179.13
Overall width	1780	70.08
Overall height	1270	50.00
Wheelbase	2500	98.42
Front track	1480	58.27
Rear track	1480	58.27

Weight (kerb)	kg	lb
Europe	1730	3814
US	1780	3924

PAINT & TRIM COLOURS

For Paint Colours, Leather Upholstery Colours and Carpet Colours see the tables in the *365 GTB/4* chapter.

The seat centres were also available in a plaid pattern cloth and these were provided with colour codes 12, 22, 23, 41, 43 and 84 to match the chosen leather colour.

The front passenger compartment, showing the very wide centre console running into the dash face, the plain-spoked leather-rim steering wheel, and the plaid cloth upholstery (on the seat centres and door panels) that was unique to this model.

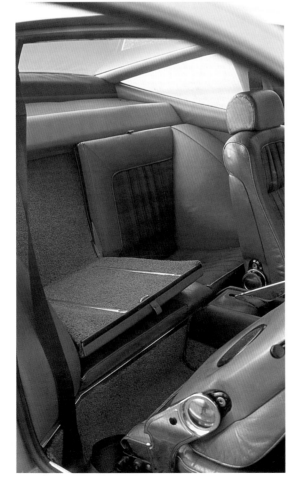

Legroom is very limited in the rear. Folding one or both of the seat backrests to provide a luggage platform is a more practical proposition.

for finer adjustment. A sliding lever on the upper side of the squab tilts it forward for access to the rear seats. The rear seating is marginal, both in headroom and more particularly in legroom, and is really suitable only for very young children – unless the front seats are well forward on their runners. Small tabs are provided at the tops of the rear seat backrests, so that they can be folded forward to provide a luggage platform. Each front seat is provided with a lap-and-diagonal static seat belt and there are mounting points for three-point rear belts. The door armrests incorporate pulls angled upwards at the front. The door-opening lever is in the trim panel, above the front of the armrest and behind the quarterlight control knob. The armrest is normally trimmed to match the upholstery colour. A circular plug in the door panel, forward of the armrest, can be removed to insert the emergency winder for the electric windows. Their control switches are in the centre console below the ashtray.

The floor and rear seat heelboard are carpeted, with inset black rubber heelmats for both driver and passenger. The range of carpet colours is given in the table on page 89 in the 365 GTB/4 chapter. The transmission tunnel console plus the front and rear inner wheelarches are trimmed in a mixture of upholstery-colour vinyl and leather as standard, the facia top and glovebox lid being trimmed in black Alcantara. The headlining is plain ivory-colour vinyl retained by cant rails upholstered in the same material, as are the rear screen pillars. The rear parcels shelf is normally trimmed in either black vinyl or to match the upholstery colour. Vinyl-covered sun visors are also provided, with a vanity mirror on the passenger's side. Also mounted on the upper screen rail is a dipping mirror.

The short chrome-plated gear lever, topped by a black plastic knob, has a leather gaiter and is mounted centrally on the transmission tunnel. The knob on US-market cars has the gearchange pattern engraved in white on its top face, to comply with Federal Safety Standard 102. First to fourth gears form a conventional 'H' pattern, with fifth outside the 'H' to the right and forward, and reverse opposite fifth.

On this model the facia and centre console are even more integrated than on the 365 GT 2+2 and thus will be described in the *Facia & Instruments* section. The handbrake is mounted in the glove tray between the front seats. The bonnet release lever is below the facia at the outer end, with an emergency ring-pull release and auxiliary power point alongside. The choke lever is also suspended below the facia on the inner side of the steering column. A pair of footwell lights is provided, operated automatically by door switches, and there is an interior roof light between the sun visors, also worked automatically by door switches or manually by a switch in the lens.

Facia & Instruments

The facia and centre console of the 365 GTC/4 form a combined unit with the side rolls of the latter running into the instrument nacelle on the driver's side and the edge of the facia on the passenger's side. The rectangular main instrument nacelle in front of the driver contains the speedometer and rev counter with, between them, the oil pressure gauge at the top and the water temperature gauge below. These are circular dials in matt black square surrounds. In the bottom left corner of the speedometer surround is the trip reset button and in the bottom right corner of the rev counter frame is the instrument lighting rheostat. The speedometer dial contains an odometer and trip recorder, plus green warning lights for turn indicators and sidelamps and a blue main beam light. The rev counter dial has warning lights for choke, heated rear window, a spare (used for a hazard warning light on German-market cars) and the braking system. The latter can be illuminated for one of three reasons: handbrake on, brake light bulb failure, or loss of pressure in either hydraulic circuit. The upper section of the centre console forms the central portion of the facia, in which there is a bank of four circular aux-

iliary dials, in square matt black surrounds, angled towards the driver. These are a clock, a fuel gauge with low level warning light, an oil temperature gauge and an ammeter. All gauges have white digits on a black background.

Below this bank of dials is a radio, with the air conditioning control knobs on either side – one for fan speed and the other for temperature. The two circular air conditioning outlets are central in the top of the facia, between the matching demister vents and low-level rectangular ones on either side of the transmission tunnel, that on the passenger's side having an output control lever. Beneath the radio is the gear lever in a square-based leather gaiter, with two slider levers on either side controlling the heating and air distribution on that side of the car. The upper one controls air flow to the circular facia-top demister and/or low-level outer footwell vents and the lower regulates the heater. The ventilation fans for the left and right sides are situated in the lower parts of the respective front wings, with ducting via their individual heater boxes to the outlets. To the top left side of the upper left slider is a toggle switch for the electric radio aerial, with a matching one on the opposite side of the console for the hazard warning lights.

Between the gear lever and ashtray is a bank of four circular black toggle switches for the left-hand-side ventilation fan, windscreen electric heating element (optional), heated rear screen and right-hand-side ventilation fan. The ashtray has an integral cigar lighter fitted below the lid. The electric window switches are mounted below the ashtray, with a fog lamp switch between them on cars for the French and Italian markets. On US-market cars produced after 1 January 1972 there is a 'Fasten Seat Belts' warning light mounted in the centre of the console above the gear lever, actuated by switches in the seat belt

The main instrument panel showing the circular dials in square surrounds, viewed through the elegantly simple leather-rim, aluminium-spoke steering wheel.

buckles. A lockable glovebox with interior light is provided on the passenger's side of the facia, with the vehicle fuse boards mounted behind cover panels on the rear face.

The leather-rimmed steering wheel has plain aluminium spokes and the central horn push is a yellow button, with black plastic rim, featuring the *Cavallino Rampante* emblem. A pair of slender chrome-plated stalks, with black plastic finger pads, project from the left of the steering column; the shorter one controls the direction indicators and the other the sidelamps plus headlamp main/dipped beam and flasher functions. A stalk on the right operates the two-speed windscreen wipers, and the washers by pulling it towards the driver. The key-operated ignition/starter switch, incorporating a steering lock, is mounted on the lower facia, to the right of the steering column shroud, irrespective of whether the car is right- or left-hand drive.

Luggage Compartment

The boot contains the twin aluminium fuel tanks, spray-coated with glass fibre. They are positioned below the floor and into the rear wings to form the sides of the spare wheel well, which has a removable cover panel. Fuel capacity is 105 litres (23.1 Imperial/27.7 US gallons). The fuel filler is on the left rear wing beneath a circular flap, opened by a lockable lever in the left inner sill panel, with an emergency ring-pull in the front left of the boot, behind the trim panel. On US-market cars a 'Fuel Evaporative Emission Control System' is fitted to comply with legislation, basically as the system described on page 90 in the *365 GTB/4* chapter.

The boot floor and sides are lined with black carpet and all plain metal surfaces are painted satin black. A light, mounted on the ceiling of the boot, is actuated by a switch plate on the self-supporting lid. Access to the boot is via a lockable lever in the left inner sill panel, behind that for the fuel flap, with an emergency ring-pull under the fuel filler flap.

Engine

The 365 GTC/4's 4390cc (267.9cu in) 60° V12 produces 320bhp (DIN) at 7000rpm and 44mkg (318lb ft) of torque at 4000rpm. The engine, type number F 101 AC 000, is the first in a revised numbering system like that of the chassis and is based on the unit fitted in the concurrent 365 GTB/4. However, this engine has two major differences and a number of smaller ones. The major ones are that it is uses wet-sump lubrication and has six sidedraught carburettors. These feed inlet ports sited between the twin overhead camshafts on each cylinder bank, reducing the overall

height of the engine. The cylinder block is similarly of the two-mounting type (on the sides of the block, in line with the third cylinder from the front) with a conventional gearbox location and a propeller shaft running in a rigid torque tube to the differential. This is also provided with two mounting points, thus the engine and transmission layout is along the principles established on the 365 GT 2+2 model.

The twin camshafts on each head run above their respective inlet or exhaust valves and each has its own slim crackle-black finished cover, with the inlet valve cam cover bearing the Ferrari script logo. The cam covers are joined by the top timing chain cover at the forward end. The camshafts are supported and driven in exactly the same way as on the 365 GTB/4, but the timing chain on the 365 GTC/4 initially had an automatic tensioner in the lower left side of its casing. The tensioner was changed to a manually-adjustable type from chassis 15259 on European cars and chassis 15181 on US-market cars.

The valves are actuated via steel bucket followers with a recess in the bucket head to accept shims, upon which the camshaft lobes operate. The inlet valves are on the inner side of each head with inlet ports between the camshafts. Fuel is fed from each carburettor by alloy manifolds, cast as part of the exhaust valve camshaft covers. The six

ENGINE

Type	60° V12
Type number	F 101 AC 000
Cubic capacity	4390cc (267.9cu in)
Bore and stroke	81x71mm (3.19x2.80in)
Compression ratio	8.8:1
Maximum power[1]	320bhp (DIN) at 7000rpm
Maximum torque[1]	44kgm (318lb ft) at 4000rpm
Carburettors: Europe	6 Weber 38DCOE59/60
US	6 Weber 38DCOE59-60/A

[1] European specification cars

TIMING DATA

Inlet valves open	43° BTDC
Inlet valves close	38° ABDC
Exhaust valves open	38° BBDC
Exhaust valves close	34° ATDC
Firing order	1-7-5-11-3-9-6-12-2-8-4-10

Valve timing should be measured with a clearance of 0.5mm (0.0197in) between the tappet thimbles and camshaft. Valve clearances with a cold engine should be 0.1-0.15mm (0.0039-0.0059in) for inlets and 0.25-0.3mm (0.0098-0.0118in) for exhausts, measured between the tappet shims and camshaft.

SYSTEM CAPACITIES

Fuel tank	105 litres (23.1 Imperial/27.7 US gallons)		
	Litres	Imp Pints	US Pints
Cooling system	13.0	22.9	27.5
Washer bottle	2.0	3.5	4.2
Engine oil	16.0	28.2	33.8
Gearbox oil	5.0	8.8	10.6
Rear axle oil	2.5	4.4	5.3

Weber carburettors fitted are 38DCOE59/60 units on European cars and 38DCOE59/60A units for the US market. The number 59 refers to left-hand cylinder bank carburettors and the number 60 to those for the right-hand bank. A petrol feed pipe runs from the tank to a T-piece at the upper rear of the engine, from where a supply pipe is taken to each bank of carburettors, running behind them. The rigid rod throttle linkages, running in roller bearings, are supported on brackets cast into the inlet valve camshaft covers and join up at the rear of the engine into a single rod assembly to the accelerator pedal. The fuel feed system is from the twin tanks via triple filters: a gauze one on the tank manifold outlet, a Fispa bowl type 128F before and a Fispa 3064-02 after the twin Bendix electric pumps, type 476087. These are mounted on the chassis frame close to the fuel tanks at the rear of the car. The pumps are self regulating to provide fuel at a pressure of about 0.3 kg/cm^2 (4psi) and operate as soon as the ignition is switched on. The post-pump filter is omitted on cars produced after October 1972.

The exhaust valves are on the outside of the vee and the gases pass into a pair of triple-branch free flow steel manifolds to each bank of cylinders, with a heat shield fitted above them. Heat shields are also fitted above the main manifold/exhaust connections. The manifolds of US-market cars are fitted with pressed steel shrouds containing insulation and have exhaust gas analysis tappings. The silencer boxes on US-market cars also have

insulated steel shrouds over the complete under-cabin silencer assemblies. European cars have manifolds with flanged connections to the silencer boxes, with push-fit tailpipe connections. The US-market silencers are all flanged front and rear. All cars have paired chrome-plated twin tailpipes, cut at an angle, so that the top protrudes further than the bottom.

The standard carburettor air filter boxes are pressed steel, painted crackle black to match the camshaft covers, with the side panel retained by three over-centre catches along each of the top and bottom edges. Each casing contains a single filter element around the perimeter and draws in air at the front through an inlet funnel, which is extended forward to draw cool air from either side of the radiator. A manually-operated flap in each intake funnel allows air to come from the front of the car in the summer position and from a cut-out in its base above the exhaust manifolds in the winter position. Intakes on US-market models are sealed by an engine oil pressure-controlled valve, which closes as soon as the engine is switched off to prevent any fuel vapour escaping. To enable the car to be started, the suction caused by the engine turning on the starter motor opens a bleed valve, which provides enough air for initial combustion; the main valve opens upon sensing oil pressure.

On each throttle control rod linkage US-market cars also have a fast idle device, which operates, like the air injection system, in the same way as described for the 365 GT 2+2 (see page 76).

More of the 4.4-litre four-cam V12 engine can be seen on this model due to the use of triple sidedraught carburettors on each bank of cylinders. The filter boxes border each side of the engine, with their intake tubes running forward either side of the radiator. Twin oil filters are mounted in the centre of the vee between the plug leads.

On European-market cars a single Marelli S129E distributor, mounted at an angle towards the centre of the car, is driven off the rear end of the right exhaust camshaft and fed by a pair of Marelli 12-volt BZR201A coils. US-market cars have a Marelli S138B distributor for each bank of cylinders, driven off the appropriate exhaust camshaft, each with its own Marelli BAE200A coil and Marelli Dinoplex AEC103A high-tension transistor ignition. From the distributors, the high-tension leads run in insulated brackets bolted to the inlet cam covers, serving each individual plug via an insulated snap-on cap. The sparking plugs, one per cylinder, are located centrally in the heads between the cam covers.

The 365 GTC/4 has wet-sump lubrication, with gear-driven oil and water pumps sharing a housing low down at the front of the engine. These pumps are driven by their own duplex chain, with automatic tensioner, off a crankshaft sprocket. From chassis 15081 on European cars and chassis 15181 on US-market models, the oil pressure relief valve is in the pump casing, instead of being forward of the twin oil filters at the top of the vee of the engine block. The lubrication circuit incorporates an oil cooler, mounted in the water radiator frame, and a thermostatic valve that only allows the oil to go through the cooler if temperature becomes excessive. A crankcase breather emission control system allows any fumes to be carried through a flexible tube from the neck of the oil filler pipe to an evaporator canister sited to the rear of the oil filters. A tube from the base of the canister returns oil to the sump, with another flexible tube running to a jet on each induction manifold, with branch tubes into the carburettor air filter housings. The normal oil pressure with an oil temperature of 110-120°C should be 5.5-6.5kg/cm^2 (78-92psi) at 6800rpm with a minimum of 4.5kg/cm^2 (64psi) under the same conditions. If the engine is running at the minimum pressure, it is recommended that engine speed should be reduced by at least 1000rpm and the cause established as soon as possible.

The water pump draws coolant through a flexible hose at the base of the radiator, via a thermostatic by-pass valve, into the engine waterways. Coolant exits at the top front of the block between the timing chain covers via a flexible hose to the top of the radiator and a branch hose to the thermostatic by-pass valve. This valve prevents water passing through the radiator until the water temperature reaches 83°C. The radiator has twin electric cooling fans, actuated by a thermostatic switch in the radiator, and the air conditioning control switch. An expansion tank with pressure relief cap is fitted in front of the radiator.

An air conditioning pump is fitted on a bracket on the right front face of the block. Drive is by vee-belt off a crankshaft pulley, from which a separate belt also serves the steering pump pulley, which in turn drives the alternator via its own belt. The air conditioning evaporator coil is mounted on the front face of the radiator, hence the interlocking of the cooling fans with the air conditioning controls.

Transmission

The overall layout of the transmission system is basically the same as that provided on the 365 GT 2+2, although the gearbox and differential casings have different external designs with additional ribbing and the gear-driven oil pump is omitted on the 365 GTC/4. The individual gear and final drive ratios are different to suit the different characteristics of the four-cam engine and the weight of the car; details are given in the table.

The gearbox is an all-synchromesh five-speed unit with a mechanically-operated clutch. This is a single-plate Borg & Beck BB9/445A, mounted on the flywheel in the bellhousing, with a spring-diaphragm pressure plate. The selector fork is actuated by a cable from the suspended pedal box assembly, which incorporates an assister spring to reduce pedal pressure. There is a tapping for the reversing light switch, operated by the selector rod, on the upper right side at the front of the gearbox. The speedometer cable drive is taken from a tapping at the left rear of the gearbox.

Drive is carried from the gearbox output shaft through a splined tubular propeller shaft via a 'doughnut' flexible joint at the rear end to the differential. Due to the shorter shaft length no central support bearing was fitted, although from chassis 16135 (European cars) and 15481 (US models) the forward end of the shaft is modified to incorporate a roller bearing support. The flanged tubular rear axle casing houses a ZF-type limited slip differential and has a support at the forward end on each side. These, coupled with the pair on the engine block, support the engine and transmission assembly as on the 365 GT 2+2. The differential casing has an oil filler/level plug on the rear face and a drain plug on the underside. The drive to each rear wheel is via a flanged one-piece maintenance-free Lobro-type half-shaft, incorporating sliding constant velocity joints.

GEAR RATIOS

	Gearbox	Overall
First	2.492:1	10.194:1
Second	1.674:1	6.848:1
Third	1.244:1	5.089:1
Fourth	1.000:1	4.090:1
Fifth	0.801:1	3.277:1
Reverse	2.416:1	9.884:1
Final drive	4.09:1 (11/45)	

Electrical Equipment & Lights

The 12-volt negative earth electrical system is served from a 77amp/hour battery, sited in the rear of the engine bay on the opposite side to the driver. A vee-belt from the power-assisted steering pump pulley drives a Marelli GCA115A alternator mounted on the top front left of the engine. The Marelli starter motor, integral with its solenoid suspended below it, is mounted on the lower right of the bellhousing. Twin air horns, mounted in the forward part of the engine bay, are activated by the central button in the steering wheel. The twin fuseboards are mounted in the rear of the glove compartment.

Lighting is all by Carello and features paired circular retractable headlamps in rectangular pods on either side of the upper nose panel. These pods, which have removable bezels for changing bulbs or adjusting the beam settings, are raised by their own electric motors when the headlamps are switched on. The lamps can be raised manually if the motors fail. The outer lens provides main beam and the inner unit the dipped beam. In the extremities of the radiator grille are the combined side/turn indicator lights, which are shaped to the profile of their surround and have a vertical inner edge. Alongside these are the rectangular driving lights, which on cars for the German, British and Swiss markets serve as daylight headlamp flashers. On all European-market cars there are small circular orange turn indicator lights on the front wings forward of the wheelarches. On US market examples there are rectangular orange side marker lamps, with chrome-plated trim surrounds, cut into the wings in the same location, with a further pair towards the trailing edges of the rear wings.

At the rear of the car are three circular lighting units, each with a chrome trim ring, in the inset matt-black tail panel. The outer lens is an orange turn indicator (red on US-market cars), the red stop/tail light is central and at the inner end is a red reflector. A rectangular reversing light is suspended below the centre of the bumper, actuated by a switch on the gearbox when reverse is engaged, with a pair of small rectangular number-plate lamps in the lower edge of the boot lid.

All cars have 'door open' warning lights in the

trailing edges of the doors, a pair of automatically-operated under-bonnet lights and one in the boot. The front side/turn indicator lenses are either orange or white, dependent upon the market destination, and French-market cars are fitted with yellow headlamp bulbs. The headlamps dip to the left on right-hand-drive cars and to the right on left-hand-drive examples.

Suspension & Steering

The front independent suspension is very similar in layout to that of the 365 GTB/4 model. There are unequal-length forged steel upper and lower wishbones, joined by the hub carrier at the outer end and mounted to the chassis via rubber bushes at the inner end. The damper, incorporating an integral bump stop, is mounted co-axially within the coil spring, which is fitted between the wishbones. Whereas the anti-roll bar of the 365 GTB/4 is connected to the lower wishbones, that on the 365 GTC/4 has a vertical link on each side to connect it to the upper wishbone.

The independent rear suspension of the 365 GTC/4 is virtually identical to that fitted to the 365 GT 2+2 model. The similar unequal-length combined forged/pressed steel upper and lower wishbones are mounted in the same manner, with a combined coil spring/damper behind the hub. A Koni type 7100-1012-OFF2169 hydraulic self-levelling unit is fitted in front of the hub, with an anti-roll bar linking the lower wishbones.

Like the 365 GT 2+2 before it, the 365 GTC/4 has power-assisted steering as standard. The ZF hydraulic pump is vee-belt driven and mounted on a bracket on the centre front of the timing

Lighting arrangements on a right-hand-drive European model. The circular repeater light on the front wing side is common to all markets except the US, where larger side marker lights are fitted front and rear.

FACTORY LITERATURE

1971
• Sales brochure for 365 GTC/4; factory reference 50/71.

1972
• Sales brochure for 365 GTC/4, identical to 50/71, but without a factory reference.
• Owner's handbook for the 365 GTC/4, factory reference 54/71, with gold/black/white cover.
• Sales brochure for 365 GTC/4, factory reference 55/71, identical to 50/71.
• US consumer information booklet for 365 GTC/4, factory reference 56/71, three different printings.
• 365 GTC/4 tyre supply control leaflet; factory reference 57/71.
• Mechanical spare parts catalogue for the 365 GTC/4, with factory print reference 59/71 and gold/red/black cover. Reprinted a number of times with various updates, modifications and supplements, including right-hand-drive variations, up to October 1972.
• Additional instructions for the US version 365 GTC/4, supplement booklet to the owner's handbook; factory reference 63/71.

1973
• Workshop manual for the 365 GTC/4 in blue ring binder; factory reference 79/73.

MAJOR ELECTRICAL EQUIPMENT

Battery		12 volt, 77amp/hour
Alternator		Marelli GCA115A
Starter motor		1.8CV
Ignition	Europe	Twin Marelli BZR201A coils
		Single Marelli S129E distributor
	US	Twin Marelli BAE200A coils
		Twin Marelli S138B distributors
Sparking plugs		Marelli CW89LP or Champion N6Y
		Gap 0.5-0.6mm (0.020-0.023in)

SUSPENSION SETTINGS

Front toe-in	5-7mm (0.196-0.276in)
Front camber	+0°40' to +1°
Rear toe-in	10-12mm (0.394-0.472in)
Rear camber	−1°20' to −1°40'
Castor angle	Fixed at 3°
Dampers: front	Koni 82T1750
rear	616-601791 plus Koni 7100-1012-OFF2169 self-levelling device

chain cover, with flexible hose connections to the fluid reservoir at the front of the engine bay on the driver's side and the ZF steering box. This is mounted on the front chassis cross-member at the base of the universally-jointed steering column.

Track control adjustment is provided on the track rod arms. The steering ball joints are non-adjustable and require no lubrication. The steering has a turning circle of 13 metres (42ft 8in). Left- or right-hand drive was available throughout the production period.

Brakes

The braking system has ventilated cast iron discs front and rear, with each disc's single caliper containing four hydraulic cylinders. The system is provided with vacuum assistance from a Bonaldi 14-07321 servo, fed by a Bonaldi 14-06341 vacuum pump mounted at the front of the right-hand inlet camshaft's timing chain cover. The pump is driven directly by a keyed shaft from the camshaft sprocket retaining nut, which has a slot in its head for the key drive.

A tandem master cylinder supplies the dual-circuit braking system, each section feeding a separate circuit to the opposing pair of cylinders on each wheel. A pressure-limiting valve is fitted in each rear wheel circuit to control rear wheel braking. Both circuits incorporate a pressure switch, so that if a loss of pressure is detected in either circuit the facia warning light is illuminated. This light also warns of 'handbrake on' and brake light bulb failure.

The handbrake, situated between the seats, operates its own set of shoes inside the disc hub on each rear wheel via a rod and cable linkage. Shoe adjustment in each rear disc is via a pair of holes (at one o'clock and seven o'clock on the right side, 11 o'clock and five o'clock on the left), through which a screwdriver can be inserted to turn a toothed adjuster. Cable length can be altered by screw adjusters close to where the cable joins the lever rod mechanism below the cabin; adjustment is also provided on the rod. The suspended brake pedal has the same facility for height adjustment as the clutch pedal.

Recommended brake pads for normal touring conditions are Ferodo I/D330 at front and rear.

Wheels & Tyres

The standard wheels are five-spoke 7.5x15in light alloy, with a satin silver paint finish under clear lacquer. The splined hub has a single chrome-plated retaining nut with triple angled ears. Cars for the US, German, Dutch and Swedish markets were fitted with special octagonal chromed hub nuts, as the triple-eared spinners did not comply with Federal Safety Standard 110 in the USA and relevant rules in the other countries. The tool kit contains a special box spanner for these markets, in place of the lead mallet supplied elsewhere.

Borrani 7.5x15in wire wheels with chrome-plated spokes and polished aluminium rims were optional. As with the alloy wheels, these required special hub nuts for the markets indicated.

The spare wheel is housed in a well in the boot floor, under a removable cover panel. The tyres supplied as standard are listed in the table.

WHEELS & TYRES

Wheels		7½Lx15in five-spoke cast alloy, knock-off hubs Optional Borrani wire wheels with alloy rims type RW4075
Tyres:	Europe	Michelin X 215/70VR-15 tubeless
	US	Michelin FR70VR-15 or 215/70VR-15

The standard five-spoke 7.5x15in cast alloy wheel with triple-ear hub nut, which is replaced for legislative reasons by an octagonal centre nut on US-market cars.

IDENTIFICATION PLATES

1. Chassis number stamped in frame above right front spring mount.
2. Engine number stamped on left side of block.
3. General data plate mounted on right-side inner wing valance panel under bonnet, with lubrication plate below it. US-market cars had the following additional data plates to comply with the Federal Safety and Emissions Standards:
4. A plate on the upper face of the steering column giving vehicle type and chassis number.
5. A plate on the driver's door shut post below the lock striker, giving vehicle type and chassis number, together with month and year of manufacture.
6. A label on the upper face of the driver's sun visor, giving tyre data and vehicle capacities.
7. Air pollution conformity label under bonnet.
8. Emission service schedule label under bonnet.

PRODUCTION

Between 1971 and 1973, chassis numbers 14179-16289. Total production 500.

Chapter 10
365 GT4 2+2

The 365 GT4 2+2 was announced at the 1972 Paris Salon and was the true replacement for the 365 GT 2+2. Mechanically virtually identical to the 365 GTC/4, the new model had a 200mm (7.87in) longer wheelbase of 2700mm (106.3in). This provided additional rear legroom, while the cabin style, with a steeply angled rear screen, gave reasonable headroom for rear seat occupants. Its design bore some traces of the 365 GTC/4 in the retractable headlamps, the external door handle design, five-spoke wheels with knock-off hubs and rear light arrangement; there were even traces of the 365 GTB/4 with a slim semi-circular indent running along the body sides. That was as far as it went, for the body was otherwise completely new, with a smooth but conservative three-box shape from Pininfarina. It is not dissimilar in profile to the Fiat 130 Coupé from the same design studio.

This model continued in production until 1976, by which time 521 examples (plus three prototypes) had been built. It was superseded by the 4.8-litre 400 series, which was bodily very similar but can be identified by the five-bolt road wheel fixing, a paired rear light arrangement and a small lip spoiler on the nose. The 400 version was the first series-production Ferrari to be offered with automatic transmission. This series continued in production with only relatively minor cosmetic changes through the fuel-injected 400i models to the 5-litre 412, introduced in 1985 and built until 1989. This span of 17 years for a single style shows the rightness of the original concept.

During the complete production span of the series, the model was never homologated for sale in North America. This was due to the relatively low production volume and the cost of satisfying increased legislation – particularly with regard to exhaust emissions and impact-absorbing bumpers. In fact from the cessation of production of the 365 GTB/4 in 1973 until the announcement of the Testarossa in 1984, no 12-cylinder Ferraris were sold new in the USA.

The lines of the 365 GT4 2+2, introduced in 1973, are a development of the angular shape of the preceding 365 GTC/4. The indent line on the body side is a styling device carried over from the 365 GTB/4, and the virtually identical rake angles of the front and rear screens make for a very balanced cabin section. Satin aluminium louvre on the bonnet is for radiator air extraction.

Body & Chassis

The 365 GT4 2+2 chassis, type F101 AL, continues the new type numbering system started with the 365 GTC/4 model. It has a 2700mm (106.3in) wheelbase, a 10mm (0.39in) narrower front track and a 20mm (0.79in) wider rear track, but apart from this it is virtually identical to that of the 365 GTC/4. Chassis construction follows normal Ferrari practice for the period, as previously described, with the same satin black paint finish.

The body, designed and built by Pininfarina, is smooth and angular, carrying little in the way of styling cues from its predecessor, apart from retractable paired headlamps, the door handles and a similar rear light arrangement on a recessed tail panel. The three-box shape provides greater headroom for rear seat occupants. The front end is dominated by the wrap-around satin-black steel bumper, with flush rectangular side/turn indicator lights above and a full-width radiator grille below, with a slim slot in the lower lip of the nose. The side indent line, on otherwise plain panels, carries the front bumper line through to the rear, where it meets the matching full-width rear bumper. The cabin features a large glass area, with slim angular rear pillars and a virtually flat rear screen, angled like the windscreen to provide a balanced profile. The body is built from welded steel panels, with an aluminium bonnet and boot lid on steel frames.

Body Trim & Fittings

The 365 GT4 2+2 features a full-width radiator opening of almost rectangular shape (slightly angled at the ends) with driving lights behind an aluminium egg-crate grille. Above, and forming the top edge of the grille opening, is a three-piece wrap-around satin black steel bumper that runs into the wheelarches. The wrap-around section on each side carries a small turn indicator lamp near its trailing edge. Flush-fitting rectangular side/turn indicator lights are mounted on either side of the nose panel above the bumper, with a triangular return onto the wing side. The plain full-width steel rear bumper is finished in satin black. A rectangular enamel Ferrari badge is fitted on the nose, between the side/turn indicator lights. At the rear, a chromed Ferrari script badge is mounted centrally close to the trailing edge of the boot lid and there is a chromed *Cavallino*

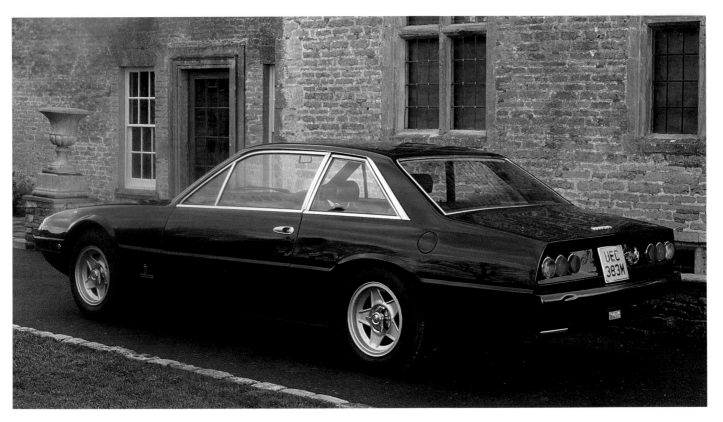

The shape of the 365 GT4 2+2 has endured the test of time, as it continued in production until 1989 with only minor alterations through the 400 and 412 series. Detail shows Pininfarina shield and aluminium script badge fitted to each front wing.

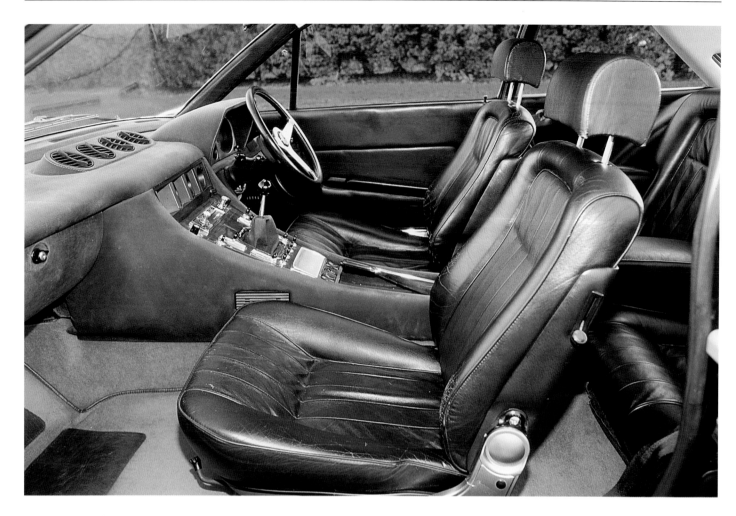

Rampante on the right of the tail panel inboard of the lights. Slim horizontal rectangular Pininfarina badges, with Pininfarina enamel shield badges above, are fitted below the indent line on the front wings. The front-hinged bonnet has a large rectangular matt aluminium louvred grille towards the front end for radiator hot air dissipation and is supported automatically by a pair of hydraulic struts when opened. The fuel filler flap is on the left rear wing below the screen pillar.

Brightwork on the body is confined to an aluminium bonnet louvre, stainless steel screen and glass surrounds, and chrome-plated arrowhead-shaped door handles with a forward pull section and the lock barrel in the trailing end. The windscreen wiper arms and blade frames are finished in satin black paint. Access to the boot is via a chrome-plated lever, mounted on the floor outboard of the driver's seat, with the matching fuel filler flap release lever outside it; the pair share a circular key-operated lock sited between them.

Plain glass is fitted and the windscreen is laminated. Two-speed self-parking wipers park on the right on left-hand-drive cars and on the left on right-hand-drive examples. The door windows are fitted with fixed quarterlights, with electric operation of the main glasses. Rear quarter windows are fixed and the rear screen is provided with heater elements for demisting, actuated via a switch on the centre console, with an 'on' warning light in the rev counter.

Paintwork

As mentioned in the chapter on the 365 GTB/4 models, a vast range of colours was available for Ferrari cars at this time and the same comments made there apply to the 365 GT4 2+2. As the 365 GT4 2+2 bodies were built by Pininfarina they should have a paint colour manufactured by either PPG or Duco. The table on page 86 in the *365 GTB/4* chapter lists the range of colours offered.

Interior Trim & Fittings

Full leather upholstery is provided to the seats, with the trim panels being a mixture of leather and vinyl. The range of colours available is shown in the table on page 89 in the *365 GTB/4* chapter. The front seats are mounted on runners with adjustment via a lever under the outer front edge of the cushion, while a knurled black plastic knob on the inner lower edge of the backrest allows its rake to be altered. A sliding lever on the upper outer side of the backrest tilts it forwards for access to the rear seats. Rear seating is the best and most

Front passenger compartment provides sumptuous accommodation in deep leather seats. Centre console and dashboard layout are very similar to the 365 GTC/4.

DIMENSIONS & WEIGHT

	mm	in
Overall length	4810	189.37
Overall width	1798	70.78
Overall height	1314.5	51.75
Wheelbase	2700	106.30
Front track	1470	57.87
Rear track	1500	59.05
Weight (dry)	1790kg	3946lb

For Paint Colours, Leather Upholstery Colours and Carpet Colours see the tables in the *365 GTB/4* chapter.

generous that Ferrari had offered in a 2+2 up to that time – not only in terms of headroom and legroom but also comfort – with individual bucket seats joined by a central armrest section. Side armrests are also provided, with oddments pockets in the side trim panel behind them. Each front seat has a static lap-and-diagonal seat belt; there are mounting points for three-point rear seat belts.

The door armrests incorporate pulls angled upwards at the front end, with a door opening lever in the door panel, above the forward end of the armrest section, which is normally trimmed to match upholstery colour. A circular plug, forward of the armrest, can be removed to insert the emergency winder for the electric windows, and a black radio speaker grille is fitted in the lower front corner of the door panel. Control switches for the electric windows are in the centre console.

The floor and rear seat heelboard are carpeted, with black rubber heelmats incorporated for both driver and passenger. The range of carpet colours is given in the table on page 89 in the 365 GTB/4 chapter. The facia, glove compartment lid and transmission tunnel console are trimmed in black Alcantara, the latter having a teak veneer top face forward of the handbrake. The headlining is plain ivory-coloured vinyl retained by cant rails upholstered in the same material, as are the rear screen pillars, which have parallelogram-shaped ventilation outlets at their base. The rear parcels shelf is trimmed in black vinyl or to match the upholstery.

Vinyl-covered sun visors are provided, with a vanity mirror on the passenger's side; the dipping rear-view mirror is mounted on the upper screen rail between them.

The short chrome-plated gear lever has a leather gaiter and is mounted centrally in the transmission tunnel console. A black plastic knob, with the gearchange pattern engraved in white, tops the gear lever. The facia and centre

Rear seating is comfortable for most people as long as the front seats are not too far back on their runners. Large glass area prevents any sense of claustrophobia.

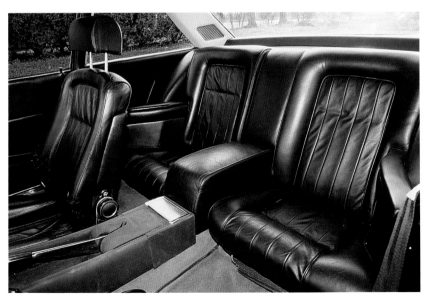

console are virtually identical in layout and configuration to the 365 GTC/4, except that the console glove tray is longer, with an ashtray at the rear end. The pull-up handbrake is mounted in the glove tray between the front seats. The bonnet release lever is below the facia at the outer end, with an emergency ring-pull release and an auxiliary socket alongside. A pair of interior lights is provided, one on the roof between the sun visors and another central in the rear roof section close to the screen. Both interior lamps are operated automatically by door switches or manually by moving the lenses.

Facia & Instruments

To all intents and purposes, the facia and centre console of the 365 GT4 2+2 is identical to that of the 365 GTC/4, apart from small location changes for some of the switchgear. The equipment in the main instrument nacelle and supplementary bank of dials in the top of the centre console has the same functions as in the 365 GTC/4. However, the centre console's switchgear, which at a glance appears the same, is different on the 365 GT4 2+2 and merits a detailed description.

Below the bank of four dials that form the top edge of the console is a radio, with air conditioning control knobs on either side of it – one for fan speed and the other for temperature. Two circular air conditioning outlets are central in the top of the facia, between the matching demister outlets, and there is a rectangular one on either side of the transmission tunnel at low level. A further adjustable outlet below the facia on the driver's side delivers air to the feet. Behind the radio is the gear lever, with a chrome-trimmed rectangular base to its leather gaiter, which has two slider controls on each side. The upper-left one is for air distribution to the circular facia-top demister and/or low-level outer-footwell vents on that side of the car; the upper-right lever performs the same function for the right side of the car. The lever at the lower left is the choke and the lower-right lever controls the heater output. The left- and right-side ventilation fans are mounted in the lower forward parts of the respective front wings, with ducting via their individual heater boxes to the outlets. Above the upper-left slider is a toggle switch for the electric radio aerial, with a matching one on the opposite side of the console for the hazard warning lights, or spare, dependent upon market. The location of the switchgear is the same whether the car is left- or right-hand drive.

Between the gear lever and ashtray is a bank of four circular black toggle switches controlling left-side ventilation fan, spare, heated rear screen and right-side fan. The ashtray has an integral cigar lighter fitted below the lid. The electric

Instrument design, with square surrounds to each dial, imitates 365 GTC/4 style. The four gauges in the centre are angled towards the driver.

window switches are mounted below the ashtray, with the switch for the auxiliary driving lights between them. A lockable glovebox with interior light is provided on the passenger's side of the facia, with the fuse boards mounted behind cover panels on the rear face. The relay boards are mounted behind a panel in the passenger footwell.

The steering wheel is leather-rimmed with plain aluminium spokes, and the central yellow horn push, with *Cavallino Rampante* emblem, has a black plastic rim. A pair of slender chrome-plated stalks, with black plastic finger pads, project from the left of the steering column; the shorter one controls the indicators and the other the sidelamps plus headlamp main/dipped beam and flasher functions. A stalk on the right operates the two-speed windscreen wipers, and the washers by pulling it towards the driver. The key-operated ignition/starter switch, incorporating a steering lock, is mounted on the lower facia to the right of the steering column shroud.

Luggage Compartment

The twin aluminium fuel tanks, spray-coated with glass-fibre, are located below the boot floor and in the rear wings, forming the sides of the spare wheel well, which has a removable cover. Fuel capacity is 118 litres (28.1 Imperial/ 33.8 US gallons). The fuel filler is on the left rear wing beneath a circular cover flap, which is opened by a lockable lever on the floor outboard of the driver's seat; an emergency release pull is provided behind the trim panel in the front left of the boot.

The boot floor and sides are lined with black carpet and all plain metal surfaces are painted satin black. A light, mounted on the ceiling of the boot, is actuated by a switch plate on the self-supporting lid. Access to the boot is via a lockable lever, located alongside that for the fuel filler flap as mentioned above; an emergency ring-pull is provided beneath the fuel filler flap.

Engine

The 4390cc (267.9cu in) 60° V12 engine produces 320bhp (DIN) at 7000rpm and 43kgm (310lb ft) of torque at 4600rpm. With wet-sump lubrication and six sidedraught carburettors, it is almost identical to that fitted in the preceding 365 GTC/4 and carries the same factory type number, F 101 AC 000. Most components and ancillary equipment are driven in the same way and fitted in the same locations. Similarly the four-point engine and transmission support arrangement is the same, with a pair of mountings on the engine

TOOL KIT

Scissor jack with ratchet handle
Set of seven open-ended spanners 6–22mm
180mm (7.1in) long pliers
120mm (4.7in) long flat-bladed screwdriver
150mm (5.9in) long flat-bladed screwdriver
Phillips screwdriver for screws up to 4mm (0.16in)
Phillips screwdriver for screws 5–9mm (0.20–0.35in)
Sparking plug spanner
Weber carburettor spanner
Oil filter wrench
Two sparking plugs
Set of bulbs
Set of fuses
2.5kg (5.5lb) lead mallet
Wheel nut box spanner (in lieu of mallet on cars for Germany, Holland and Sweden)
Emergency warning triangle

Although fairly shallow, the boot provides adequate volume and a sensible shape, making it a practical proposition to carry four people's luggage. The spare wheel sits beneath a panel in the boot floor.

Engine bay layout is almost identical to that of the 365 GTC/4, as both models use the same specification of 4.4-litre V12 (type number F 101 AC 000). The canister behind the twin oil filter bowls is the oil vapour condenser, for the crankcase emission control system.

ENGINE

Type	60° V12
Type number	F 101 AC 000
Cubic capacity	4390cc (267.9cu in)
Bore and stroke	81x71mm (3.19x2.80in)
Compression ratio	8.8:1
Maximum power	320bhp (DIN) at 7000rpm
Maximum torque	44kgm (318lb ft) at 4000rpm
Carburettors	6 Weber 38DCOE59/60

TIMING DATA

Inlet valves open	43° BTDC
Inlet valves close	38° ABDC
Exhaust valves open	38° BBDC
Exhaust valves close	34° ATDC
Firing order	1-7-5-11-3-9-6-12-2-8-4-10

Valve timing should be measured with a clearance of 0.5mm (0.0197in) between the tappet thimbles and camshaft. Valve clearances with a cold engine should be 0.1-0.15mm (0.0039-0.0059in) for inlets and 0.25-0.3mm (0.0098-0.0118in) for exhausts, measured between the valve pads and camshaft.

SYSTEM CAPACITIES

Fuel tank	118 litres (28.1 Imp/33.8 US gallons)		
	Litres	Imp Pints	US Pints
Cooling system	13.0	22.9	27.5
Washer bottle	2.0	3.5	4.2
Engine oil	18.75	33.0	39.6
Gearbox oil	3.1	5.5	6.6
Rear axle oil	2.5	4.4	5.3

and a further pair on the differential casing. This engine always featured the manually-adjustable timing chain tensioner provided on late series 365 GTC/4 models.

The fuel feed system is from the twin tanks via twin filters, a gauze one on the tank outlet and a Fispa bowl type before the twin Bendix electric pumps (type 476087), which are mounted on the left side of the chassis frame just forward of the fuel tanks. The pumps are self-regulating to provide fuel at a pressure of about 0.3 kg/cm^2 (4psi) and operate as soon as the ignition is switched on.

The exhaust system is similar in layout to that of the 365 GTC/4, although longer due to the increased wheelbase, with flanged manifold front connections to twin silencers and push-fit connections to the tailpipe assembly, which incorporates a further small silencer. Heat shields are fitted above and to the rear of the manifolds, with a pair of shields above each twin silencer assembly under the cabin.

The standard carburettor arrangement and air filter boxes, with a manually-operated summer/winter flap in the intake pipe to each bank, are as fitted to the 365 GTC/4 model. The only substantial specification difference on the 365 GT4 2+2 engine is the provision of twin Marelli S138B distributors, each with its own Marelli BZR201A coil, instead of the single Marelli S129E unit on the European-market 365 GTC/4 models.

The 365 GT4 2+2 engine lubrication system, blow-by arrangement, cooling system (apart from the header tank location to the right of the radiator), air conditioning pump and drive, vacuum brake servo and hydraulic steering pump drives are all identical to those described for the 365 GTC/4. On the 365 GT4 2+2 the oil pressure relief valve is always incorporated in the pump casing. The normal oil pressure with an oil temperature of 110-120°C, should be 5.5-6.5kg/cm^2 (78-92psi) at

6800rpm and a minimum of 4.5kg/cm² (64psi). If the engine is running at the minimum pressure, it is recommended that engine speed should be reduced by at least 1000rpm and the cause established as soon as possible.

Transmission

The overall layout of the transmission system and the type of components used are basically the same as on the 365 GTC/4. However, individual gear and final drive ratios are different to suit the greater weight of the 365 GT4 2+2 (see panel).

GEAR RATIOS

	Gearbox	Overall
First	2.590:1	11.137:1
Second	1.706:1	7.336:1
Third	1.254:1	5.392:1
Fourth	1.000:1	4.300:1
Fifth	0.8145:1	3.502:1
Reverse	2.240:1	9.632:1
Final drive	4.30:1 (10:43)	

The only difference between the two systems is on the propeller shaft, which is longer due to the increased wheelbase. A solid shaft is used, with sliding splined ends which connect direct to the gearbox and differential pinion shafts, without the rubber 'doughnut' coupling of the 365 GTC/4. The increase in length necessitates additional support for the shaft midway along its length, achieved by flanging the torque tube so the inner part of the flange provides a bearing housing for the central roller bearing.

First to fourth gears form a conventional 'H' pattern, with fifth outside the 'H' to the right and forwards, and reverse opposite fifth.

Electrical Equipment & Lights

The 12-volt negative earth electrical system is served from a 77amp/hour battery, sited in the rear of the engine bay on the opposite side to the driver. A vee-belt from the power-assisted steering pump pulley drives a Marelli GCA115A alternator mounted on the top front left of the engine. The Marelli starter motor, integral with its solenoid suspended below it, is mounted on the lower right of the flywheel bellhousing. Twin air horns, mounted in front of the radiator, are activated by the central push-button in the steering wheel. Specifications for the major components are provided in the table. Twin fuseboards are mounted in the back of the glove compartment and relay boards behind a panel in the footwell on the passenger's side.

The lighting equipment is by Carello and features paired retractable headlamp units in rectan-

Front lighting in open configuration, seen here with orange turn indicator lens – cars for some markets have a full white lens. The triple circular lens rear light arrangement is identical to that on the 365 GTC/4.

gular pods. These pods, which have removable bezels for changing bulbs or adjusting the beam settings, are raised by their own electric motors to reveal the circular light units when the headlamps are switched on. The lamps can be raised manually if the motors fail. The outer lens provides main beam and the inner unit the dipped beam. In the extremities of the radiator opening, behind the grille, are square driving lamps, which on cars for the German, Swiss and French markets serve as daylight headlamp flashers; French models have yellow glass. On Australian, Austrian, British, Irish, Italian and South African models these are fog lights. Combined slim rectangular

MAJOR ELECTRICAL EQUIPMENT

Battery	12-volt Marelli 6ATP15, 77amp/hour
Alternator	Marelli GCA115A
Starter motor	Marelli MT21T
Ignition	Twin Marelli S138B distributors
	Twin Marelli BZR201A coils
Sparking plugs	Champion N6Y

side/turn indicator lamps, with a triangular return section that wraps around the corner of the wing, are mounted on the nose panel above the bumper. These either have plain white lenses or combined orange/white lenses, dependent upon market. Small circular orange indicator repeaters are sited on the side sections of the front bumpers.

In the inset tail panel are three circular light units, each with a chromed trim ring. The outer lens is an orange turn indicator, the red stop/tail light is central and at the inner end is a red reflector. A rectangular reversing light is suspended below the centre of the bumper, actuated by a switch on the gearbox when reverse is engaged, with a pair of small rectangular number plate lights in the lower return edge of the boot lid.

All cars have 'door open' warning lights in the trailing edges of the doors and automatic under-bonnet and boot lights. French-market cars are fitted with yellow headlamp bulbs.

Suspension & Steering

The front and rear independent suspension systems, materials and layout are identical to those of the 365 GTC/4 model. The unequal-length upper and lower wishbone assemblies are joined by the hub carriers at the outer ends and mounted to the chassis via rubber bushes at the inner ends. The front dampers, incorporating an integral bump stop, are mounted co-axially within the coil springs, which are located between the upper and lower wishbones; an anti-roll bar connects the upper wishbones. Independent rear suspension uses a combined coil spring/damper unit

SUSPENSION SETTINGS

Front toe-in		+2 to +3mm (+0.079 to +0.118in)
Front camber		+0°40' to +1°
Rear toe-in		None
Rear camber		−1°20' to −1°40'
Castor angle		Fixed 3°
Dampers:	front	Koni 82T-1824
	rear	Koni 82N-1825 plus Koni self-levelling device

behind the hub and an hydraulic self-levelling unit in front of the hub; an anti-roll bar links the lower wishbones.

As with the 365 GTC/4, the 365 GT4 2+2 features power-assisted steering as standard equipment. This is identical to the system provided on the earlier model and with the same components mounted in parallel locations.

Track control adjustment is provided on the track rod arms. The steering ball joints are non-adjustable and require no lubrication. The turning circle is 13.2 metres (43ft 4in).

Brakes

Braking is virtually identical to the system provided on the 365 GTC/4, with ventilated cast iron discs front and rear, each with a single caliper containing four hydraulic cylinders. Vacuum servo assistance is provided in the same way and uses the same components.

A tandem master cylinder is provided, each section feeding a separate circuit to the opposing pair of cylinders on each wheel, with a pressure-limiting valve in each rear wheel circuit. A pressure switch is connected to both circuits; if a loss of pressure is detected in either circuit the facia warning light is illuminated. This light also warns of 'handbrake on' and brake light bulb failure. The handbrake arrangement is identical to that on the 365 GTC/4, albeit with longer cables due to the longer wheelbase.

Recommended brake pads for normal touring conditions are Texstar T259 at front and rear.

Wheels & Tyres

The standard wheels are five-spoke 7.5x15in light alloy, identical to those of the 365 GTC/4. The splined hub has a single chrome-plated retaining nut with three angled ears.

Cars for the German, Dutch and Swedish markets were fitted with special octagonal chrome-plated hub nuts, as the triple-eared spinners did not comply with safety rules in these countries. The tool kit contains a special box spanner for these, in place of the lead mallet for other markets.

WHEELS & TYRES

Wheels, front & rear	7½Lx15in cast light alloy
Tyres, front & rear	Michelin XWX 215/70VR-15

IDENTIFICATION PLATES

1. General vehicle identification plate on right engine bay valance panel, with engine oil plate below.
2. Chassis number and type stamped in frame near right front suspension mount.
3. Engine number and type stamped in top centre of block, near rear of engine.
4. Vehicle type and chassis number plate on top of steering column shroud in cabin.

FACTORY LITERATURE

1972
• Sales brochure for 365 GT4 2+2; factory reference 69/72.
• Owner's handbook for the 365 GT4 2+2, factory reference 75/73, with green/black/white cover.

1973
• Mechanical spare parts catalogue for the 365 GT4 2+2, with factory print reference 78/73 and green/yellow/white cover.
• Sales brochure for 365 GT4 2+2; factory reference 88/73, identical to brochure 69/72.

PRODUCTION

Between 1972 and 1976, chassis numbers 17091-19709. Total production 521 (plus three prototypes).

The standard five-spoke road wheel with triple-ear hub nut. Although Borrani wire wheels were still available as an option, they were very rarely fitted to these cars; Ferrari customers were coming to accept the move away from wire wheels, and the elegance of the alloy wheels that succeeded them.

Chapter 11

Close Relatives

The cars covered in the preceding chapters are the front-engined series production models manufactured by Ferrari (and all designed by Pininfarina). Models that do not fall within this category are relatively few, as series production was really on stream at Ferrari by the mid-1960s. Customers could still specify detail changes, as long as these did not stray too far from the normal specification.

However, some cars fall outside the normal production range. Apart from factory prototypes for the production cars, there were other creations by various coachbuilders, some of which were period and others later rebodies. An illustrated *résumé* of these special-bodied cars follows, preceded by pictures of the 330 America that was the last evolutionary step in the 250 GT series but used the 4-litre engine found in the 330 models covered in this book.

During 1965 Pininfarina produced a 330 GT 2+2 with 500 Superfast-style bodywork for HRH Prince Bernhard, on chassis number 06267, which is often wrongly included in 500 Superfast chassis listings. In 1966 Pininfarina, in collaboration with Ferrari, produced two examples of the road-going mid-engined 365P model, on chassis 08815 and 08971. This was notable for its three-seat arrangement with a central driving position, a layout resurrected by McLaren during the 1990s for its F1 road car. There were also the two front-engined Pininfarina-designed 330 GTC *Speciale* models, built in 1967 on chassis 09439 and 09653, together with four mid-engined design studies by Pininfarina – the 250 P5 and P6 of 1968, plus the 512S and Modulo of 1970. In 1969 this coachbuilder also produced a one-off metallic blue 365 GTB/4 hard-top on chassis 12925 (sometimes

Although fitted with a 4-litre engine, the 330 America of 1963 was the final derivative of the 250 GT series and therefore falls outside the parameters for detail coverage in this book.

wrongly quoted as 12585). It featured a white vinyl-covered roof panel, stainless steel roll hoop, zip-out rear screen, a lengthened tail and longer wrap-arounds to the bumpers. Initially this car had the headlamps under Plexiglas covers but was converted to a retractable headlamp arrangement early in its life.

A number of cars received special bodywork from various coachbuilders. These included a 330 GTS (chassis 10913) that was converted to a targa roof in the USA for American collector Bill Harrah. Incidentally he also had a Ferrari 365 GT 2+2 engine fitted into a Jeep Wagoneer, this engine later finding its way into a Ford Model T hot rod in California. One 330 GT 2+2 (chassis 07963) was re-bodied as a station wagon by

Apart from tail badging, the 330 America looks identical to a Series II 250 GT 2+2. Badge treatment could vary, with the '330 america' script positioned centrally on the boot lid (right) or on the right (below).

Vignale for Luigi Chinetti and another (chassis 05805) as a spider by Nembo. A 365 GT4 2+2 (chassis 18255) was converted to a station wagon by Felber in Switzerland, as was a 365 GTC/4, with a further variation on the station wagon theme being constructed by Panther Westwinds in England on a 365 GTB/4 (chassis 15275). Felber also rebodied a pair of 330 GTCs as 'Spider Corsas' and another 365 GTC/4 (chassis 16017) as a beach car. Although these cars were designed by Felber, the construction was carried out by Panther Westwinds. Michelotti rebodied two 330 GT 2+2s (chassis 06109 as a spider and 09083 as a coupé) and later rebodied at least four 365 GTB/4s with differing body styles, which were called NART spiders. All four were for Luigi Chinetti, NART being the initials of his North American Racing Team. The Fly Studio in Modena modified a 365 GT4 2+2 (chassis 17405) to incorporate a T-bar roof with rear quarter panels that ran to the tail of the car, while Piero Drogo's Carrozzeria Sports Cars in Modena rebodied a 330 GT 2+2 (chassis 07979) with a very angular and flamboyant body for Italian nightclub owner Norbert Novarro. Apart from these mainly period confections, a number of 275 GTBs and 365 GTB/4s were decapitated to become spiders. In the 1980s this was much in vogue, as the spider version was more valuable. Some 330 GT 2+2s have become donor cars to construct 250 GTO replicas.

Chassis number 09653 is one of two 330 GTC *Speciale* models by Pininfarina. The nose, featuring retractable driving lights, is virtually pure 365 California, but lacks the central bonnet bulge and has an extra cooling intake below the quarter bumper.

Distinctive rear of Pininfarina's 330 GTC *Speciale* features buttressed roof pillars and squared tail treatment, with bullet-lens lights taken from the 500 Superfast and 365 California. Door handle style is unique to this design.

This 330 GT 2+2 station wagon, chassis number 07963, was Vignale's last Ferrari body, shown at the 1968 Turin Salon in gold over green. As with many of the one-off bodies of the period, this example was constructed for the Chinetti family.

Michelotti-bodied 365 GTB/4 NART Spider, chassis number 15965, at Le Mans in 1975. It practised, but was withdrawn from the race – along with the other NART entries – after a dispute between Luigi Chinetti and the race organisers.

The 365 GTB/4 NART Spider, chassis number 15965, in more recent times, with targa top removed and a new coat of red paint. A NART badge has been added to the front wing, but NART lettering no longer appears on the tail.

A further Michelotti interpretation on the 365 GTB/4 NART Spider theme was created on chassis number 16467. The standard 365 GTS/4 provides a comparison of lines from the two styling houses of Michelotti and Pininfarina.

The unique 365 GTB/4, chassis number 12925, with fixed hard-top and zip-out rear window, produced by Pininfarina in 1969. It also has a longer tail than the standard model, together with wrap-around quarter bumpers.

One of the two mid-engined 365 P *Tre Posti* (three-seater) models produced, this being chassis number 08815 seen in the USA in the mid-1970s. It has a central driving position, and body lines very close to those of the production Dino series.

In more recent years chassis number 08815 has undergone a change of colour. Rear view shows cooling slots for mid-mounted 4.4-litre V12, and the large stainless steel wing fitted to this 365 P to aid high-speed stability.

The wooden body buck for the 365 P, used to check panel shape and size during the construction process. The three-abreast seating meant that the car is rather wider than a Dino, but the similarity is striking from this angle.

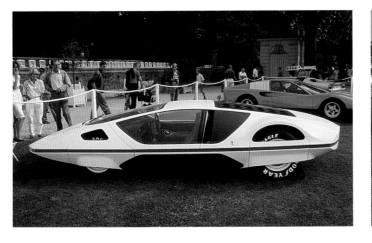

The Pininfarina 512 Modulo concept car from 1970. In the background can be seen the same designer's P6 concept car from 1968, showing clear styling pointers towards the first mid-engined 12-cylinder Ferrari road car, the 365 GT/4BB.

The 512S, like the Modulo, is a one-off Pininfarina concept car from 1970. As with the Modulo, its 5-litre V12 engine is mounted longitudinally behind the cabin. The wedge profile was increasingly in vogue during this period.

Chapter 12

Competition Derivatives

The 275 GTB/C

When, in July 1964, Ferrari was refused homologation for the mid-engined 250/275 LM in the GT category as a development of the 250 series, the logical step was to look to developing a competition version of the forthcoming 275 GTB road car. The main challenger for the 1965 season was to be the AC Cobra, also front-engined, so a competition version of the 275 GTB should have been competitive, given that it had independent suspension all round and a ten per cent increase in engine capacity over the preceding 250 GTO. That had still managed to take the GT crown from the Cobra in 1964, albeit with some controversy. Thus late 1964 and early 1965 saw Ferrari produce three 275 GTB competition derivatives – on chassis numbers 06701 GT, 06885 GT and 07217 GT – with the intention of competing in the 1965 GT Championship.

However, much to Ferrari's disgust, in April 1965 the Fédération Internationale de l'Automobile also refused to homologate the 275 GTB because the example submitted was considerably below the dry weight stated in the sales literature for the road car, from which it was developed and which was on sale by that time. After the 250 LM fracas, an offer was made by Ferrari to the FIA to accept homologation at the weight stated in the sales literature, but the FIA refused this offer. As a result, a justifiably angry Ferrari announced that it would not make any further requests and would not participate in the 1965 GT championship. This stance brought the FIA back to the table, as any form of competition needs more than one serious contender to justify its position and maintain public interest. Behind-the-scenes negotiations saw both sides climb down from their positions, to reach a compromise and agree on a figure approximately midway between the two extremes. Ferrari re-submitted its application at the beginning of June 1965, with a weight of 2165lb, which was accepted by the FIA in time for the Le Mans 24 Hours later in the month. However, by this time the battle on the track in the GT category had been lost. Due to the polit-

An early 'short-nose' 275 GTB Competition model, chassis number 07641, with appropriate California license plate. The enamel badge on the front wing side is that of NART (North American Racing Team).

PRODUCTION

Prototype (1964): chassis number 06021GT.

'Speciales' (1964-65): chassis numbers 06701GT, 06885GT, and 07217GT. Chassis 07185GT was converted to a similar body and mechanical specification by the factory in 1966.

First 'short-nose' series (1965): chassis numbers 07271, 07407, 07421, 07437, 07477, 07517, 07545, 07577, 07623 and 07641.

Second 'long-nose' series (1966): chassis numbers 09007, 09015, 09027, 09035, 09041, 09051, 09057, 09063, 09067, 09073, 09079 and 09085.

Visually the only differentiating feature from the standard 275 GTB is the row of louvres in the rear wing, although this example also has an outside fuel filler cap not visible in this view.

ical manoeuvres, only one of these 275 GTB/C, chassis 06885, ever saw competition during 1965. It ran in the prototype class in the Targa Florio and at the Nürburgring, as a GT at Le Mans, where it finished third overall behind two 275 LMs, and at Nassau in the Bahamas at the end of the year. Of the other two examples built, 06701 GT was used for testing, but neither it nor 07217 GT had a contemporary competition career.

These three 275 GTB/C *Speciale* models, as they have come to be known to differentiate them from a standard-bodied 275 GTB/C, were built by the Ferrari competition department. Each one has unique details and visually it is the general body shape – a 330 LM berlinetta-style nose allied to a 275 GTB cabin section and a 250 GT Lusso-style bonnet air intake – that unites them. Not only were these cars visually different from their kin, they were very different under the almost paper-thin aluminium skin. Engine specification was virtually pure 250/275 LM, with dry-sump lubrication and six carburettors, and chassis tubes were smaller and lighter than on the standard road car. Interior trim was minimal on the facia and doors, but there was a plastic roof lining and a pair of GTO-style aluminium-framed bucket seats; the rest of the interior had bare surfaces painted in satin black. Extremely basic, but these were built as pure racing cars, following in the tradition established by the legendary 250 GTO. Had homologation been forthcoming when initially submitted, then they may well have continued the winning ways of the GTO and would probably be thought of today as the '65 GTO.

During 1965 a series of ten competition berlinettas was constructed by the factory's racing department for customers, based on lightweight aluminium-bodied road cars. All were originally of the 'short-nose' variety, with the seven-point engine/transmission mounting system and wet-sump lubrication, and were much closer to the road version than their predecessors. The only major differences were the thin aluminium sheet used for the bodywork, minimal sound deadening and trim material, a fuel tank of 140 litres (30.8 Imperial/37.0 US gallons) mounted in the front of the boot (with the spare wheel fixed vertically behind it), higher-lift camshafts and six Weber 49DCN/3 carburettors. Engines were checked carefully and balanced during construction, to ensure optimum performance. The fuel tank location necessitated raising the rear parcels shelf (this is not readily apparent) and often there was a quick-release aluminium filler cap in the right rear wing or sail panel. These 'C' versions normally ran on wire wheels, the front ones usually being 'outside-laced' (ie, the spokes also run from the outer part of the rim to the hub and not just from the inner part as is normal practice). The factory build sheets for this series of cars carry no suffixes to the description, or any other note to indicate that they are anything but standard production cars. Some examples had bumpers, a few had rectangular driving lights cut into the lower front wings (under clear plastic covers), and others had vertical slots in the trailing end of the rear wings – or a mix and match of these features.

For 1966 the competition development was extended and additional features homologated, although an error in the submission meant that

Two views of 275 GTB/C 'Speciale' chassis number 06701 clearly show the many differences between this example and the normal street version of the 275 GTB, including the elongated nose with covered driving lights and brake cooling duct intakes, fuller wings, side/turn indicator light location, and rear wing louvres. It is currently fitted with these later-style ten-hole alloy wheels, whereas when sold new it had the 'starburst' pattern ones.

the six-carburettor arrangement was omitted from the application, thus all this series of cars was originally fitted with three carburettors. These would be the last Ferrari GT cars built by the factory competition department – the later 365 GTB/4C and 512 BB/LMs being built at the *Assistenza Clienti* in Modena – and also the last competition Ferraris to be fitted with wire wheels, again with outside lacing on the front ones. They were all produced after the cessation of two-cam 275 GTB production and their build run overlapped that of the early four-cam models. Whereas the factory had been reticent about noting anything competition-oriented on the 1965 cars, with this series the 'C' became part of its official title, as it had been with the three 1964/65 *Speciale* models.

The rudimentary gauze air filter over the carburettor intakes on chassis number 06701.

These views of 275 GTB/C 'Speciale' chassis number 06885 are worth comparing with those of chassis number 06701. The rear wings are much fuller, with a straighter line to the top edge running into a more pronounced rear spoiler, and there are quick-lift jacking points front and rear. The yellow paintwork is the colour of Belgian importer Ecurie Francorchamps, under whose banner this car won its class and finished third overall at Le Mans in 1965.

At a glance they appear the same as any other 'long-nose' two-cam 275 GTB, but they are very different animals. The aluminium sheet used for the body is about half the thickness of that found on the normal optional aluminium body and even thinner than that of the 250 GTO, making it extremely susceptible to damage – even from somebody leaning against it. Whereas previously the bumpers had been attached to the chassis, on this new series they were much lighter units fitted to the body, making damage from an unwittingly placed foot a real possibility. As larger-diameter, wider Borrani wheels had been homologated (7x15in type RW4010 front, 7.5x15in type RW4011 rear), the profile of the wings, particularly at the rear, is more bulbous to accommodate

them. The only glass is the laminated windscreen, all other windows being Plexiglas. Non-structural frames for the bonnet, boot and doors are drilled for additional lightness and the interior has a vestige of upholstery material, without any sound-deadening quilt, so that it appears quite standard. The floor pan is light aluminium – too light to bolt the lightweight seat frames to, so they are fixed through the floor on to special chassis support mounts. Twin aluminium fuel tanks, spray-coated with glass-fibre, have a total capacity of 140 litres (30.8 Imperial/37.0 US gallons) and are sited in the base of the boot on either side of a well for the mandatory FIA 'suitcase', which formed part of the regulations at the time. The spare wheel is mounted horizontally at the front of the boot.

The engine received modifications to increase power output, to provide better lubrication under competition conditions and to reduce weight. The engine block was still of the four-mounting type, but without rubber mounts, with the second type of driveshaft arrangement to the transaxle (ie, with the larger-diameter driveshaft incorporating universal joints at each end). The transaxle received a magnesium alloy casing, close-ratio gears, a strengthened limited slip differential and a choice of final drive ratios as tabulated on page 38 in the *275 GT Berlinetta* chapter.

To keep everything in the engine well lubricated and at the right operating temperature, dry-sump lubrication was employed. The oil reservoir was in the front wing, on the opposite side to the driver below the battery, and an oil cooler was mounted in the nose forward of the radiator. The system is essentially the same as that used on the 275 GTB/4. To reduce weight, the sump plate, clutch bellhousing, camshaft and timing case covers were cast in magnesium alloy. Performance modifications included a special crankshaft, forged racing pistons on special connecting rods giving a compression ratio of 9.3:1, a high-lift camshaft and Nimonic steel valves, the exhaust ones being sodium-filled for better heat dissipation. On the induction manifolds sat triple Weber 40DFI13 carburettors, with unique rearward-curved velocity stacks within the air filter box, while on the exhaust system there was a larger-bore separate twin pipe per bank arrangement from the manifold collector headers.

The net result of this was a very capable competition GT car, which had many class successes in the late 1960s, including a trio of consecutive GT class victories at Le Mans – in 1965 with *Speciale* chassis 06885, in 1966 with chassis 09035 and in 1967 with chassis 09079. Apart from the first two outings of chassis 06885 – in the Targa Florio and at the Nürburgring in 1965, when it was entered as a prototype by the factory – the remainder of the 275 GTB's competition career was in the hands of private and concessionaire teams. It may not have achieved the glorious results of the 250 GTO, but even in the short intervening period things had moved on tremendously in terms of the type of car that was necessary to capture overall victory, and such a car certainly would not be user-friendly on the road. As a gauge it may be worth looking at those Le Mans GT class results once more. In 1965 the GT class winner was third overall, but had slipped to eighth overall in 1966 and 11th overall in 1967. The disparity between pure racing cars and modified road cars was increasing rapidly although, as will be seen with the 365 GTB/4C, reliability in endurance races sometimes yielded unexpectedly good results.

The 365 GTB/4C

The Ferrari 365 GTB/4C was the factory's final competition flirtation with a front-engined road car and came about mainly at the instigation of

The second-series 'long-nose' 275 GTB/C (this is chassis number 09067) of 1966 is visually very similar to the standard road car, like its 'short-nose' predecessor from 1965, but the aluminium used for the bodywork is very thin and the bumpers are mounted directly to it instead of the chassis – so the front nudge bar fitted here would not fulfil its purpose!

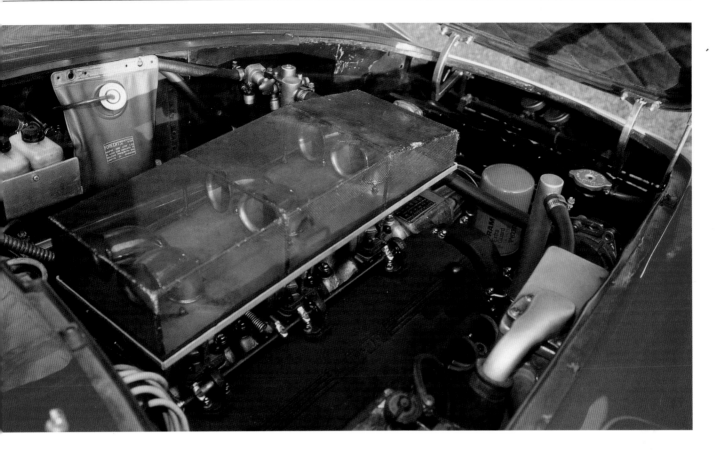

The engine bay of chassis number 09067, showing the triple carburettor assembly with curved trumpets in their gauze cage, unique to these second-series 275 GTB/C models. The engine has dry-sump lubrication instead of the wet-sump system of the two-cam road variants.

American importer Luigi Chinetti. He persuaded Ferrari to build him an alloy-bodied example on chassis 12547 specifically for the Le Mans 24 Hours in 1969 – although another two years would pass before the first series of competition-prepared examples would be built. The car was finished at the very last moment and run in during Chinetti's drive from Maranello to Le Mans for the practice sessions. After this sterling effort it was crashed in the first practice session and took no further part in the proceedings, but not before showing a good turn of speed and potential for further development. After repairs it eventually made its racing debut at the 24 Hours of Daytona in January 1970, only to retire in the 15th hour with a broken clutch. The second car modified by Chinetti, chassis 12467, ran in the Sport category of the 1971 Le Mans 24 Hours and, although only 33rd in qualifying, ran like the proverbial train to finish fifth overall. Had it been homologated in the GT category it would have won it easily, but it did take victory in the Index of Thermal Efficiency.

It is likely that these performances – allied to the ever-increasing cost of competing in the prototype class for concessionaire and private teams and their pressure on the factory – prompted Ferrari to initiate the construction of the first series of 'C' cars. This began at its *Assistenza Clienti* workshop in Modena during summer 1971, ready to run in the Tour de France Auto that autumn.

This first series comprised five cars. Their all-aluminium bodies, without bumpers, featured a shallow chin spoiler, small aerodynamic fences on the forward top edges of the front wings and slightly flared front and rear wheelarches to accommodate the homologated wider wheels – 8in or 8.5in at the front and 8.5in or 9in at the rear. The only example to retain these lightly flared arches is chassis 14429, which never had a competition career. The other cars in the series were campaigned actively in succeeding years and received the homologation updates of their younger relatives, including more radically flared wheelarches covering wider wheels and tyres. Small rectangular air scoops are provided near the trailing edge of each sill, to duct air to the rear brakes. Paired headlamps are fixed and mounted behind rectangular Plexiglas covers, which are shaped to the nose profile, allowing covered space below the headlamps for rectangular auxiliary lights if required. All windows, except for the laminated windscreen, are Plexiglas. The fuel tanks were identical to the road car, with the fuel filler under a flap on the left rear wing; however, as with other elements of the car, this arrangement was updated to bag tanks with a quick-release filler on the right rear wing.

Inside the car there is only a minimum of upholstery and almost no sound-deadening quilt. The facia is bare metal, with a satin black crackle finish, although the glove locker lid retains the standard model's Alcantara finish. The seats have cloth centres with vinyl bolsters and there are four-point safety harnesses together with a

The first 365 GTB/4 developed for competition under the direction of Luigi Chinetti is chassis number 12547. Apart from 'go-faster stripes', decals, side exhausts and outside fuel filler, its all-aluminium body appears much as any standard production Plexiglas-front road example.

360mm (14.2in) diameter leather-rim steering wheel. The door panels and transmission tunnel have a black vinyl covering, with a grey diamond quilt to the centre and passenger's side of the firewall to reduce engine heat transmission to the cabin. A similar quilt finish acts as the headlining, while inner sills, inner rear wheelarches and rear shelf have a thin black felt covering. All other surfaces, apart from the sometimes silver-finished six-point-fixing roll cage, are painted satin black. Any unnecessary details were omitted, even down to the quarterlight catches and sun visors, while the internal door release is a plastic-covered cable.

The engine differed very little from a standard, apart from having been carefully balanced and assembled. An aluminium cold air box, 155mm (6.1in) wide by 100mm (3.9in) deep, was fitted

around the velocity stacks of the six Weber 40DCN21 carburettors, which had no starter choke assemblies and different jetting to the standard car. The exhaust manifolds were carefully tuned, with larger-bore pipes running into a pair

Under the bonnet of chassis number 12547 the only significant visual difference is the crackle-black cold air box, which draws air to the carburettors direct from the grille opening in front of the radiator. This arrangement featured all subsequent series 365 GTB/4C models.

Interior of chassis number 12547 is very similar to production examples apart from the black crackle dashboard finish and cloth seat centres, although the latter could be specified as an option on road cars.

PRODUCTION

Pre-series: Chassis number12547, an aluminium-bodied car, was the first 365GTB/4 to race in international competition under Luigi Chinetti's North American Racing Team (NART) banner. He subsequently had an earlier example, chassis 12467, modified to competition specification.

Series I (1971): Five cars, chassis numbers 14407, 14429, 14437, 14885 and 14889.

Series II (1972): Five cars, chassis numbers 15225, 15373, 15667, 15681 and 15685.

Series III (1973): Five cars, chassis numbers 16343, 16363, 16367, 16407 and 16425.

Luigi Chinetti instigated the preparation of four more 365 GTB/4s to competition specification during this period. They were chassis 13367 and 13855, prepared by Sport Auto in Modena, and chassis 14065 and 14141, prepared by Traco Engineering in California. In 1975 he had a further small series of 365 GTB/4s rebodied by Michelotti and one of these, chassis 15965, practised at Le Mans that year. The last period preparation of a 365GTB/4 for competition was carried out by Ecurie Francorchamps in Belgium, on chassis 16717.

A few contemporary amateur drivers converted their cars to varying degrees of competition specification and other examples have been converted subsequently. However, only the cars listed above are generally considered to be genuine competition examples.

of straight-through exhaust pipes for each cylinder bank, exiting under each door.

The 15in wheels – 8in or 8.5in front, 8.5in or 9in rear – were retained by a single central octagonal nut to a standard hub and ventilated brake disc; the brakes used the standard road car's servo system. The suspension was provided with stiffer springs and shock absorbers (Koni 82P1833 front, 82P1834 rear), anti-roll bars of larger 24mm (0.94in) diameter at the front and 22mm (0.87in) at the rear, and a little more negative camber.

The Series II cars produced in early 1972 were all fitted with the larger-wheelarch body to accept newly homologated 9x15in front and 11x15in rear wheels. Manufactured in lightweight magnesium alloy by Campagnolo, these replaced the Cromodora wheels fitted to the road cars. Body material reverted to steel, with the aluminium doors, bonnet and boot lid of the road cars, but window glass was unchanged from the Series I examples. An aluminium undertray was homologated as a sump guard at the same time, to provide smooth airflow beneath the engine bay. The flexible rubber-bag fuel tanks had a combined capacity of 120 litres (26.4 Imperial/31.7 US gallons), with an aluminium quick-release filler on the right rear wing. An external battery cut-off switch and fire extinguisher switch were provided on the right front wing, to comply with new safety legislation. Interior layout remained unchanged.

Mechanically there were no significant differences from the Series I cars, apart from the provision of a fuel break tank. A pair of Bendix blue-top pumps drew fuel from the main tanks and a further pair delivered it from the break tank to the carburettors on a loop circuit. Shorter steering arms,

which reduced the number of turns from lock to lock from 3.25 to 2.9, were homologated but otherwise everything on the suspension and steering side remained virtually the same.

The Series III cars appear virtually identical to Series II cars, but only the bonnet and boot lid are aluminium, the doors being steel, as fitted to road cars starting from chassis number 15701. Push-fit fuel filler caps are set into a recess in each rear wing, feeding the flexible bag tanks. The chin spoiler is a narrower but deeper unit below the radiator opening. However, by this time racing teams were trying their own aerodynamic tweaks, although none strayed too far from the standard layout, proving that the factory package was aerodynamically sound. The windows are all glass and the interior layout is identical to the earlier series.

The engine underwent several changes that increased horsepower, with different pistons and new connecting rods providing a higher compression ratio, while higher-lift camshafts and changes to the valve timing gave a further boost in output. A wider and deeper cold air box improved the breathing, with larger carburettor main jets, while 38mm (1.5in) or 42mm (1.6in) diameter exhaust manifolds were available, each having its own optimum valve timing set-up.

The suspension was provided with externally-adjustable Koni shock absorbers, type 8201T front and rear with different load ratings. Front and rear anti-roll bar diameters were increased to 26mm (1.0in) and 23mm (0.9in) respectively, that at the rear being rigidly mounted instead of with the normal rubber bushes. At the same time the front wheels were given slightly less negative camber and a greater castor angle. Servo assistance to the

An example of each of the three series of 365 GTB/4C. At the top is chassis number 14429, the only one of the five aluminium-bodied Series I cars to retain its original body configuration – it had no period competition career and thus did not receive the updates of its relatives involved in racing. In the centre is a Series II steel-bodied example, chassis number 15681, in the colours of Maranello Concessionaires as raced at Le Mans in 1972. At the bottom is an attractive corporate livery, that of the Thomson electrical appliance manufacturer, on a Series III example (chassis number 16363), as worn at Le Mans in 1973.

brakes was omitted and a twin-circuit (separate front and rear) braking system with tandem master cylinders was installed. The brake calipers were modified to accept pads of twice the normal thickness to reduce the number of pad changes in endurance races.

In the three series of cars produced, all of the first series had left-hand drive, while one example each of the second and third series was right-hand drive. During the course of their competition careers, early cars were often modified to later specification, so it is not unusual to find cars from the first two series with a mixture of later features, which are best described as period modifications adopted during their competition careers. Some 365 GTB/4Cs had quite extensive and successful competition careers. At Le Mans in 1972 they filled fifth to ninth positions in the overall classification and the top five positions in the GT category, with victory and second place in the Tour de France Auto the same year. In 1973 and 1974 they again took GT honours at Le Mans, with sixth and fifth places in the general classification respectively, while it was as late as 1979 that one of the most memorable results was achieved. This was in the 24 Hours of Daytona, when the pairing of John Morton and Tony Adamowicz took second overall in the general classification – in a six-year-old car! The result was all the more memorable and poignant because Otto Zipper, the team manager, died just before the race and the car carried a diagonal black band across the bonnet as a sign of respect.

The 365 GTB/4C had numerous good placings in endurance events over the years, those mentioned being the highlights. The 1979 24 Hours of Daytona second-placed car, chassis 16407, was still being campaigned in 1981, 12 years after an example had first appeared at the 1969 Le Mans and eight years after the model ceased production in 1973. Rarely does a car remain competitive for such a period of time with relatively little ongoing development; its blend of power and reliability has made it one of the all-time GT class classics.

Appendix

PERFORMANCE COMPARISONS

Model	0-60 mph (sec)	0-100 mph (sec)	Max speed (mph)	Source	Date
275 GTB (2 cam)	6.4	12.5	159	AS	3/66
275 GTS	7.2	18.8	145	R&T	9/66
275 GTB/4 (4 cam)	6.2	14.5	166 est	C&D	10/67
275 GTS/4 NART	6.7	15.0	155	R&T	9/67
330 GT 2+2 Series I	6.3	15.5	152 est	C&D	3/65
330 GT 2+2 Series II	6.8	16.8	151	SCG	1/67
330 GTC	6.8	16.7	153 est	C&D	7/67
330 GTS	6.9	17.1	146	R&T	8/68
365 GTC	6.3	14.7	151	AC	29/5/69
365 GT 2+2	7.1	15.7	151	AS	1/70
365 GTB/4	5.8	12.65	174.73	AS	10/71
365 GTB/4C	5.8	12.6	186	R&T	11/74
365 GTC/4 (US)	7.3	19.3	152	R&T	7/72

Abbreviations: AC = *Autocar*, AS = *Autosport*, C&D = *Car and Driver*, R&T = *Road & Track*, SCG = *Sports Car Graphic*

PRODUCTION ENGINE TYPES

Model	Engine type	Capacity cc	Power (DIN) bhp	rpm	kgm	Torque lb ft	rpm
500 Superfast	208	4943	400	4750	48.5	350	4750
365 California	217B	4390	320	6600	37	267	5000
275 GTB (2 cam)	213	3286	280	7600	30	217	5500
275 GTB/C	213	3286	290[1]	–	–	–	–
275 GTS	213	3286	260	7000	30	216	5000
275 GTB/4 (4 cam)	226	3286	300	8000	32	231	6050
330 GT 2+2	209	3967	300	6600	33.2	240	5000
330 GTC/S	209/66	3967	300	6600	33.2	240	5000
365 GTC/S	245/C	4390	320	6600	37	267	5000
365 GT 2+2	245	4390	320	6600	37	267	5000
365 GTB/4	251	4390	352	7500	44	318	5500
365 GTB/4C	251	4390	400+	–	–	–	–
365 GTC/4	F 101 AC 000	4390	320	7000	44	318	4000
365 GT4 2+2	F 101 AC 000	4390	320	7000	43	310	4600

[1] Approximate power output

PRODUCTION AT A GLANCE

All road cars of this period were assigned odd chassis numbers, including the competition derivatives.

Model	Production period	Chassis numbers	Numbers built
500 Superfast	1964-1966	05951-08897	36
365 California	1966-1967	08347-10369	14
275 GTB (2 cam)	1964-1966	06021-08979	454[1]
275 GTB/C	1966	09007-09085	12[2]
275 GTS	1964-1966	06315-08653	200
275 GTB/4 (4 cam)	1966-1968	08769-11069	330
275 GTS/4 NART	1967-1968	09437-11057	10
330 GT 2+2 Series I	1964-1965	04963-07533	625
330 GT 2+2 Series II	1965-1967	07537-10193	474
330 GTC	1966-1968	08329-11577	598
330 GTS	1966-1968	08899-11713	100
365 GTC	1968-1970	11589-12785	168
365 GTS	1969	12163-12493	20
365 GT 2+2	1967-1971	11051-14099	800
365 GTB/4	1968-1973	12301-17615	1284
365 GTS/4	1969-1973	14365-17073	122
365 GTB/4C	1971-1973	14407-16425	15[2]
365 GTC/4	1971-1973	14179-16289	500
365 GT4 2+2	1972-1976	17091-19709	521[3]

The dates and figures given above exclude prototypes, unless noted.
[1] This figure includes the '*Speciale*' models and series I competition examples, details of which can be found in the *Competition Derivatives* chapter. The factory classifies 06021 as the first production 275 GTB, but this was also a competition prototype
[2] See the *Competition Derivatives* chapter for details
[3] Plus three prototypes

PRODUCTION CHASSIS TYPE NUMBERS & DIMENSIONS

All chassis are of welded tubular steel construction.

Model	Chassis type number	Wheelbase mm	in	Track front mm	in	Track rear mm	in
500 Superfast	578	2650	104.3	1397	55.0	1389	54.7
365 California	598	2650	104.3	1405	55.3	1397	55.0
275 GTB (2 cam)	563 (to early '66)	2400	94.5	1377	54.2	1393	54.8
275 GTB (2 cam)	563/66 (from early '66)	2400	94.5	1401	55.2	1417	55.8
275 GTB/C	563 (to '65)	2400	94.5	–	–	–	–
275 GTB/C	590A (from '66)	2400	94.5	–	–	–	–
275 GTS	563	2400	94.5	1377	54.2	1393	54.8
275 GTB/4 (4 cam)	596	2400	94.5	1401	55.2	1417	55.8
330 GT 2+2	571	2650	104.3	1397	55.0	1389	54.7
330 GTC/S	592	2400	94.5	1401	55.2	1417	55.8
365 GTC/S	592/C	2400	94.5	1410	55.5	1414	55.7
365 GT 2+2	591	2650	104.3	1438	56.6	1468	57.8
365 GTB/4	605	2400	94.5	1440	56.7	1453	57.2
365 GTB/4: 8in rim	605	2400	94.5	1453	57.2	1466	57.7
8½in rim		2400	94.5	1465	57.7	1478	58.2
9in rim		2400	94.5	1478	58.2	1491	58.7
365 GTC/4	F 101 AC 100	2500	98.4	1480	58.3	1480	58.3
365 GT4 2+2	F 101 AL	2700	106.3	1470	57.9	1500	59.0

Index